ED CUTTS

Designer, Boatbuilder, & "Cutts Method" Inventor

WAYNE BROWN

LEEWARD PUBLICATIONS

First published by Leeward Publications LLC
Ed Cutts Designer, Boatbuilder, & "Cutts Method" Inventor
Copyright © 2014 by Wayne W. Brown

First paperback edition published 2014 by
Leeward Publications LLC
P.O. Box 693
Fairfield, CT 06824

Library of Congress Cataloging-in-Publication Data
Brown, Wayne W.
ISBN 978-0-9892766-0-3
LCCN 20-13917221
1. Biography. 2. Boat building. 3. Boat design.

Cover designed by Rob Johnson Toprotype Inc.
Interior designed by 1106 Design
Printed in the United States of America

TABLE OF CONTENTS

INTRODUCTION

When interviewing Ed Cutts in 2002 for *Tidewater Times* magazine, I discovered he had worked at the Henry B. Nevins Boatyard, well-respected builders of fine yachts at City Island, New York. He told me the government of Finland had invited him, and his son Eddie Jr., to their country to lecture on a new boat building technique. He mentioned the "Cutts Method," which he invented. This was a surprise to me.

His Cutts & Case boatyard in Oxford Maryland, he said, could build with this method a lighter, faster wooden boat without metal hull fastenings and without frames. I watched him and he was serious, but I harbored many questions. It seemed at first as if he had kept his building method a secret, within his cloistered, scenic boatyard. This is set in the small historic town of Oxford on Maryland's Eastern Shore. I had rented daysailers here, as a teenager, in the 1940s long before he took over Wiley's boatyard. This quiet town was an unlikely location for technical breakthroughs.

Ed had learned designing from the famous yacht designer L. Francis Herreshoff, fourth son of the great Nathanael Herreshoff. Some of Ed's boats, which he had designed and built, were at his dock. Others were in Long Island, New York, for the boating season.

For my article, he revealed nothing of his early life and background, his designing and building career. How had he discovered a revolutionary boat building method? Was this as great an improvement as he said? Except for boaters who lived nearby, owned his boats, kept boats at his yard, or sailed in the Upper Chesapeake Bay, this builder/designer was a man of mystery.

When Ed told a few events from his life, I began to see some of the challenges he had faced, along with breakthroughs and successes. I often told him, "Someone should do a book on you, Ed." A few months later, he said, "Well, nobody has yet. Why don't you?" So, I started on this biography in 2004.

With frequent trips to Oxford, we soon became good friends. My wife, Carol, and I lived nearby between St. Michaels and Tilghman Island. Regular interviews with Ed continued over the years, after we moved to Virginia in December 2005, through the launching of his last sloop and up to his Crossing the Bar in 2009. I enjoyed Ed's robust humor and opinions, his wisdom and knowledge as he spoke on diverse and varied subjects. His comments usually concerned boats.

Ed had some engineering training, but like Edison, whom he admired, he also studied on his own. Once he worked at Grumman Aviation while boat building on weekends. He designed a secret method to lay down the lines of a new boat. He talked about the Cutts Method, the R & D behind it, and how to use it in building and major rebuilding, which should interest many readers. His love of speed drew him at an early age to motorcycles, which he started collecting, as did his two sons, who now run the boatyard.

I feel fortunate that I could write the story of Ed Cutts — a vigorous, opinionated, talented, inventive, often humorous, and unique individual. He was quietly brilliant and fully dedicated to the future of wooden boats. I believe we should all know more about Ed, his life, and his work. I hope the readers will agree.

Wayne Brown, 2013

Chapter One
BOATS AND BEGINNINGS

In 1972, Edmund A. Cutts had been co-owner of a boatyard called Cutts & Case in historic Oxford, Maryland, for almost seven years. He was used to visitors stopping by. Some wanted boats repaired or to tie up at his dock, but many were just looking around at the power and sailing craft and enjoying the beautiful boatyard. Towering chestnuts and pines shaded the red sheds in the scenic yard of four and a half tranquil acres. Facing the docks were white spruce, red cedar, locust, and magnolia.

On this day, a visitor from Maine parked his car and walked around looking carefully and intently. He was visiting building-boatyards in the East to gather notes for a planned publication. The visitor was Jonathan Wilson. A friend, about to open a wooden boat-building school in Maine, had recommended the Cutts & Case boatyard. A tall, lanky man with wind-blown hair and dressed in faded clothing came out the door of a shed and strode purpose-fully toward the newcomer.

Wilson later wrote, ". . . when I told him I was a small boat builder in search of kindred souls, he smiled (tolerantly) and welcomed me in. It was Ed Cutts. I discovered immediately that I was not talking with an everyday boatyard/marina operator;

indeed, I got the feeling (fast) that I had met up with my first real genius." (*WoodenBoat*)

In his historic old house, Ed showed Jon models and drawings of boats and spoke about his background and consulting with L. Francis Herreshoff. Then at the dock they looked at three of Ed's sailboats, discussing design choices and joinerwork. Inside a large shed Ed showed his visitor a 46' ketch under construction.

An account of this meeting appeared years later in Jon Wilson's editorial for the September–October 1987 *WoodenBoat*. "I had not only found a kindred soul," Wilson wrote, "I found one of the elders of the kinship. . . . I was rendered speechless by the rest of what was represented by Ed Cutts." That issue also had an excellent article, "A Lineage of Craftsmanship" with a subtitle: "Ed Cutts Strives for Innovations that will Help Wooden Boats Endure" by Winston Groom.

Ed Cutts's journey to designing and building wooden boats in the classic tradition was not only challenging but also often frustrating. Early in his career he struggled. Perhaps Ed's strongest trait throughout his life was his determination to reach a goal, in spite of rejections and delays — strong currents and headwinds.

Some people know what they want to do in high school or college or after going to work. Ed Cutts decided he wanted to build wooden boats when he was around ten years old. He didn't change his mind. His interest and early talents continued to develop because his father, Vernon Vane Cutts, introduced Eddie to boat building. His dad shared his knowledge of famous yachts and racing classes, encouraged his son's drawing, and helped him improve his boat models. Vernon, whose own father was a carpenter, was skillful at carving models and could do mechanical repairs on family boats.

When the Cutts family sat at the dinner table, Vernon Cutts spoke about crossing the Atlantic and growing up in Westchester.

But, there were taboo topics. Ed recalled he seldom talked to his family about his first marriage or about family tragedies.

Vernon was born in February 1881 in Brimington, Derby, England. According to the 1881 census, his father John Cutts was born in 1855 in North Wingfield, Derby, and worked in an iron foundry as a wheelwright. At some point he mastered precision carpentry techniques at a carriage-building firm. In 1887, John and his wife Sarah decided to sail to America with six-year-old Vernon. To board the ship, they traveled about 100 miles to Liverpool.

A cacophony of sounds from passengers, peddlers, cranes, horses, wagon chains, hovering gulls, and boat horns greeted the Cutts family. Coming from inland, Vernon was surprised by the salty, fishy air from the Mercy River. The 455' ship was motionless, a floating, peaceful behemoth.

With two funnels and four masts, *Britannic II* loomed like a sleeping giant over the milling crowds and loading activities at the port. Launched in 1874, the *Britannic* and her sister ship the *Germanic* were the newest White Star Line liners. (Bowen, Parker)

Once aboard, Vernon and his parents discovered cramped sleeping quarters with double-decker beds. For meals, socializing, and reading, however, they used large assembly rooms filled with chairs, sofas, and tables fastened to prevent sliding in rough seas. This ship was the first to pipe fresh air below decks for everyone, not just First Class.

The ship crossed to Dublin, where it took on more passengers. The *Britannic*, built by Harland and Wolff of Belfast, was a well-liked steamer of 5,004 tons, able to do 16 knots with her single-screw propulsion. For three years, 1876 to 1879, she held the speed record on the North Atlantic crossing, for a time of 7 days, 12 hours, 47 minutes on her winning run.

In photos of the 1880s, *Britannic*'s foremast and mainmast had square topsails furled on three yards. An early poster to encourage safety-conscious travelers had fore and aft sails rolled up on the mizzen and spanker booms. Canvas could be unfurled for speed, steadiness in rolling seas, saving coal, and emergencies. After the advent of steam engines in the 1840s, captains, experienced with sail, were cautious about using the early engines for long voyages. Therefore, transoceanic steamships carried plenty of sail until early engines proved themselves. Because of the continued reliability of the giant steam engines, White Star Lines launched the *Teutonic* in 1889 without sails or masts.

When the *Britannic* landed passengers at Castle Gardens at the southern tip of Manhattan, John H. Cutts signed his name as "laborer," as did many other passengers. The Cutts family took a New Haven ferry with large paddle wheels. Paddle-wheel boats, called "Paddlers" in England, once sailed ocean routes. Shipping line founder Samuel Cunard's ships continued for many years to have paddle propulsion because he believed the passengers felt safer seeing and hearing the metal-encased paddles. On deck, Vernon was interested in the paddle propulsion and in watching New York City move past, before they entered Rye Town's large harbor where they disembarked.

In Port Chester, John Cutts started to build wagons and carriages. He and his wife Sarah Cutts had a troubled marriage and had planned to divorce after arriving in America. Sarah, however, continued living at home, because she could see that her son, just starting school, needed her.

The following year the storm of the century hit on March 12th. "The Blizzard of '88," as it is known, started off coastal New Jersey and then sped to Philadelphia. Twenty inches of snow and sleet landed on New York City. Moving vehicles halted, blocking everything while pedestrians fought the blinding blizzard and deepening snow. Drivers abandoned wagons and carriages to ride their horses home. In some cross streets, the winds created snow drifts to the second floor. Unable to walk home, 3,500 people took shelter in the Castle Gardens Immigration Center for two nights. People crowded together to survive in large city buildings.

In New York Bay tugboats hauled damaged schooners and cleared huge blocks of floating ice. Nine pilot boats were lost in New York harbor, along with seventeen pilots.

The massive blanket of overhead communication wires and live power lines, in cities like New York and Washington, crashed to the ground. Boston and Philadelphia were hard hit as was Montreal. In Port Chester, John Cutts and his family waited out the storm, which continued for thirty-six hours, before the cleanup could begin along with food deliveries. (Cable, Lyons)

Vernon often said his father built beautiful carriages, and quoted him saying, "I would build anything to stay alive." This included furniture, dray wagons, milk wagons, and even sledges to haul ice. At nearby Rye Lake, men cut blocks of ice to store for the summer.

Sarah Cutts raised Vernon and kept him in school while she protected him from his father. John was a fine carpenter but not an easy man to live with. From an early age, Vernon helped his father in his shop. Once, after working for weeks on a project, Vernon and his mother thought at last they would have enough food, for they had skimped and stretched what supplies they had. John left to deliver a new carriage. His return was a shock. "My father came home wearing new boots and a fine new outfit — and no money!" Vernon said. "We were devastated!"

John and Sarah Cutts did divorce when Vernon was eleven, and she left him with his father. She moved to New England where she remarried. Her letters to her son suddenly stopped because she was afraid to tell her new husband of her previous marriage. When John also remarried, life may have become easier for Vernon with a woman in the house once again. Since Vernon's school did not enforce attendance, his father sometimes kept him home to help him in the shop.

"The building work was all important because it put food on the table," Vernon later told his own children. "Sometimes my hands were raw from using sandpaper and planes. If I got any blood on the wood, my father would beat me." Vernon, however, managed to keep up with his studies and graduated from high school. He went to work full time for his father, who was then building milk wagons. Because automobiles were being manufactured in greater numbers, people needed fewer carriages. Later, John constructed wheels for Studebaker milk wagons.

When he was twenty, Vernon delivered a new milk wagon to a large dairy in Rye. While there, he asked, "Do you have some work I could do?" They hired him to handle the horses. He was glad to move out of his father's house into a barn apartment at the dairy. His employer, Charles Adams, owned two dairy farms at Rye Lake and distributed the milk. Vernon began a casual friendship with Susie Adams, the farmer's eighteen-year-old daughter. Soon both wanted to marry, so Vernon asked her father, as was the custom, but Adams refused.

Discouraged, Vernon went to Texas where he worked for a year while thinking things out. When he returned, he worked again at Adams's farm on Rye Lake and continued to see Susie, whom the *Port Chester Journal* described as "a radiantly gorgeous young lady." But, wealthier young men were interested in her and her sisters. Vernon was at a disadvantage. The paper reported, he "brandished a gun" to frighten off other suitors, but it didn't state that he threatened them. He probably wore a six-shooter in a holster, like the men he had met in Texas at the turn of the century. Adams promptly fired him.

Vernon rented an apartment in Yonkers and landed a position with the Borden Condensed Milk Company in 1903. He developed a secret plan for the day following Christmas and kept in touch with Susie. When her father left for work, Susie walked to Port Chester to meet Vernon who had a carriage. They rode to the

Methodist Episcopal Church where the minister married them. Then Vernon sent a telegram to Adams asking for his forgiveness.

This wasn't forthcoming. Adams promptly shipped her trunk with a note, "Never come to Port Chester again." The *Journal* headlines read, "Consent Refused, Love Finds a Way. Like Lockinvar of Old He Bears His Bride Away." In Yonkers, Vernon and Susan lived at Bartholdi Place on the Hudson River. In October 1904 they had a son who was baptized Vernon Jr., but they called him Buddy. (*Port Chester Journal*)

As fishing was his major hobby, Vernon installed a motor in his 27' sailboat, *Starbright*. In June 1911, after Susan gave birth to Gladys, her second child, they moved to Racine Avenue. By 1913, Vernon was a milk inspector at the dairy. Changes were underway at Borden, because foresters were clearing land in Croton for a new reservoir to supply New York City. The state took the land so people and dairy farms had to move. The Borden Condensed Milk Company, with the bald eagle trademark, built a new plant in Roslyn, Long Island, and Vernon moved his family to Brooklyn for a shorter commute.

When Susan Cutts gave birth to a third baby, Clifford, in February 1914, she suddenly died. Vernon hired a woman to care for the three children. Vernon was visibly grief stricken by this tragedy. His good friend Joe Fegan often took him fishing, trying to lift his spirits. Although Vernon enjoyed his children, he continued to feel devastated.

A year later, Joe invited Vernon to a musical show saying it would cheer him up. Vernon watched one singer in particular and was surprised when Joe said it was his sister, Adelaide Fegan, using a professional last name of Arnold. Dinner that evening started a relationship.

Vernon's first daughter, Gladys, once told her son Richard Somerville of an early, jarring incident. "When Vernon remarried in 1915," Somerville said, "he brought this woman up to the house and said to those three kids, my mother, Vernon Jr., and the baby Clifford, 'This is your new mother.' " It sounded abrupt and sudden. "They had lost their own mother only about a year before," Richard said. "It should have been more discrete." Buddy was eleven years old and Gladys was about seven.

Adelaide's family hailed from Dublin. Her grandfather Joseph Fegan, a bookkeeper, married Isabelle Brown, and their first child Edward Fegan was born in 1854. The family, with Joseph's two brothers and his sister Nellie, who would later have a significant influence on the family, crossed the ocean. They settled in Kings County, Brooklyn.

Edward Fegan rose to become a court stenographer in the Rockaway Courts, and later he successfully advised people facing court appearances when they couldn't afford a lawyer. He married Kate Williamson, whose father was a captain. Daughter Adelaide was born in 1886, followed by a brother Joe, and a sister Loretta in 1893.

Their married aunt, now Nellie Tierney, couldn't have children, so she asked Edward if she could raise one of theirs as her own. The parents agreed to this and chose Adelaide, who moved to New Rochelle where she lived as an only child. Her wealthy aunt invested successfully in New Rochelle real estate and farmland.

Nellie Tierney took Adelaide to the theatre, and sponsored singing, music and dancing lessons, probably in nearby New York City. Mrs. Tierney died in 1904 when Adelaide was about eighteen. After being tricked out of the property her aunt had left her, Adelaide moved back with her own parents. She attended theatre auditions and was soon a member of John C. Fisher's *Mamselle Sallie Company*.

On tour she sent postcards to her family from cities around the country — Birmingham, Alabama, to Cape Elizabeth, Maine; from San Antonio, Texas, to Victoria, British Columbia. While the touring shows were musical theatre and reviews, the company may also have performed scenes from operas. The family heard that Adelaide understudied a featured role in *Aida*. In 1909, after performing in Cleveland, she moved back with her family in Brooklyn. She continued to perform in the New York area, while learning the real estate business from her parents.

Adelaide explained to Vernon, her new husband, "Conditions in the theatre were changing for the worse, because there were unethical producers and managers." She was disillusioned. "Although I loved singing," she said, "I decided to leave show business."

The marriage brought Adelaide immediate responsibilities and some problems. She loved little Clifford like her own child and treated the older children as her family. But, Buddy, the eldest, resented her.

In 1917, Adelaide gave birth to Martin, and, after two years, to a second boy William. But, in 1921, the Cutts family suffered another tragedy. Seven-year-old Clifford died from Bright's Disease. Within two weeks Adelaide's two sons, Martin and Willie died from diphtheria. Their deaths were years before the advent of miracle drugs.

The next year, Adelaide Cutts had a baby girl, whom they named after her mother. They took baby Adelaide to a Presbyterian church as a compromise, because Vernon was Church of England and Adelaide was Catholic. In 1926, the milk company promoted Vernon, so the Cutts family was able to buy a house on 89th Street in Woodhaven, Queens. On New Year's Day in 1927, Edmund Anthony Cutts was born, Vernon's seventh child. He had three surviving older siblings.

As Eddie grew older, health issues were paramount with his parents, so he was kept at home whenever sickness like influenza was making the rounds. The house was warm in winter and the meals were nutritious. As Eddie began school, he often joined his parents and Gladys in the living room after an evening meal, where they talked, read papers, and listened to the radio news. Sometimes, Vernon would say, "Three small caskets stood over there." Then he would silently stare into the distance. Eddie noticed his mother crying after the mention of the tragedy and felt the grief himself.

On a windy spring Saturday in 1933, Vernon drove his family in his brown Studebaker south from Queens toward Brooklyn. He turned before the bridge over Jamaica Bay and parked beside a small boatyard. A bottom-up boat, like a small whale skeleton, exposed its structural backbone and rib-like frames. It sat at the top of the ways, near the shed opening, and slightly elevated from their car. At the bow, a man was adjusting a clamp. Vernon told his six-year-old son, "This boat is larger than last year's boat. He is building it solid but rough — as a work boat to take out fishing parties." His father called his son "Manny" and said he was like a little man. The lad accepted this special name from the dad he loved. His mother used his real name — Eddie. Adelaide, then an attractive, serious woman of forty-nine, showed as little interest in the boat as did eleven-year-old daughter Addie. The boatbuilder drilled a plank as they watched. The salty scents of lumber, paint, and tar intrigued the boy.

The family stopped at the boatyard to check on the boat-building progress whenever they drove over the Bay Bridge to Rockaway from their house in Queens to their shore property. Every spring Adelaide checked for winter damage at their summer guesthouse in Howard Beach facing the Atlantic. The family lived there in the summer. She had inherited four buildings from her mother. After a work week as a manager at Borden Condensed Milk Company, Vernon did carpentry, painting, and plumbing repairs as needed. When he had time, he went fishing.

Their guesthouse at 108th Street and Rockaway Boulevard housed two summer shops downstairs, an Armenian shoemaker and a butcher. Upstairs were cozy seaside rooms and a shared kitchen. Nearby at 103rd Street, Adelaide's sister Loretta also managed a rooming house with stores. In Far Rockaway, Uncle Joe Fegan and Aunt Marie had an apartment building. Gladys sometimes took her half brother Eddie out for ice cream or an amusement ride. They saw little of "Buddy," who then had his own family.

Eddie often carried a model boat, copied after sail and power yachts, which his father had carved. On his father's models, Eddie fastened sails to the spars, while his dad taught him sail nomenclature, rigs, and reef points. Eddie soon made his own boats, which were rough. Over the years his skills improved as he created more beautiful models.

One day on the beach twelve-year-old Adelaide announced to Eddie she was going to swim to a sandbar. It ran parallel to the shoreline about 140 feet from the beach, depending on the tide. Seven-year-old Eddie couldn't swim, but Adelaide was a capable swimmer and pulled him out over the deepest water. They sat in the shallows of the sandbar, looking at the crowded beaches and the amusement rides on their left. Suddenly, Addie spotted a girlfriend on the beach and said, "I'm going to swim in." She ran splashing into deep water, and the boy watched her swim off.

"She forgot she took me there," Ed vividly recalled. "She didn't know anything about tides. Kids don't know about that. It was a long way off." He shouted. Nobody seemed to hear him over the wind and the breaking surf. "At low tide on the bar I could walk around, but the tide was coming in. It could be six feet and more." He shouted and waved his arms like a semaphore, but no one noticed. Growing tired, he watched and waited for his sister. The incoming tide moved up his body as he stood. "I was going to drown," he said.

"There happened to be a man on the beach looking out at the water, and he didn't believe what he saw. He was a strong swimmer and came out and grabbed me across the chest and took me back." On the beach, Eddie spit out salt water. The rescuer walked off before Eddie could thank him.

Eddie never told his parents. He did ask his sister why she left him, and she answered vaguely, "Because . . . ," and trailed off into silence. "That was typical of her," Ed said. "My mother didn't understand my sister too well, and neither did I. For a time, I wondered if she was trying to get rid of me. I almost drowned out there, if it hadn't been for that man." He wished he could have thanked him. When Eddie learned to swim the following year, he was proud. "I taught myself to swim like a fish in shallow water," he said.

Vernon often told Eddie, "I know where something interesting is being built. Would you like to come along?" Eddie usually got to the car first, as boatyard visits continued over the years. Eddie felt at home with scents of cedar, varnish, canvas, and caulking material. In 1934, at the Purdy yard in Port Washington, they both admired the 60' cruiser *Shadow Fay*, just launched. Vernon pointed out unusual design features and exceptional joiner work. Each year they visited building boatyards. They kept out of the builders' way but observed what they could.

Joe Fegan's boat, a 24' double-ended cabin cruiser, was not for kids. They could get in the way. But, when Eddie was eight and a half, the men invited him to come along as they fished for fluke and flounder outside the New York harbor entrance. As they cruised out, Eddie's first trip in a boat widened his eyes and exhilarated his senses. Boat handling and seamanship interested Eddie the most. He helped baiting hooks and kept out of the fishermen's way. He squinted into the distance at interesting boats. Vernon knew many boat classes, sometimes the builder's name, or even the name of a famous yacht.

One day approaching from the ocean, they all saw a black two-masted steamboat. It turned into New York harbor, looking huge with smoke coming from a single funnel. Vernon said, "It's the newest Corsair. It belongs to J. Pierpont Morgan of the New York Yacht Club." They took turns with the binoculars watching the yacht, even longer than a football field with end zones — as mysterious and powerful as Mr. Morgan himself.

Boatyard visits continued as the boy became nine and ten. Vernon sometimes drove into Fyfe's boatyard at Glen Head in Hempstead Harbor to see beautiful new ships under construction. Shipyard sounds often merged — band sawing, a router, flags snapping in the breeze, the complaining whine of a crane, the screech of a block and tackle — echoed by laughing and herring gulls.

Perhaps, this was the significant day that Eddie Cutts reached a decision he wanted to share. "Dad, this is what I want to do in life — build boats." Vernon said that sounded fine because he knew Eddie loved boats. As they walked off, he put his arm around the boy's shoulder.

At home, Adelaide wasn't thrilled at the news. Ever the business woman, she hoped Eddie would become a lawyer, banker, or doctor. "You'll change your mind as you get older," she said. Eddie heard this repeatedly growing up.

The thirties was a time of struggle for the country and for Americans. Eddie knew that banks failed and companies closed down following the Stock Market Crash. The Depression continued into the late thirties until military-based industry began to gear up and accelerate production. At a time when many people earned only $12 a week, Eddie was proud his father made $52. In 1937, Eddie, then ten, saw a man dancing in the street by himself outside his house. He asked, "What's the matter with him?" His parents said, "Nothing. He just got a job for $16 at a department store in Jamaica." Eddie understood the Depression more clearly.

The Cutts household had good meals, but everyone watched the expenses and minimized waste. Adelaide was an early entrepreneur, and as her granddaughter said later, "Ahead of her time." She managed the money, saved for tax payments, and shared with her whole family. But the household wasn't always peaceful. Alone behind closed doors, the couple sometimes argued. Eddie heard that his mother didn't share the income from her properties with his father, but "squirreled it away."

Eddie's early boat building began in the basement with his friend Rudy, "who wore thick glasses like the bottom of a glass milk bottle." Rudy's eyesight was hardly encouraging for precision work, but the two ignored fine measurements. "We built by eye, but it was fun," Ed said. They wondered how they could plank the little boat and yet spend no money. Then, on trash day they found linoleum that someone had thrown out. "Our boat had a round bottom, which is why we needed linoleum," Ed said. When completed, the appearance was far from nautical because the hull featured large red dahlias.

The boys loaded the rowboat on a bicycle and tied it to the handlebars. With homemade oars on the second bicycle, they walked to Jamaica Bay to launch the red-flowered skiff. Eddie climbed onto the thwart, positioned the oars in the thole-pins, and Rudy pushed him out for a trial run. "We had it all pitched up," Ed said, "but, of course, it leaked like hell. Rudy stayed on the beach hollering for me to come in because he wanted to go rowing." The co-builder took his turn to test the leaky skiff. "He took off and then the strangest thing happened," Ed said. "The boat was going along, and he wasn't rowing. He had stepped through it! He was walking on the bottom, and it was as if he were wearing the boat." Eddie was predictably upset as they left the boat and bicycled to the ocean beach. When the boat vanished a few days later, they suspected someone had taken it because of the Depression. Eddie and Rudy had better luck with model boats.

At Christmas, Eddie unwrapped a Lionel double-cockpit metal Chris Craft, about 16 inches long with a spring-wound motor. One weekend he cycled to Jackson Pond where he and his friends sailed model boats. Navigating a bump in the road, Eddie watched the boat slip and hit the ground, breaking the propeller. Adept with tools, Eddie measured suitable metal to cut out and make a new propeller, which worked just fine.

By 1939, when young Eddie was twelve, pleasure-boat construction practically stopped as defense industries had the first call on materials and skilled labor. Some racing classes like *Lightnings* and *Stars* continued in production as long as yards had wood and metal fittings.

If not making a model, Eddie drew a yacht he particularly liked, sometimes working from a boating magazine photo. He also made model war planes, Navy ships, and Army tanks from kits. His parents were proud of all his abilities. "They knew I was capable. If they saw me doing something, they would back off and let me do whatever I wanted to do," said Ed, in his senior years. He paused to consider this. "I was a little bit spoiled. I could hardly do any wrong. And they didn't hound me, although my mother was always remonstrating about being decent and saving money. She had learned about business from her mother and was penny conscious."

Distant war reports came into their home via the *New York Daily News*, the *Journal American*, and their large Majestic radio that stood on legs. The family followed what Germany and Italy were doing in Europe and Africa, secret meetings between Roosevelt and Churchill, and also Japan capturing much of China. Eddie read the newspapers, but the wars were far away. They didn't interest him as much as the planes, tanks, and boats involved. In early 1940, when German U-boats appeared in Atlantic shipping lanes, President Roosevelt announced he was countering with a "Neutrality Patrol" of US cruisers patrolling the East Coast. Later, the President declared a "Limited State of Emergency." As Republicans, Eddie's parents had little love for Roosevelt, who had won a third term in 1940. Although opposed to isolationists, Vernon didn't want Roosevelt's name mentioned in the house.

The family knew when the United States seized all German and Italian ships in US ports. After a German submarine sank a US freighter out of Mozambique on May 27th, Roosevelt announced there were Axis ships in the Western Atlantic. The security of a vast, protective ocean diminished for US citizens. The international climate was uncertain and precarious as thirteen-year-old Eddie walked the few blocks from his house at 8019 89th Avenue, Woodhaven, to his high school, PS 171 in Brooklyn.

He complained to his parents about the dry school curriculum, saying, "They aren't teaching me what I want to know." Vernon and Adelaide Cutts knew this meant wooden boat building. His mother called this kind of talk "foolishness." In his own quiet way, Vernon continued to encourage his son's ambitions, talking with him about famous yachts and taking an interest in his wooden models. At the local library Eddie read *Popular Mechanics*, *Popular Science*, and *Motor Boating and Yachting*. The librarians sometimes gave him magazines to keep.

More than ever, Eddie's eyes were on the Navy. "The smaller Navy boats are made of wood," he informed his family, friends, and teachers. "I want the chance to work on these captain's gigs, mine sweepers, lifeboats, and launches." One high school teacher knew all about Eddie's ambitions. As school ended for the summer of 1940, she told him about a high school that had opened "to teach maritime sciences and boat building." Eddie was jubilant to be accepted at Metropolitan Maritime High School in Manhattan.

Along the Far Rockaway boardwalk that summer, Eddie saw that the few lit lamps were blacked on the ocean side, for this was the law. Enemy submarines along the coast could use town sightings to locate ports and freighter routes. Vernon put up Blackout Curtains in the guesthouse and at Woodhaven because of possible air attacks. News cables clicked about the new military draft. Eight days later, the country learned about a "Lend Lease" of fifty commissioned flush-deck destroyers going to Britain to defend freighters against German submarines. In exchange, England gave the US 99-year leases for air and naval bases from Trinidad to Bermuda.

Eddie traveled to his new Manhattan school by an elevated train, which became a subway after crossing the Williamsburg Bridge. The curriculum in the eighth grade was similar to high school. Seniors took a wooden boat-building class, but try as he might he couldn't get in. Used to getting his way, Eddie did try to circumnavigate the school rules without luck. He took classes on theories of mechanics and physics. He liked learning about marine subjects like engines, propellers, and displacement, but gradually he became critical. "These were glossed over too quickly," he said. "I wanted to know how things worked in detail and not just in theory."

At home, however, he began a project that was detailed and exacting. He converted his bicycle into a "motorcycle." With instructions from *Popular Mechanics*, he mounted an old Maytag two-stroke washing-machine engine, which ran on gas. When completed, he skipped school the next day, claiming to be sick, and snuck out of the house to test it.

"There was a light rain, and I was coming down Jamaica Avenue," he said. "At that time it had cobblestones like little loaves of bread. You have to be careful, but in the middle, to make it worse, were trolley tracks. The trolleys were in constant use, so the tracks were as shiny as chromium. When I got down to PS 197, where I had attended lower school, there was a big policeman on the corner. He put up his hand to stop me, and I tried, but my wheel got caught in the trolley track, the bike fell on its side and skidded into him. He took me out of the rain into a nearby shoemaker's shop, where he often stopped for coffee." Eddie told him he had motorized the bike, which impressed the policeman. But, he had a message for the young cyclist. "He said if I didn't get rid of that blasted thing, he would personally send me to reform school!"

Eddie knew he would have to sell the motorized bike, but it wasn't finished. For better control, it needed a clutch. Ed designed this and made metal parts to adjust tension under the drive belt.

Then he needed a small wooden roller. He thought about this. Then, he remembered seeing Rudy's mother, a German lady, making strudel with a large rolling pin. "I convinced Rudy," he said, "that if we cut off the end of her rolling pin and put it on the engine for a clutch, that she would never know." After Rudy furtively smuggled it out of the kitchen, the young engineer cut off a section and fit it into his clutch assembly. On trial runs, over quiet streets, the wooden clutch worked. Ed had succeeded. He soon sold the "motorcycle" for thirty dollars to a friend.

The clutch caper was a double success. Rudy's mother never mentioned her shorter rolling pin. If she knew, she kept the secret.

Chapter Two

Navy Service
and Civilian Life

AT HIS NEW MANHATTAN high school Eddie Cutts excelled at general boat-oriented courses. He already had a grasp of mechanical drawing from his boat drawings at home. Of course, he had regular school subjects to learn, but being there, with the boating environment and the advanced courses for higher grades, made him feel good.

In his second year at the Metropolitan Maritime School, Eddie followed the major news of the World War in Europe. He knew volunteer American flyers called Flying Tigers went to Burma that summer to help China in its long war with Japan. He heard when the US suspended oil shipments to Japan. Americans, however, had focused more attention on England and the war in Europe so were surprised when December 7th shook the country with Japan's attack on the Pearl Harbor Naval Base. President Roosevelt made an impassioned speech to the nation. The next day Congress voted to declare war on Japan. Germany and Italy declared war on the US.

Following school on December 8th, Eddie brought home pictures of President Roosevelt. Knowing his father disliked the Democratic President, Eddie took them to his mother and said, "I want to put them up some place because we are at war." Adelaide agreed. Soon after this, Gladys dropped in with her two boys and her husband Alexander Somerville, who walked up to the President's photo. "I won't stay in a house with a picture of Roosevelt," he said, and promptly turned his family around to leave. He blamed Adelaide without knowing what had happened. Family relationships were far from perfect.

The universal draft was in effect, but Ed's older half-brother Buddy was exempt because he was thirty-seven with two children. He continued his job at Borden and became an Auxiliary Policeman, at a time when others were volunteering as Air Raid Wardens and Plane Spotters.

Eddie read that the Brooklyn Navy Yard was accepting apprentices. Having lost many hundreds of shipyard workers to the armed forces, the Yard was understaffed. Eddie quickly shared this news with his parents. "It's right up my alley, because they build wooden boats. The life boats, liberty launches, and gigs are all wood." As usual, his parents agreed to this.

Eddie took the required aptitude test. While the results were fine, they didn't point to wooden boat construction. "They decided I should be a machinist because I can run a milling machine and a lathe, and can read micrometers and do close work," he said. "And I can understand what they're talking about."

To work in the Navy Yard, the required age was sixteen. Eddie was fifteen. "It was not a secret many of us were too young, but everybody went off to war, so they needed help desperately." To avoid any violation of Child Labor Laws, the Navy Yard scheduled high school classes, twenty hours a week, on academic subjects. For the other half-week they sent Eddie and others to machinist training. After completing this, they went to the Navy Yard's machine shop. The instructors took Eddie's group to see the new Navy ship they would work on.

"I was confronted," he told his family, "with a ship so large and formidable that with the scaffolding and work structure you could not tell where you were standing. We are helping to build the Battleship *Iowa*. It's lying on its side in its huge dry dock. It looked like the Empire State Building on its side." His parents were impressed.

Eddie, now called Ed at the Navy yard, was slim but strong at 125 pounds when he machined huge scuttling valves. "They weighed over 500 pounds," he said, "and had to be lifted by a hydraulic crane into a huge milling machine." He and the other young men machined and faced the last of the forty valves, which he described as "bronze and half the size of a Volkswagen."

At the Dairy Bar, he told his friends who envied his adventurous work, "Sixteen-inch shells weigh a ton, so if you keep firing tons away, something happens to the trim of the ship." He explained how these valves changed the trim and ballast by letting water in and out of special tanks.

When *Iowa*'s last valve was completed, they worked on smaller parts for other ships. "Many of the young builders played hooky from their classes," he said with a wide grin, "and later on I did too." He didn't want to sit in a class, when there were ships to build. Possibly, Ed was among the high-school age builders dropped for skipping classes, but he had another explanation. "I wanted to earn more money," he said. "They didn't pay very much." As a result, he wasn't present when the Navy Yard launched the *Iowa* on August 27, 1942.

His military service records revealed Ed studied engine mechanics and marine and aeronautical engines at Woodrow Wilson Vocational High School. "The big steam reciprocators and large steam turbines, the boilers and boiler systems, all those things were extremely interesting," he said. "They were as big as a house."

In the winter of 1942 with his sixteenth birthday weeks away, Ed went out with his father and found a car after his own heart — a 1933 Plymouth convertible with running boards and a rumble seat. Eddie added his $30 from the sale of his motorbike and other earnings to what his father paid. Now, he could tiptoe out of the house at night to take secret practice runs around the block, preparing for his driving test.

After the engine course, Ed landed a job as an assistant garage mechanic also doing fender and bodywork. He did this for a year. He was searching for a better paying position when a friend, Brand Meier, told him about an opening at a machine shop. So in April 1944, Ed started at Ludlee Plastic Engineering in Sheepshead Bay, where he worked, as he said, "to .001-inch tolerance." The company manufactured high-pressure metal dies for companies making plastic buttons, which were replacing bone and metal. His parents disagreed on whether he would be better off in high school.

In the summer, Ed met a pretty local girl named Jeanne Yanitelli, and they both fell in love. At the beach, with Jeanne or with his family, he saw planes heading out to sea on late afternoons. "They were out of Floyd Bennett Field and some would fly down the beaches," he said. Coast Guard boats patrolled off shore. Overhead he could see blimps and light planes of the Civil Air Patrol. All were searching for submarines.

Although Vernon was patient and good natured, sometimes Ed and Addie heard their parents' voices raised in heated arguments. Though unable to hear clearly through the closed doors, Ed understood what was going on. He had known, for years, how his dad was unhappy with the carpentry, painting, and house repairs, after a full work week. "I loved the two of them," Ed said, "and they fought all the time. They argued over finances because my mother was in all kinds of business. She was sharper than my father." Adelaide Cutts, a skilled business woman, handled the money from the family-owned buildings. But, she was always concerned with providing for her children's future. Ed knew this, but also knew how much work his father did. "He was a good dad and always took care of us."

Vernon Cutts and his second wife Adelaide whom he had married in 1915.

Cutts Family

In spite of Adelaide's success as a singer and actress, neither Ed nor Addie had theatrical aspirations. "My mother was beautiful when she was young," Ed said, "but I don't think Addie was. She was just an ordinary girl, just as I wasn't handsome, but just a regular guy. But my father was handsome — he looked like General MacArthur and carried himself well."

Ed often joined his parents listening to war reports of Edward R. Murrow, Eric Sevareid, Howard K. Smith, and others. "When I became older, I was really into following everything going on." The daily papers and *LIFE* magazine informed the Cutts household of bombed cities and fast changing battle lines. Sometimes it took a week or longer to learn the outcomes because of slow communications and censorship.

Eddie planned to join the Navy at seventeen, before he could be drafted into the Army, and wondered if he would serve on the *Iowa*.

On a rainy Saturday night in October 1944, Ed and his friend Charlie Brady went to their favorite hamburger place. In Charlie's old Ford, they drove to Howard Beach, turned left to Weiss's Restaurant on Jamaica Bay to order their hamburgers. They knew Mr. Weiss, who was standing near onions and pastry pyramids.

Afterwards, they ran to the car as the rain storm worsened in intensity. The sky was black. They headed north in poor visibility with darkened stores and scattered streetlights. At a movie entrance, people took shelter under a dim marquee with blurry unreadable letters. As they crossed Jamaica Avenue, over the pelting rain and engine sounds, Ed thought he heard a voice calling, "Eddie, Eddie." He wasn't sure. He squinted out the side window at figures on sidewalks through moving lenses of water, unclear and blurry. He knew no one living there. Charlie kept steadily driving to the wipers' rhythm.

The next day Ed heard that Jeanne had been killed the night before, near the spot where he heard his name called. He learned later that an older gentleman had hit her. "Visibility was very bad, and he had an old car." He hadn't known which movie she was working at. "She was only trying to make Christmas money so she could buy gifts for everyone. She was one of the most extraordinary people — and she was only sixteen when she was killed. My God, everybody was devastated." Almost sixty years later, he stared ahead, silent, eyes tense, and remembering. One could see how grief had struck him head on. After Jeanne's death, Ed said he felt shaken and wondered what to do.

It wasn't long until he joined the Navy on December 29th, 1944, three days before his eighteenth birthday. Following basic training at Sampson, New York, the Navy sent him to NAATC

Aviation Ordnance School in Norman, Oklahoma, for another eighteen weeks. At San Francisco's Mare Island Naval Shipyard, he repaired and set up bomb racks and machine guns. The war ended on August 13, 1945. Ed remembered that it was two days later when he boarded the *USS Pelias* (AS 14) bound for the Naval Base at Pearl Harbor, Hawaii. This Griffin-class submarine tender had been converted from the former luxury liner *SS Mormacyorka*. The ship continued to observe blackouts at night as a precaution, Ed said. At Pearl Harbor he worked on bomb racks and machine guns for Navy and Marine Corps aircraft. These were: Douglas Dauntless dive bombers, Consolidated amphibious patrol bombers (PBY flying boats), and Grumman Hellcat carrier fighters. On August 28, Ed's official records show he transferred to Carrier Aircraft Service Unit.

His assigned carrier had been part of the Naval force at Japan during the signing of the Peace Treaty. The *USS Cowpens* (CVL-25) had been converted from a light cruiser and carried thirty planes. The trip ended when Ed and other men disembarked at an amphibious base on Manus with an airstrip. On this Admiralty Island the Japanese had once constructed extensive tunnels and underground bunkers. Manus was in the Palau chain near Guam, as was Peleliu where there were huge casualties.

It was more than a year after final mopping up, Ed said, when he and other Navy men were assigned to the volcanic island. The far end of the island was heavy jungle, so no one had any reason to go there. During sweltering September days — they were on the Equator — off-duty men swam in the ocean. One time Ed and others were swimming when they saw spouts of water here and there. "We figured fish were jumping," he said. But, the mysterious spouts kept up. This seemed to happen around where the men were swimming. Suddenly, a swimmer shouted, "Someone is shooting at us!" In the immediate response, men rushed ashore and over the sand, yelling and swearing.

"I can tell you that Jesus wasn't the only one who walked on water," Ed said. "We got out of there as fast as we could. That's about as near as I came to getting a hole through me." Word spread around, and swimming came to a halt.

The evidence that hostiles remained on Pelau answered some curious thefts. "Guys would come out at daybreak," Ed said, "and see their things missing from the wash lines and would think other military units took them." Japanese solders were infiltrating the base at night. "They would steal food if they could get it, thinking the war was still on." As a result, the military brought in a retired Japanese admiral who persuaded them to "surrender with honor."

Ordnance Technician Cutts was sighting machine guns on warplanes. He lined up the target through the barrel and fired to check accuracy. With peace and less ordnance work, the Navy assigned him duty as a gunner on a PBY that was flying circular patrols. These flying boats were the work horses of the Naval Air Service. Ed's plane was an earlier model more suitable for a museum. Instead of metal wings, this plane's wings were canvas covered. But, it had metal under the two overhead motors — for engine mechanics to walk on and to prevent fire. "It was a good plane with almost no glitches, but it shook you to death," Ed said.

He often talked with the pilot and sometimes sat briefly in the co-pilot's seat. One time Captain Goldberg told Ed he had dropped a cigarette into the low walkway that ran aft. "I have to find it, so take over." Climbing off his seat, Goldberg said, "Just keep her steady on course." Then he vanished. Ed grasped the wheel of the noisy vibrating plane, which weighed over 17,000 pounds, with a wingspan of 104 feet. "All I could think was I mustn't crash with six other guys aboard," he said. "So I held it as steady as I could." Finally, Goldberg climbed back with a butt in his mouth and casually took over. Years later, after he had learned to fly, Ed decided the Captain "must have put the plane on autopilot to play a trick on me."

In 1946, the Navy began shutting down the base and removed reservists like Ed Cutts. As the base emptied, the Navy loaded barges with damaged planes and materials and dumped these outside the Palau reefs. They were shutting down the base, Ed said, and didn't want anyone to find and use military property. Coral reef destruction was not an issue then.

Ed came into the Naval Training and Personnel Distribution Center in Shoemaker, California. The base is no longer there, but at the time they called it "Fleet City," and it included a Naval Hospital and nearby Sea Bee Base. Men awaiting discharge filled openings such as mess detail, but Ed landed laundry duty. On July 22, 1946, the Navy moved Ed to his former ship, USS Pelias, berthed at Mare Island, San Francisco. A month later, he received an honorable discharge and discharge pay of $219.19. He rode to New York by a troop train with smoke and cinders coming in open windows.

At home once more, Ed Cutts planned to find a boatyard job. He reasoned it shouldn't be difficult, following his machine-shop, Brooklyn Navy Yard, and ordnance experience. He had a special fondness for City Island. "It was," he said, "the Mecca for boat building. Almost everyone on the island was connected to the yachting industry." He applied at the Nevins, Consolidated, and Minneford yards where crews were actively building boats. No one offered him a job. He soon discovered why the odds were against him.

"After the war, the shipyard workers came back," he said. "They had been replaced to keep those yards working, and a whole new apprentice group had been taught. The thousands who had worked in the shipyards before wanted their old jobs again, and the law backed them up." There were more experienced boat builders looking for work than there was work. "I looked and looked," he said, "but there was nothing."

Like many veterans, Ed Cutts came from doing skilled technical work in the military and found closed doors as a civilian. He applied at all area boatyards building recreational boats, including: Bruce and Knudson, the Bunch Yard, Chute and Bixby, and William Wood Jr. He also went to Fyfe's and Purdy. At each place he told them that he wanted to learn and was willing to start at the bottom. There were still no openings. "I was sort of down-hearted," he said. Even with special skills, he was jobless, unwanted as a trainee, and living at home.

Ed had been out of work some months when his cousin Muriel visited the Cutts' house with her husband Fred. They noticed Ed's despondent manner, which surprised them. They heard him say, "I've got to find something!" which he had been repeating to himself for many weeks. Fred, who was a lead compositor for a Manhattan printing firm, studied Ed for a moment.

"How would you like to learn typesetting?" he asked.

"Well-l-l," Ed drew out the word. He thought how this would be a way to earn some salary. He could still visit yards on weekends and draw boats in his free time. Fred was carefully observing him. Ed asked, "Do you really mean it?"

"I do. If you want to learn the business, I can help you."

"Okay, why not? Anything's better than nothing."

Fred promised to teach him typesetting when they had any free time, but he warned, "They'll keep you running all over the place." And they did. Ed traveled Manhattan by bus, subway, and elevated trains, but mostly by foot, carrying packages of printing orders. As promised, when Fred had the time, he taught his cousin typesetting.

"Somehow it came easy to me," Ed said. "In those days you set lead type on a Linotype machine, or a Monotype, or a Ludlow for headlines, or with hand setting." Ed discovered he was good at typesetting. After two years he became restless again, wanting a better salary. Based on what he had learned, he moved to a Long Island City printer. "The company was doing an artistic type of printing. That appealed to me because I liked the beauty of things well done." Making choices about how to do the layout interested him. "It was graphic art, and drawing boats was also a graphic kind of art."

The foreman, a seventy-five-year-old German, was a good man, but many found him difficult. Ed got along well with him, watched and learned, and eventually was doing the foreman's work. When the older man suddenly decided to leave, the owner and managers talked about hiring a new foreman, and then noticed Ed turning out good work.

"They found me doing design work and making sure the presses were ready to run. For example, you try to use similar colors so you don't have to keep washing them." As a result, they promoted Ed to foreman at twenty-six. A welcome salary increase allowed Ed to buy a car, but he kept his Indian Scout motorcycle.

Ed was still living with his parents, so he was saving money for the future. He had a good relationship with his parents; his mother was happy with his salary and skills, and his father appreciated his boat designs and encouraged him to get a little boat of his own. Ed not only saw how much his relatives liked Vernon, but he also heard many stories of his father's outgoing thoughtfulness.

Many family members had fond memories of Vernon. Gladys' son, Dick Somerville, remembered his grandfather, who would sometimes drop in for a visit. "He usually arrived by himself. He was a good guy, about six feet tall and lanky. He had a stern face, and people listened when he talked. He smoked a straight pipe, and Mom used to give him tobacco. He was somebody you could sit down and talk with."

Buddy's son, Bob, recalled the time Vernon helped his father repair a 15' open boat. "They put a new keel on it, and I remember my grandfather drilling a shaft hole. They ran the shaft through, and it turned out great. He was a very talented man." At their Long

Island summer place, Bob often went crabbing or fishing with his grandfather early in the morning. "He was a real gentle fellow, and he was intelligent just like Ed. He didn't try to impress you."

Vernon's wife Adelaide wasn't as well liked. Gladys told her son Richard that the meals were small at the Cutts'. "You could starve to death in that house," she said. Ed Cutts, at seventy-nine, defended his mother, saying that even with food rationing during the war, the food was good. "My mother put everything on the table, but she thought very carefully about waste. Gladys didn't starve to death. It was just that you didn't have to go on a diet if you lived there. It was good food, top notch, all fresh — but she was stringent with it. Meals were a little on the lean side, but if you ate the meals, they were healthy. You didn't gain weight." Ed's mother, although frail in her senior years, lived into her nineties as did Vernon.

Buddy's daughter Virginia Erickson recalled her first and only ride on a motorcycle when Ed came over to their house in Ozone Park. "I was a teenager of sixteen or so, and he must have been in his early twenties when he asked if I would like to go for a ride, and I said sure. This was in the days before helmets." She didn't know if they went above the speed limit, but said, "It was just kind of breathtaking for me. We rode around the meadows before Kennedy Airport was built, and I had the time of my life." She returned from the ride with wind-blown hair, quite a while later. "Well, of course, my mother thought I was long since in a ditch somewhere."

While working in the printing company, Ed toured boatyards on Saturdays, looking for an opening. "Boat building was a strange business," he said, "because a company would get an order for a boat, and then if it was a good-sized boat, they would have to find people to work. When the work was over, you were let go." At Purdy's the largest boat built in Port Washington was nearing completion in 1950. Phil Rhodes had designed the 81' 10" auxiliary diesel ketch, originally named *Constellation* but launched as *Blue Swan*. Ed saw it when he visited the boatyard.

Fiberglass boat manufacturing was spreading and was then practiced on the North Shore. Lunn Laminates in Glen Cove came out in 1949 with *Challenger*, an 18' fiberglass daysailer. The 1950 New York Motor Boat Show, which Ed attended that year had twenty-two different models of fiberglass boats. Cape Cod Shipbuilding was producing Herreshoff's popular *Bulls Eye* in fiberglass. Naturally, Ed focused on the wooden boats, ignoring the others.

In 1951, J. H. Bill Dyer produced at his yard a 42' fiberglass, double-ended ketch named *Arion*, designed by Sidney Herreshoff. At that time it was the largest fiberglass auxiliary sailboat. Fiberglass (originally spelled with one "s") manufacturing methods were changing constantly with new materials. The early practical use began in the military. Dyer had built military landing-craft hulls of fiberglass, so he could draw on this experience with a successful Dyer Dhow in 1949. Fiberglass powerboats still had to win over boat buyers, but skiffs for outboards were selling around the world.

While hoping to build boats, Ed's social life centered on the beach and also the ice cream parlor on Jamaica Avenue. Among a dozen regulars, he liked one girl in particular. "She was dating someone else," Ed said, "and I was too at the time." His current interest was the niece of the printing company's owner who worked at the company. On a date, he confided to her that some time in the future he would be leaving his printing job to build boats. "Would you consider joining me when I do?"

"Oh no," she said. "I can't leave my aunt. I'm sorry, but that's how I feel."

"Well, if you think more of this damn company," Ed replied. "But I have to see what the world has to offer." The friendship foundered.

Ed decided to pay more attention to Marguerite Buttner, whom he termed "pretty and smart." Her friends called her "Maggie."

On a chilly, rainy night he dropped by the Dairy Bar to discover that she was the only one of the regulars there. So he invited her out to dinner. "I took her to Lundy's, a good restaurant near Coney Island, for a lobster dinner. Having enough money, I could take her places where her boyfriends couldn't, which gave me an advantage over the competition." Maggie responded with genuine interest when Ed talked about boats and his future ambitions. He took her to the 1953 New York Boat Show, where she saw he was drawn to a book that grabbed his attention. He spent time looking through it, so she bought this for him. *The Common Sense of Yacht Design* by L. Francis Herreshoff became a crucial part of Ed's design education and training.

As Ed studied the boat designs and descriptions, he often thought of the author. At that time, Francis Herreshoff lived and worked in Marblehead, Massachusetts, where he designed boats and wrote for *The Rudder* magazine. Earlier in his career he had worked with Boston naval architects Burgess, Swasey, and Paine. Herreshoff's designs were built at the boatyards he liked, such as George Lawley's yard in Neponset, which shut down after the war. But his favorite yard had been the Herreshoff Company in Bristol, Rhode Island.

After R. F. Haffenreffer bought the yard in 1926, Francis Herreshoff still sent clients there. In 1939, the boatyard landed a government contract to make Navy Patrol Torpedo (PT) boats. Some pleasure-boat building continued in other boatyards until they ran out of wood and hardware. Defense industries were in full production with the threat of war spreading to the United States from England and Europe. Many boat building companies also built for the military.

The Herreshoff yard went out of business in May 1945, when the demand for PT boats had ended. Soon, after that, the War ended. This was Ed's favorite yard, and he often spoke of it. "The greatest builder of them all was Herreshoff in Bristol, Rhode Island.

They had a great tradition of building America's Cup contenders, yachts designed at first by Nathanael Herreshoff." His fourth son Francis and his older brother Sidney designed boats built, later, at the Herreshoff Company.

Ed Cutts, while continuing his printing work, in his free time studied the construction plans and design information in the Francis Herreshoff book. He was ecstatic about the volume, which encouraged his own drawing and which taught how a great designer worked and thought. "It was the only book of wooden boat building worth a damn," Ed said. "That's if you had enough moxie to read between the lines and to read the drawings. His stuff was superb."

Ed had many questions. He wanted to learn, he said, "why certain choices had been made." How had Herreshoff arrived at something? This analysis was important. Ed was trying to train himself to think like the great designer. As Ed worked to improve his own designs, more questions would come up as he studied the book. Now, he had a new goal — to meet with the famous author.

Ed planned a trip north to talk to Francis. He didn't write ahead, he said, because a letter from a stranger might not get an answer. But, if he went to Marblehead, he might meet Herreshoff to say hello, and then follow up with a letter. Ed told Marguerite and his parents, "It will be a good opportunity to see what they're building up in Massachusetts."

Chapter Three

L. FRANCIS HERRESHOFF
AND NEVINS

On a beautiful Saturday in the fall, Ed drove his Indian Scout through Connecticut and and north to the Boston Road, his destination northeast of Boston — Marblehead on the Atlantic between Salem and Swampscott. The custom work on the small cycle, which he had polished, often caught the sun. As he drove, the wind hitting him made him look thinner. Although close to six feet, he was wiry and strong. On his head were sun goggles but no helmet. He was enjoying the ride and had previously traveled as far as Canada on this Indian, lending his other motorcycle to a friend.

In Marblehead, a man gave him directions and pointed to what he called "the Castle," a gray building on a hill. Approaching, Ed saw three turrets and a roof with battlements like a small medieval fortress made of gray stones. Ed parked his motorcycle near the stone steps, collected himself, and quickly combed his hair. Daunted by the looming fortress, he considered leaving. As a stranger, who was he to bother this famous marine architect? "Drawing on moxie," as he phrased it in later years, he climbed the stone steps and knocked on the heavy oak door, studded with bolts. "Certainly I had gall," he said, "for I was only twenty-seven, to go and knock on the great, thick door of that formidable castle."

When the door opened, standing there was the owner — a tall impressive man of good posture without an ounce of fat, with a trim medium goatee and mustache, which gave him a military look. He wore casual khaki clothing. Ed recognized the yacht designer at once from photographs. "Oh, Mr. Herreshoff, my name is Eddie Cutts, and I read your book, and I couldn't pass through without telling you how much I enjoyed it."

Herreshoff thanked him and then looked down at Ed's Indian in the driveway. He said he loved motorcycles and had owned some. He invited Ed to come in. They first talked about Herreshoff's yachts before Ed asked for advice. "I study drawings of yachts as carefully as I can. For years, I have hoped to design."

Showing interest in his visitor, Francis Herreshoff listened patiently before he spoke. "If you are serious about designing, you should find work in a boatyard and learn by building boats. A designer will never be exceptional, if he doesn't build his own work." Ed inscribed those words in his mind and then asked questions about things in the book. Later, he drove down to the boat-filled Marblehead harbor where he walked into some boatyards. Relishing the building work going on, he noted the different class and one-design boats, some of which were new to him. He burned up the highway going south, feeling triumphant and lucky.

When he arrived home, he told his parents and his girl that he never really thought Herreshoff would invite him in or answer his questions. He was elated, and they were happy for him while wondering what the future held in an overcrowded field.

Eight years after leaving the Navy, Ed Cutts was in love and ready to marry. In December 1954 when he proposed, Maggie accepted. "I gave her the best little ring I could afford," he said.

Boat designer and author
L. Francis Herreshoff,
fourth son of Nathaniel
Herreshoff.

Provident Journal

"We got along well, right from the start." They had a church wedding early in 1955 and moved into a Port Washington apartment.

Following Herreshoff's advice, Ed made regular boatyard
rounds in Brooklyn, Nassau, and City Island. Still, no one was hiring. At McMichael's in Mamaroneck, a man working there whom
he knew named Doug Soper told Ed there was a used wooden
sloop for sale — a *West Coast Mercury*, designed by Neunes. After
taking it out for a trial spin, Ed was sold. The sails were good, the
hull looked fine, but an underwater check revealed that the keel
needed strengthening. He bought the sloop and sailed it to the
Glen Cove Marina and, after hauling it out, removed the keel. To
put in two additional keel bolts, he went to nearby Charlie and

Andy's boatyard to borrow a long bit. Charlie Davidson asked him how wide the keel was, and Ed replied it was two inches at the bottom.

"For sure, you're going to come out through the side of that damn thing," Davidson said.

"I don't think so, because I'm going to be very careful. It's important how I sharpen the bit so it doesn't walk away on me." When Ed began his drilling, Charlie was there to observe, fully expecting the drill to appear. With great care Ed lined it up on the keel and then drilled. The first hole went as planned, so he drilled the second, which he checked. Turning to face Charlie, he said, "Smack in the middle, both times."

The yard owner's face was a picture of astonishment as he leaned over to examine the wood. "Do you know, kid, I'd hire you in a minute?"

"Would you really?"

Charlie nodded, which was the answer Ed needed. On Monday he told the printing company he would be leaving. His first boat-building work, since his Navy service, was here. But, it came with a dramatic plunge from his printing foreman's salary. Maggie tried to change his mind. "What will this do to our budget for the house and the expected baby?"

"I'm going to build boats. I can't be a printer all my life, Maggie." His voice was firm. "This is my chance, and some day the pay will be much better." She saw Ed's determination, and she did want him to be happy.

Boatbuilding was what Ed had dreamed of since he was a little kid. Repairing boats at Charlie and Andy's Boatyard was a first step. He thought nothing could stop him now. Ed regretted an earlier decision when he left the Navy. There had been a post-war program called "52-20" under which the government gave military veterans $20 a week for one year to help with readjustment.

"I had felt slightly guilty about such stuff," Ed said, "so I had never applied for it. Now, I could have used it."

On weekends, Ed sailed his sloop from Great Neck to City Island where he visited the shipyards. If luck was with him, he would find a boat owner who needed an on-the-spot repair. The extra income helped. While there, he liked to check out the large yachts underway or at moorings. One boat he often saw was a famous 33.6' yacht named *Foto*, in which noted photographer Morris Rosenfeld covered major East Coast races.

Ed and Maggie wanted to have a house. After they talked of this desire, and their limited savings, Ed spoke to his mother who agreed to help out. Ed thought of Northport, a picturesque town northeast of Huntington, that had its own protected bay off Long Island Sound. Most important for Ed, the town was convenient to North Shore boatyards. Driving through town in the spring, he saw a street with houses starting to go up. He liked one available lot at the end of the cul-de-sac on a rise. He returned with Maggie who found the location suitable for raising a family. They approved the builder's plans for a 975-square-foot ranch house. Although away from the water, Ed made sure there was room for him to build a future shed for boatbuilding.

Watching the building activity, Ed was pleased to see carpenters doing diagonal tongue-and-groove construction. As they framed his house, the men were putting asbestos shingles on other neighboring houses, so he went over to the foreman. "If you'll give me cedar shingles, I'll put them on the house myself." The company approved, and soon the cedar shakes arrived.

As Ed began work, a man appeared with tools and told Ed he was a house carpenter. "I came over to help you shingle as a good neighbor." His name was Stanley Waszczak. "He was a friendly guy, enthusiastic and a little boisterous," Ed said. "We enjoyed working together and did a beautiful job in half the time."

The couple moved into their new home. The basement, with its 8' ceiling, became Ed's design room with ships' lanterns and overhead beams. He thought of this as the captain's room on a square-rigger.

When he had time, Ed sailed in his sloop. "It was an especially nice little boat and a good sailer, but it was built of plywood, and that turned me off building any boats with plywood," he said. "It was nearly impossible to keep it looking the way I expected the boat should look, no matter how much I worked."

Charlie and Andy's was a big yard, but it didn't rank near the top yards. "Some small boats were being built, but most had to be fixed, so you learned a lot," Ed said. They assigned him to painting, varnishing, and a variety of repairs, but most important to him was observing the builders.

Ed had anxiety about the two-dollar-an-hour salary. For many fields, eighty dollars a week was a fair starting wage in 1955. Maggie understood that boat building was what her husband had to do in life. Although they were receiving help from Ed's parents, she worried about paying the bills for an expanding family. When the healthy baby arrived, he was named Eddie Jr. after his father.

Now that Ed was working at a boatyard, he wanted to visit Francis Herreshoff again. "He had been so gracious to me before. He didn't know, other than our conversation, if I had any particular talent." On his next trip he would bring some of his boat drawings.

After phoning ahead, Ed Cutts drove his car to Marblehead and again parked by the castle, no longer daunting and intimidating. Francis, who had bought it in 1945 from the builder, told Ed it was copied from Eric the Red's Greenland castle, where his son Leif Erickson had lived.

Carrying drawings in cardboard tubes, Ed Cutts followed Herreshoff into the Great Room with its vaulted ceiling, rafters, and massive fireplace. The designer sat in a slightly-worn easy chair, while Ed took an upright seat. At the back of the room, wooden steps led to a design room and office upstairs. It contained a machine shop where Herreshoff manufactured signal cannons and repaired antiques. Stone steps went to the first-floor galley and dining area. Ed never saw these other floors.

Francis Herreshoff folded his arms on his chest and listened to Ed's questions about his articles in *The Rudder* magazine. His answers cleared up anything that had confused Ed. Then, Ed opened boat drawings one at a time and asked the designer for his comments. Herreshoff studied these, questioned things he didn't agree with, and said what he specifically liked. Ed leaned close and learned what he could. He recalled Herreshoff's thoughtful attitude and generous assistance. And he discussed his own methods, said Ed. "If something seemed a little foggy to me, he explained it."

When Ed said he was now repairing boats in a small yard, the conversation shifted to leading boatyards. Francis said he liked the custom yachts made by yards like Purdy, Lawley, Nevins, and Herreshoff. "Rufus Murray, who was in charge of all construction at the Herreshoff yard, came down to City Island to work at Nevins," Francis said. "And he brought several good men with him. Nevins would be the best place for you to work." Ed silently resolved to get there, somehow or other, and felt encouraged as he drove off. He planned to return to the Marblehead castle from time to time, because now he had a teacher and mentor.

Back in Northport, Ed improved his construction plans and drawings. On weekends in 1956, he drove with his toolkit to marinas, trying to pick up side work from any boat owner in trouble. One Saturday morning, he passed the huge Nevins yard at 204 City Island, where a sign announced an opening for an apprentice with experience. Early Monday morning, he was first in line at the office door. "I could then hurry back to my Glen Cove job," he said. Because he could do precision metal work and general boat repairs, the Nevins interviewer hired him.

The first day at Nevins, Ed met Mike Sullivan, overall Supervisor, and Nils Halvorsen, Loft Supervisor, to whom he was first assigned. Nils gave Ed various jobs and kept his eye on him to evaluate this newcomer's ability and potential. The Nevins yard had a history of building well-known racing classes and America's Cup boats. "Henry B. Nevins really loved boats," Ed said. At this time, Carl Havgaard was head of the yard.

Rufus Murray, who had started working at the Bath Iron Works, went to Herreshoff and became Head of Production. During the First World War he went to Luders in Stamford, Connecticut. Tom Nye, Historian at the City Island Museum, New York, said that during WWII, boatyards had "temporary job assignments based upon the need of certain yards to fulfill government contracts. Key people within the industry were sought and asked to take positions. Luders needed Murray's expertise building Subchasers and other military craft."

Ed heard from fellow workers how, after the war ended, the Nevins representative found Murray sitting in a restaurant bar, looking discouraged, and walked up to him. "An owner of a large boatyard in City Island wants to build great yachts like you did at Herreshoff. How would you like to work for him as supervisor?" Murray responded like a spinnaker catching the wind. The rest is boating history.

This meeting set Nevins in motion to become a builder of the first rank, Ed said. "Henry Nevins found it expensive, but he gave Murray and new men the salaries they had been used to or better. Murray deserved this new position, because he was experienced as a supervisor, was a hard worker, and he was Irish." Ed smiled at his joke. He liked the Irish because his mother was Irish.

Rufus Murray brought in Mac McLain who had been the Machinist Foreman at Herreshoff's. And he set up his system of crew bosses, which he had learned at the Herreshoff boatyard. Each department head in different work specialties had seven men working under him. This is what Henry Nevins wanted him to do. The boatyard began building a number of custom yachts concurrently. "Rufus Murray supervised all the work and immediately changed the quality of the boats and the way things were done," Ed said, with enthusiasm. "Nevins became one of the finest yacht-building companies anywhere in the world. But it was nowhere near the size of the Herreshoff Company, which at one time had employed three hundred men — the greatest of all boat-building companies in the United States, or anywhere else in the world."

Tom Nye said Murray brought methods he had used at Herreshoff. For example, when building more than one boat of the same design, Murray had them "building hulls, framed and planked, upside down, and then turning them right side up to finish." Later, Murray became the Nevins vice president. "While Murray, as proficient as he was, offered much to the Nevins Yard success, he did join a staff of first-rate shipwrights, who on their own right were among the best in the industry," Nye said.

Rufus Murray died in 1943. When Ed Cutts began working there, in 1957, the system of crew bosses continued in place, along with Murray's high standards. Nils Halvorsen moved Ed to various bosses, or "whips" as they were called, when they were short handed.

In his seventies, Ed remembered their names like family members. He wrote these down: "Bill Hodges, Bill Towers, Adolph Trahan, Jerry Moen, and the LaBlanc Brothers." Other bosses, unknown to Ed, had outside crews doing cradles, painting, and hauling work. Ed estimated that the yard had about fifty-five men when he was there.

With Nils watching and advising him, Ed did a variety of jobs as an apprentice and trainee. He was learning skills, while his abilities developed to meet the high standards of the yard. When Leo and Tom LaBlanc needed help building spars, Nils assigned Ed to work in their loft. This measured 52 by 175 feet in order to work on spars for the large yachts they constructed. "We built some of the most beautiful masts you ever saw in your life," Ed said. "We used Western spruce, which didn't have a knot, and it was just gorgeous stuff as if it had been made in heaven." The advantage of spruce compared to other woods, he said, was the high compression strength and the light weight. He remembered the LaBlancs were meticulous. "If we were making spars for 12-meter boats, they would build the shape the designer wanted. There might be a pear-shaped section, or there might be a rectangular section, according to what the designer specified," Ed said. "There was a methodology that was generated a hundred years before, and the expectation was perfection.

"Many of the glues hardened with a color similar to the spruce, so you would have to squint closely with an eyeglass to detect a seam. When the spars were very long, they were pieced together with long scarfs as strong as the mast itself. There were no fastenings used on these," he said. "Electric wires were inside for lights, and the sail track was screwed on the back side."

Ed also worked in the cabinet shop next to the spar loft. "The work was beautiful, and it was carried down and fitted into the boat." They left everything a little oversize on the sides for final installation, he said.

Nevins made their yacht hardware, said Ed. "Bronze does better in salt water, but brass is used where you want it to shine like gold and where highest strength is less important.

"Nils Halvorsen had worked under Murray who taught him, by osmosis, all he needed to know." Ed had fond memories of Nils, a short man, known for wearing two pairs of glasses at once. "His eyes appeared small because of the reversed magnification. However, he could quickly spot beautiful work, as well as anything less than perfect. He would get real close to study it." After a period of monitoring Ed's work, Nils told his superiors he would like the young fellow to work with him, and they agreed. He took Ed up to his 110-by-125-feet loft, to help with lofting.

Ed tried to be as precise as possible, but this wasn't easy. "You had these tiny plans, and you had to decide certain things during the building. The lines of a boat are subject to the wobble of a man's hand. In lofting you get much closer to the truth of the lines. You could have an error of drawing with one side of a pencil line or the other side. It could be a 32nd of an inch, so now when you blow it up in scale, sixteen times, you can spot it right away as a ½ inch error or greater. So it could be corrected in full size on the loft floor."

Nils Halverson puts down molding for framework at the large Henry B. Nevins loft.

City Island Nautical Museum

As Ed became more experienced, he noticed that not all of the designs were of the same quality. "Nils would build whatever design you gave him, and he would build it beautifully. Even if it was mediocre, he would build it just as carefully as a grand piano." Ed also benefited from Nils talking to him confidentially on what he thought of different boat designs. Nils took a liking to Ed and invited him to his home to discuss their work and to meet his wife.

In his first year at Nevins, Ed brought some of his boat drawings to Nils, who quietly studied them. "He asked why I did this or that, nodding in understanding and agreement when I explained. Sometimes he questioned, but he was always helpful, kind, and very encouraging." Was Nils Halvorsen another mentor? "Yes absolutely," Ed said with emphasis. "He taught me things Murray had taught him. I tried to learn everything I could, and I would ask him hard-to-explain questions. He would tell me what he knew — and he knew an awful lot."

Foreign-made yachts sometimes motored in to Nevins for provisioning or special work, and these gave the Nevins people a chance to compare them with their own boats. Ed joined in looking at these boats for design differences and workmanship. There were companies in Europe at that time producing beautiful boats, but he believed Nevins work was better. "Our finished boats were like the finest furniture. The English boats were well made, but not quite on a par with Herreshoff or Nevins. Even the Germans sent some boats over that were not quite up to par," he said. "That's how good we were at the time." Ed spoke with quiet sincerity and with obvious company pride if not exaggeration. "It was the most marvelous thing for me not only to be at Nevins, but also to be there with the very best in the world, working directly with them.

"Nils put me in these different places so I could learn," he said. "So I would understand the whole works. Everything was business. There were no long bull sessions." He said that Nils "insisted that the work be good. He was so generous to me and so important to me and I loved him." Nils at that time was getting on in years, while working with his two glasses and his face usually just above the loft floor for greater accuracy. That was the way he appeared in photographs.

When General Sarnoff, founder and head of the National Broadcasting Company, had his 85' motor yacht built at Nevins, Ed helped build the cabins and install the engine. At the launching of *Electron*, Sarnoff gave a bottle of whiskey to each of the builders, including Ed.

For two years, Ed continued at Nevins, gaining this valuable experience, but his apprentice salary was a problem. Family responsibilities increased when baby Linda joined two-year-old Eddie. "I was enthralled to be working under Nils, but my wife was not enthralled with my paycheck," Ed said. His salary was still $80 a week. The long trip to City Island, with two tolls, was an additional expense on a tight budget, but Ed knew that working under Nils and top supervisors was a priceless reward. He would hold on a little longer.

There came a time when Owens Corning Glass approached the Nevins Yard to test out a new type fiberglas (spelled with one "s" in the early days). "They chose Nevins, being a high-tech yard, with a great reputation," Ed said. He knew nothing about this material when Nils assigned him and others to work on it. They wanted Ed to collect data on this, because they felt he had an analytical ability.

Nevins was building seven Sparkman and Stephens mahogany yawls, called the *Nevins-40*, although Ed said they measured 39' 9" length overall (LOA). There was a great deal of interest in these new racers, but they were constructed in a closed shed, out of bounds to visitors and photographers. Before they were all sold, Sparkman and Stevens ordered another seven built. At this point, the yard announced seven were to have standard canvas decks, but the other seven would have decks of the new fiberglas formulation, if the owners agreed. Owens Corning covered the expense to make sure their product worked in these early trials.

After the application to the full deck on one sloop, Ed and the others went home, expecting it would harden overnight. The next morning, instead of a beautiful finished deck, Ed and the others discovered what he called, "a sticky mess like molasses." The manufacturer's technical people arrived, blamed it on a bad batch of resin, and took a sample back to study.

"We had done everything in exact accordance with instructions. Personally, I was horrified and disgusted," Ed said. "We scraped it off and tried a different formula. This looked better when it dried, but unfortunately it proved to be dangerous. The deck was treacherously slippery when wet. They discovered it was necessary to add sand."

From a historical viewpoint, Ed was in on the ground floor of the first marine fiberglas deck. But he hated it. He asked Nils to take him off the project, and added, "I came here to learn the beautiful art of wooden boat building." He was angry, disappointed, and being honest. As Ed remembered, he was the only one of the boatbuilders to speak out against the new product. They loved wooden boats as he did, but they stuck it out. Nils understood and assigned him to the standard-deck yachts.

Putting canvas decks on other S & S yawls was fine with Ed. "A special loose-woven duck was used," he said. "This was set in white lead over a painted deck. It was painted, immediately, with thinned paint, to wick the white lead up thru it. It was an excellent method, if done right, and the labor was not expensive.

"When I thought of the loss of skill that would be instigated by working with horrible 'slops,' I was disenchanted immediately," said Ed. From that time on Ed could never consider building with fiberglass, but other boatbuilders switched. Owners of fine, well-designed fiberglass boats may disagree with him, but many will understand and share Ed Cutts' love of wooden boats for their lines and classical tradition, workmanship and joiner work, and sailing qualities.

Some great wooden-boat designs would become available in fiberglass, one example being the *Herreshoff 12½* manufactured by Cape Cod Shipbuilding. This was an early fiberglass production boat from a popular design with great lines and excellent sailing qualities by Nat Herreshoff.

With no sign of a salary increase after two years, Ed was geared for more responsibilities at a new boatyard. He desperately wanted to design boats. This desire led him to drive to a busy Port Washington boatyard when he had the chance. In appearance, Ed was what people called lanky, but it was a solid hardness coupled with fine coordination and a steady hand. As he walked from his car in long strides to find the owner, his windblown hair was a distinguishing feature, as was a prominent sharp nose.

Thorsten Peterson examined Ed's sail and power-boat drawings. After learning he was a Nevins man who wanted an opportunity to design, Peterson hired him at a good salary with a promise of design work. Nevins was highly respected in the entire boating community, as Ed well knew, and Peterson's attitude clinched it. Ed explained, "All anyone had to say was, 'I'm a Nevins man,' and people knew what you could do since you were working on the finest boats."

Now Ed had the difficult task of explaining his leaving to Nils Halvorsen, who was the one most responsible for Ed's lofting abilities and for placing him under expert "whips" who had trained him. For so many years Ed had wished for such an opportunity, so he knew how much he owed to Nils. At the meeting, Ed thanked him for his expert guidance. He came to the difficult part. "I'm sorry, Nils, but I really can't afford to work here, with two young children and a house." Nils understood Ed's reasoning, and the two parted with a handshake as good friends.

Ed knew he still needed Francis Herreshoff's guidance and advice to keep improving his designs. "I went frequently to show him what I was doing because he was my mentor." At the Marblehead Castle, an expensive foreign car was often parked out front, and one time this was a gull-wing Mercedes. "Francis liked beautifully designed vehicles and once owned a Ferrari," Ed said, "but he lived simply and quietly, and never married."

Sitting in his comfortable armchair, Herreshoff resembled a military officer of a bygone era, with his mustache and trim goatee making his face appear longer. While he would wear stylish clothing when going out, he greeted Ed in casual clothing, adding a sweater in cooler weather. He would cross his arms, looking relaxed and alert, and wait for Ed's probing, design-oriented questions. His eyes, sharp and penetrating as seen in photos, indicated his great intelligence. During these meetings, light came from electrified copper torches on the sides of the huge fireplace and from overhead rafter lights, but not much illumination came in the small gothic windows, as Ed remembered. In this replica of Leif Eriksson's castle, Ed enjoyed the atmosphere of this banquet room, but didn't recall any paintings or photographs on the gray walls. It was as austere and classic as its owner.

"He was a funny fellow in some ways," Ed said. "He wouldn't hide his knowledge from me, exactly. On the other hand, he wouldn't advance it unless I questioned him. I would ask how to determine this figure or that dimension in a design, and he would tell me exactly how he determined it. But he wouldn't offer the information just to make conversation."

Ed gave an example of a typical question and Herreshoff's answer. "In a 40-foot auxiliary, in order to have a fast boat, what do you think we should shoot for, knowing what the construction weights are going to be? What do you think its displacement should be? And he would say, 'Well, I did a boat for so and so, and I always wished I had made it a little lighter, and I thought I could have made it lighter by doing such and such.' That's how we went along, with him saying, 'Perhaps if he had chosen slightly different scantlings.' Francis would tell me of different things that he knew, such as formulas that his father Nathanael had generated, or other formulas that he had used. One Herreshoff family standard was ¼-inch planking for every 10 feet of boat. This scantling was calculated for longitudinal strength."

The Marblehead meetings gave Ed a priceless education of what worked and exactly why — such as design choices on successful boats. And he learned from the thought-out opinions and advice on his own drawings. Many beginning designers would have liked this opportunity.

"He was surprised at the questions I asked, but it's how one learns, of course," said Ed. "Francis took his ideas from his father. The closer I could get to the psyche of Captain Nat the better. I wanted to see how he looked at it."

Ed admired Nathanael Herreshoff for his record of great boats, including five America's Cup yachts that were unbeatable. Speaking of the differences between father and son, Ed said, "Francis did not mind sitting at a drawing board three or four days to get something right." But, Nathanael didn't have to do that. "Most people don't know that he had three or four draftsmen at the shop. His drawings weren't for publication or for a magazine," Ed Cutts said, somewhat pointedly. He learned from Nathanael whenever he could, so it is not surprising that Ed made it an early rule not publish designs. But, Francis made his plans available to boatbuilders.

A former Marblehead resident and excellent racing sailor, John Haug of Bailey Island, Maine, said of Francis, "The main thing about him was he was far more interested in designing a good boat than designing a boat for some racing rule that can win in a race. He was interested in a good wholesome boat." Haug added that Francis had never designed anything of fiberglass, which he hated. Francis was known for candid and salty opinions. *The Rudder* magazine quoted Francis as saying, "Fiberglass is frozen snot."

Ed Cutts could also be critical. "I like to call fiberglass boats 'plastic boats.' You know how things made of plastic were cheap and not very good?" He smiled.

Boat companies making boats with the new material had different construction methods, sometimes named in their advertising. In 1955, Herter advertised "Chrome Fiberglas boats, runabouts, canoes and cruisers." In 1956, Wizard's brochure said they were, "one of the oldest, largest and most experienced manufacturers of Fiberglas Reinforced Plastic Boats in the world." Ed's "plastic" comment was right on course.

⚓

Chapter Four

LONG ISLAND BOATYARDS AND EARLY DESIGNS

THORSTEN PETERSON had two boatyards on the North Shore of Long Island, one in Port Washington for building and a larger yard in Glen Cove for repairing and rebuilding. Ed Cutts, who went back and forth working at both, said, "It was all according to where he wanted you.

"Thorsten found out that I was a budding designer and could draw quite well. He first asked if I could design a little boat, a skiff for rowing or an outboard. He probably wanted to see what I could do," said Ed. "He then gave me bigger things to draw for him, and he was pleased with what he saw." Now, Peterson could accept orders requiring an in-house designer.

Ed designed rowing shells for training crews, and after drawing these at home, he helped to build them at the yard. "We had standard, thwarts-hip rowing dimensions for the shells," he said, "but lengthwise they weren't as big because they were for teaching people — individually or two at a time. They were beautiful little things with outriggers and sliding seats. The oars were the same dimensions as the racing boats, and spooned." Francis Herreshoff's brother James had invented the sliding seats.

Sometimes boat owners wanted changes such as a new configuration of a keel, which Peterson assigned to Ed. "If a client had some trouble, I would figure it out," he said. "It could be rigging, chain plates, a mast step or anything."

Customers liked Peterson as did the workers at his boatyards. "He was as interested as we were in what we were doing, but not in a critical or derogatory way. If someone was doing beautiful work, he was delighted, but Peterson himself couldn't draw or drive a nail straight," Ed said. "He didn't have any accent, so I think he must have been born in this country, unless he came over as a child. He was a strange old duck, stocky and a little bent over. He had a funny little facial twitch, that we used to joke about, but everyone liked him."

Peterson often used the drinking fountain in the main shed. Holding a cup of water, he would look around to see what the men were doing before going back to his office. "We called him 'Thirsty Thorsten,' but we never saw him drink alcohol," Ed said.

His daughter Agnes helped in the office. Ed described her as "tall and willowy and movie-star gorgeous. She didn't seem to feel she was anything special, but everyone was in love with her from afar. When she married a policeman, we were all upset."

Peterson's yard built no sailboats, and Ed thought he knew the reason. "Peterson felt there was more money in building power boats, and also less agony. Basically, you built a nice hull and put an engine in it, and then you were finished. But with a sailboat of the same size, you weren't yet begun."

News went around the yard that Wheeler Yachts was going out of business and that Peterson was meeting with them. From the early 1930s this company had produced cabin cruisers called *Wheeler Playmates* in the 30' to 44' range. They had a classic, cabin-cruiser look with brightwork and brass, compared favorably with other manufacturers' boats, and were affordable. When the company closed down, some Wheeler hulls went to Dawn Shipbuilding, and what remained in the yard went to Thorsten Peterson. Ed remembered stacks of lumber, design work, completed patterns, and some partially finished cabinetry.

"We built these Wheelers for Thorsten, one after another. These were below the quality of boats being turned out by Nevins, but were attractive yachts, well-furnished and equipped for comfortable off-shore cruising."

Ed and the other shipwrights were building hulls, finishing cabins, and adding engines and all the interior work. This routine continued for a long time. Ed gradually became disheartened because he wasn't designing, so he analyzed the situation. He decided the boatyard was overextended and focused on completing these yachts. "I could see that Peterson didn't have the inclination or the time to take orders for new designs." Although earning a decent salary, he wanted to keep moving ahead with his dream, so he began looking around for a yard needing a boat builder/designer.

On Saturday mornings, Ed forayed to marinas, tool kit in hand, looking for small repair work from boaters anxious to get out on the water. One weekend when scouting around, he heard a North Shore yard had received an order for club tenders that they couldn't accept, not having a designer on staff. Ed drove to the Seaman Seacraft boatyard in Locust Valley.

Owners John and Albertson Seaman learned of Ed's experience at other yards, liked his designs, and hired him as a builder/designer. Bert Seaman asked him to design two yacht-club launches of about 25', open with motor amidships and seats on all sides. "The sailboats were on moorings," Ed said, "and six or seven people riding out would fill up half the launch with big sail bags and equipment."

Ed told Albert Seaman he couldn't draw the plans at their yard, but wanted to work in his own design studio. He estimated two weeks' work, and they agreed to this. When Ed completed the drawings, he joined others and began the building. The specs were 24' 4" LOA, 7' 3" beam, and 22" draft for the boats, with teak decks and seats. Ed never learned which clubs bought them, but he hoped they were maintained well. The production of these craft continued as they were popular.

Customers know that Ed was always concerned with properly maintaining a boat, and he could go into lectures on the subject. "I didn't know if they used canvas covers on the launches or stored them in a shed. They required the standard care of an open boat where rain can get in. If nobody cares, in the winter, two feet of snow can pile up," he continued. "What hurt me, time and time again, was the work we did to make all the boats as nearly perfect as we could, and then to see how the boats were cared for."

Glen Cove Marina sold them through an ad with photograph in *The Rudder*. When his designs appeared in the magazine, Ed was surprised. While many marine designers would be glad of the recognition, Ed Cutts had mixed feelings. "It could lead to more work for Seaman's and for me. Or it could be copied with slight alterations by other yards." Being copied was one reason for his not wanting to publish boat drawings.

The basement of his home was comfortable for designing and drawing boats, without distractions and without travel time. To Ed it suggested the great cabin of an old sailing ship, and he was comfortable. "Many times, I worked as a boatbuilder by day and designed boats for people at night. I had so much energy I couldn't decelerate myself."

Ed built *Lightnings*, a popular 19' racing class, which Seaman's was turning out for yacht clubs. Olin Stephens had achieved his goal of a boat suitable for family and racing. He had designed the first prototype in 1935 and worked on modifications with the Barnes Brothers of Skaneateles, New York.

In 1960, Boris Lauer-Leonardi, editor of *The Rudder* magazine, ordered a cabin cruiser from Seaman Seacraft. He wanted it to be

31.5' with a round bottom chine-design. Francis Herreshoff had designed his last boat but it wasn't fast. Lauer-Leonardi told Ed he wanted more speed and a comfortable cabin to cruise the New England coast with his wife.

"I always try to find out what a client has in mind because I can design a boat to do almost anything," Ed said. "That's if they tell me correctly what they want. If it's to be a good boat, you're going to be very careful with everything you do dimension-wise with measurements and calculations. I didn't like diesel [engines] because of the weight. They need more batteries because they have to crank at a 15-1 pressure ratio." For this client he wanted to keep the engine light for a better cruising speed. "I just drew it," he said, "and was glad to get back and help them build it." He worked with another builder named John Hickey, and said, "He did fine work."

The Rudder was one of the boating publications Ed liked to read. "Boris had a nice way of writing — a good style, pleasant and poetic, that people liked." When the magazine carried an article by Francis Herreshoff, Ed studied it like a student at Aristotle's feet. Whenever Boris came to check on the building progress, Ed took the opportunity to talk to him about boats, learning what he could. "We talked about the old Herreshoff yard and about Francis. I hadn't told him I knew Herreshoff when we talked about his designs and famous boats."

Boris sometimes visited Herreshoff in Marblehead when he was gathering material for publication. At the Castle, to discuss future articles, he described his new cruiser being built. "There's a young fellow who designed my new yacht," Boris said. "He has a tremendous interest in boat design and in your work and the Herreshoff Company. I'd like him to meet you. His name is Eddie Cutts."

"I know Eddie Cutts," Francis said, "because he comes up to see me. The stuff that Eddie brings me is the best stuff that anyone has ever brought me." In recalling this conversation, Ed could have exaggerated, but Francis did like his drawings. There was an opposite side to the coin when Gregory Mcdonald, of the *Boston Globe*, interviewed Francis. He was seventy-six years old and a man known for colorful opinions. "At the present time," he said, "there isn't one designer in the whole world that's any Goddamned good. No one knows how to draw." (Mcdonald) Perhaps, Francis Herreshoff either exaggerated or was in a bad mood. Others may have heard different comments at different times.

After hearing Boris's account of the conversation, Ed was elated. "It was super encouraging. Herreshoff was the best. You need encouragement like that as a young man. Someone's got to give you a kick in the rear. That was a real boost. Now, I was not afraid to begin producing. I was on cloud nine."

In 1961, when Ed and Boris took the new cruiser for a trial run, Boris was surprised the 6-cylinder Chrysler Crown pushed the yacht 18.8 mph. "When the Seaman Brothers saw how the boat went," Ed said, "they immediately asked me to design a bigger and faster 33' boat." Ed drew this. He also designed a 29' power boat for a customer named Clark, who owned a car museum in Southampton. "People like that would appreciate beautiful work," Ed said. "I did lots of stuff for people I don't remember, little boats or whatever they wanted." When not assigned to other work, Ed continued building *Lightnings* that Seaman's built eight at a time.

Changes were taking place at the Northport house. In 1961, when Eddie Jr. was five and Linda about three, they had a new baby brother, Ronnie. Outside, Ed had constructed a garage to hold his two motorcycles. His next project would be a boat-building shed.

After two years at Seaman Brothers, Ed met a racer who wanted a small fast sailboat, so he drew a 23' racing sloop with a compact, two berth cabin. The customer liked it, so Ed negotiated with Bert Seaman to rent a shed near the front of the yard. It was in the winter when he ordered the wood, made the molds, and started on the backbone. Building his own boat after a full eight hours for Seaman's, added up to a work day of twelve or thirteen hours, he said. "I was full of energy then and had to keep going."

One day, in early 1962, he was shocked to learn his customer had to "drop out." This was a blow Ed hadn't anticipated, although they had only a handshake agreement. Now, he would have to find a new customer to avoid building on speculation, which he couldn't afford. At the Glen Cove Marina, Ed often talked with Alfred Meyer, who was a well-known boat sales representative. Ed knew Meyer was a good judge of a boat's characteristics and called him "extremely knowledgeable." Members of yacht clubs and boaters consulted Meyer to see what was available.

"I need to find someone for this little sloop," Ed said, showing Meyer his designs. "It should be able to do well racing." Meyer checked around and before long introduced Ed to a couple who wanted a wooden boat to race. Helmut and Helga Fontanes were experienced sailors. They liked the drawings, looked over the partially framed hull, and told Ed they wanted it.

Ed Cutts continued working into the night and on weekends to build the sailboat, but after a few weeks he wondered how he could speed the building and still continue his present daytime job. The Fontanes wanted delivery in time for summer racing. Ed was working mostly by himself, and sometimes John Hickey helped him. Although Ed's day work paid the bills, he now realized he would have to build it full time to be ready for the early yacht club races.

He explained to John and Bert Seaman why he had to leave his daytime job, saying he was "available for emergencies, if you need me to change a design or to help with construction, for a few days." This arrangement was fine with the brothers. "They were good to me," Ed said, "and I did what I could when they had trouble."

Manfred Michaelis, Helga Fontanes's cousin who worked at Seaman's, helped Ed build on weekends. At last, the boat and spars were ready, and the sails arrived. When they launched *Cygnet*, Ed observed she sat in the water "exactly as planned" and handled well in trials. The owners soon realized she was fast. In her first weekend race at Sea Cliff Yacht Club she came in 12th out of about 20 entries. She took 2nd the following week, and then won the third race. "Out of ten or twelve races, I won three or four times that year," Helga Fontanes said. "It is a very, very fast boat for its size, and she's very, very seaworthy."

The 1962 Sea Cliff Yacht Club Invitational Race was approaching, bringing in top racing skippers from yacht clubs to the north. With the owners' approval, Ed Cutts and Al Meyer shared the helm and sail handling on this important race. As the race progressed, the little boat pulled ahead. "One time we went around a buoy

The first boat that Ed Cutts built on his own was *Cygnet*. He designed it for the racing rules with cruising accommodations.

Benjamin Mendlowitz

very close," Ed recalled. "No one was breathing down our neck at the end. We knew we were first. As I remember, we beat most all the boats over the finish. They were astounded that this small boat walked away from the whole fleet to win under the handicap-rating system." Helga Fontanes said there were *Meridans*, *Tritons*, and maybe *S Boats* in a field of forty to fifty boats. When asked who was captain on this race, Ed said, "It wouldn't have made any difference anyway, but I suppose I was."

Now that Ed was having some small success, he wanted to concentrate on designing. But, he was building the club tenders and *Lightnings*. This work continued half a year until spring of 1963. "I still had a mortgage on the house," he said, "which seems tiny today, but it was large at the time." He told Al Meyer he would like to find work so he could design at night without being tired from boat building all day. "Do you have any suggestions?"

Meyer soon got back to him. "Eddie, I have a friend who is a boss at Grumman Aviation on Long Island. I asked him if he would be interested in a man who has designed and built boats, who understood lines and the care required. He said he would love to have a person like that." When Ed talked to Grumman, they hired him because he could do precision work in metal and wood and because he understood boat shapes.

Ed told the Seaman Brothers of his planned move. "They were nice fellows and didn't want me to leave," he said. "I never had a disagreement with them."

At first Grumman had Ed making metal patterns for the Olympic class *Flying Finn*. Machined to a 2/1000-inch tolerance through all the hull shapes, these would guarantee that the boats would be identical and conform to these master shape patterns in any country building them.

Once again, Ed began getting some design work on his own. He was glad to have more energy and time for this after his Grumman work. There, he worked on the NASA *Apollo* nose cone. "I made the patterns, usually wood and plastic, for the Grumman design. I was proud of that, although I don't think pride is a good thing. The Bible speaks against that." He paused a moment and took a deep breath. "But we need a boost for our abilities if we are going to do good work."

Following this project, he machined steering nozzles for the original NASA Moon Landing Vehicle, which they called the *TFX*. At Grumman, Ed Cutts was using the latest advancements in metals and materials.

In good weather Ed would ride his BMW motorcycle to work at Grumman, and often, when he returned, "the kids would be lined up wanting to get a ride." Ed would take his children and then the neighborhood children for rides down the street. Among the kids would be the daughter of the neighbor who had helped with the house shingles. "Little Mary Ellen Wasczczak would ring the bell and ask, 'Can Linda come out and play?' She was so little you would open the door and not see her at first," Ed said with a warm smile. His hand indicated about three feet. "I always kept Mary Ellen for the last. I thought the world of her as a little kid."

Mary Ellen remembered that Ed encouraged her at about five years of age, to go to the end of the line of kids. "Then Ronnie, the youngest Cutts, and I would get on. We'd put Ronnie in the middle 'cause he was a little guy, and I'd get on the back, and we would go for a nice long ride down town, the beach or whatever, and back.

"So he was very special," she said. "Mr. Cutts and I had this special little bond. I almost felt that he was my dad in a previous life — because I had an instant love for him and his ways. He was magical and always joking and singing songs and making me laugh. Such a loving spirit.

"He always was fun," she said. "On Halloween, he dressed up in a sheet, hid in the bushes, grabbed us as we were running, scared the living heck out of us, and then squirted us with whipped cream," she remembered. She was about six and living on Madison Street. "He called it Mad Street because everyone was crazy."

During this period, Ed went sailing on his little Marconi-rigged sloop, but he objected to that nomenclature. "Marconi never had anything to do with sailboats, so I don't know why they call it that. It's really a Leg-of-Mutton rig," Ed continued. He thought the name was originally used because of "Guglielmo Marconi's tall radio towers, which suggested a tall non-gaff sail." He didn't like an alternate name Bermuda rig that appeared in yachting magazines.

Over the years Ed sailed with Al Meyer, who owned beautiful boats, including three designed by Nat Herreshoff. "There was the 27' 'S' Boat. It had a curved mast, a tiny jib, and a big main," Ed said. "It had a little more guts to stand up to the breeze and was one of the most raced classes of all time." He also sailed on Meyer's *H23* and also on a 35' racing sloop, and believed that Meyer had about twenty boats one after another. When one needed a repair, Ed would take care of it without charge as repayment for Meyer's help in finding early clients and helping him at Grumman.

"Although Meyer never did any boat building, he was a keen judge of boats," Ed said. "He knew what was right or wrong in the structure and shape, and he was able to spot trouble before it happened." When Meyer wanted to check out a boat for himself or for a client, he would take trips as far as Massachusetts. Ed sometimes accompanied him — an experience that increased his own knowledge of boats.

It seemed like a coincidence after Ed's wartime armament work on Navy aircraft that his next assignment was machining exterior panels for the Grumman F-111 fighter. "Contoured panels were very tricky stuff and were hard to position so they would fit the contours of a particular plane," he said. "They couldn't be off at all. We had Navy inspectors at Grumman, and they simply wouldn't accept anything less than perfection. Some of the panels were the size of a sofa, and some were smaller engine contours. A panel could have been curved in all directions. That's contour, and that's why it's hard to position them."

Many of these metal plates were expensive — Ed guessed thousands of dollars worth of work before they came to his section for drilling. The Chief Inspector, Steve Baylis, noticed that Ed never had a throw-away. "He asked me how I was positioning these contours because once a hole is drilled, it's either dead right or dead wrong. There is absolutely zero room for error. So I showed him how I had figured out a precise method of registering these various-sized panels." Baylis listened to Ed, and after consulting with the Engineering Command, told the metal workers how Ed was doing the operation. "We never had another throw-away," Ed said. "As Maggie would tell you, I got a raise in salary. After that, I came up with several other innovations for Grumman. They just seemed normal to me. They were saving time and money, and each time I got another raise." Before long, the engineering department moved Ed to a desk where he studied the operations, analyzed reasons for problems, and looked for solutions.

"When I was there, I felt rested at the end of the day," Ed said, but of course he was sitting down writing a lot of the time. He continued, "But when you worked hard for yourself, you had to really sweat." This was true when he constructed, evenings and weekends, an 18' x 30' boat shed, with a cement floor, that was attached to his house.

At the Glen Cove Marina, Al Meyer had a customer Abe Oberlin, who couldn't decide on a boat. His first boat had been a *Bulls Eye*. "It was a great little boat," Oberlin said. "But then I purchased a *Schott*, which was a very tender boat — tipsy in a strong wind. The *Bulls Eye* was very stable. It was built for Cape Cod and rough waters and was designed by Herreshoff." Oberlin considered an *International 30* from Norway, but changed his mind and ordered another boat through Meyer. "This boat came in, and

I admired it," Oberlin said. "Then I told him it's not the boat for me and to sell it."

Meyer could see what this customer really needed was a boat built to his own specifications and said to him, "Let me introduce you to a boatbuilder I know who builds great boats."

Oberlin, co-owner of a large dress company, told what happened. "Ed Cutts came over to my house in Baldwin Harbor, and we made a deal that night for a 30' sloop." Ed made the sketch into a drawing with the specified cockpit and cabin dimensions. Oberlin liked it and gave Ed an advance to begin on it.

In January 1965, Ed completed the designs, made a half-hull model, and ordered cedar for planking and oak for frames. Once again he was building a boat mostly by himself. The hull was taking shape in his shed, but he had to be careful about hammering and noisy machines at night because one neighbor complained. On weekends, with help from builder Manfred Michaelis, Ed accomplished more. He wanted to build a boat of Nevins quality, so he made the joinerwork and everything as perfect as possible. Occasionally, he recruited Maggie to help by holding boards. Eddie was nine and Ronnie was four, but they helped with small jobs and carrying lumber. "They felt they were helping, and that was good," Ed said, with a warm smile.

When Mary Ellen would go and watch Ed building the new boat, he sometimes gave her a wood plane. "I would plane the floor boards the boat was sitting on, and he would be planing the bottom of the boat," she said. "I wanted to be with him and doing what Mr. Cutts was doing, and he would find a way to allow me to do that without ruining anything. I'd be planing away and he'd be singing *Barney Google with the Goo-Goo-Googely Eyes* — and making funny faces. I would rather be with him than with friends."

Daughter Linda was six, and her bedroom had a hinged window next to the boat shed. "When I went to bed at night, the bed was right underneath the window," she said. "I would stand on

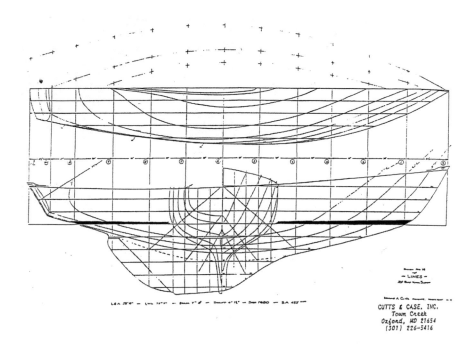

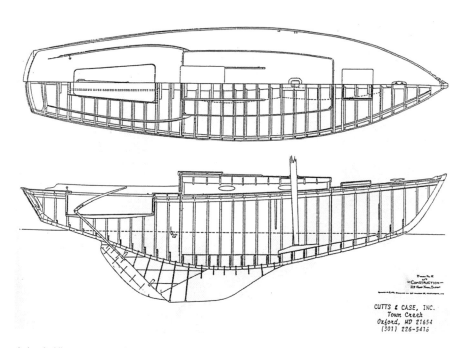

Joie de Vivre construction plan of Ed Cutts.

the bed, and we talked, although I was too little to see him. And he would pass me chocolates through the window. It was fun."

Ed's sister, Addie Durstewitz lived nearby on Long Island and regularly brought her family to visit Ed and Maggie in Northport. When Addie's son Jeff was nine to fourteen, he always looked forward to a special ride with his uncle. "Riding on that BMW touring bike was a big thrill for me as a kid," he said. But Ed also played another role for this boy. "My father was in the merchant marine so I didn't see him very much," Jeff said. "He was gone about 80 percent of the time. Therefore, Uncle Eddie was a surrogate father for me, to a certain extent, more so when both families lived on Long Island forty miles apart. Occasionally I stayed with them in their house for a week at a time."

Jeff sometimes saw his Uncle Ed making bronze hardware. "He was such a fanatic that he even had his own forge in the

In his Northport shed, Ed often had visits from his kids and the neighboring children. This is four-year-old Ronnie who liked to watch and help out.
Cutts Family

basement. It was a small furnace that was hot enough to melt metal. He had to make sure that everything was exactly the way it was supposed to be." Ed always made his spar hardware but gave some things to a foundry.

When Jeff was thirteen, he sometimes helped his uncle in the shed. Ed appreciated the boy's interest. Often needing some help, he would assign Jeff to stack lumber or to hold the end of a plank for planing. "I always tried to keep the kids interested," Ed said. "They all felt they were helping, and that was good. Little Eddie was astute about building stuff. He caught on very fast. Ronnie also caught on quickly, watched me constantly, and tagged after me. He was always my shadow as the smallest kid. I took Ronnie every place with me." This was like Ed's own childhood when his father played a significant role with companionship and encouragement. "In my grandfather's day Vernon was the cook," Jeff said. "I remember going to Sunday dinners at their house in Queens. Uncle Eddie and Aunt Maggie would be there with the whole family sitting around the table. It was usually roast duck. Uncle Eddie picked up cooking from his father." On family get-togethers in Northport, Ed Cutts enjoyed preparing the fine meals.

The 30' hull was framed and Ed was doing the planking. He realized he would soon need to find another customer if he wanted to keep working. Unknown to him, at the Glen Cove Marina, an impressive tall man was looking over wooden sailboats with Alfred Meyer. John Case, formerly a high executive at IBM and at Fairchild Camera, owned a large yacht but also wanted a medium-sized sailboat. One small sloop, different from the usual designs, caught his attention; he looked over its mahogany cabin and ample cockpit. "What a beautiful little boat," he said.

"A friend of mine built that, and he does beautiful work," Meyer said. "It's a very fast boat and has won a lot of races."

"I'd be interested to know what the designer could do with a larger boat."

It was mid-spring of 1965, when Meyer phoned Ed Cutts. "Can I borrow a model of a larger sailboat to show a client of mine who liked *Cygnet*?" Ed brought him a half-hull model of *Joie de Vivre* for John Case to inspect. Later, Case drove over to Ed's house, where he saw the 30-footer, which was almost fully planked — single carvel planked on the bottom and double planked above the water line.

Case sat down with Ed in his Captain's Cabin. "What I want is a boat, 32 to 34 feet, that is not too difficult to handle." He wanted to single-hand the boat and told Ed the number of people he might want to take for a sail. "And another thing, I like double-enders."

"I do too," Ed said. "Well, Mr. Case, why don't you let me draw what I think we're talking about — a masthead sloop about 33 feet overall?"

Following the meeting, Case told Meyer, "I like Cutts's skill and enthusiasm." Al Meyer relayed this to Ed. "I told John Case you built from models like Nat Herreshoff. I said you would certainly have your own yard some day the way you were going. But I don't know if he's interested in anything like that." Meyer had some final advice. "This man is a multi-millionaire. If he wants to do something, stick with him."

Ed completed his drawing and phoned John Case, who invited him to dinner at his place on Centre Island, Oyster Bay. Case was impressed and later told writer Roger Vaughan, "He was at my door with a set of plans four days after I called him. Cutts said if I signed a contract he would quit Grumman and get going on my boat. So I signed." (Vaughan)

"I don't know where we are going to build it," Ed told Case. "If you're in a hurry, we might have to give it to another builder."

Case, who had seen Ed's careful workmanship on two boats, said, "I want you to be in on the building."

"Right now I'm committed to completing work on the 30-footer. There's the deck, cockpit, cabin and spars to do." Ed had to level with him as he strolled around the living room to study models and photographs of the boats Case had owned up to his present 53' ketch *Little Revenge*. He turned to his host. "With all these boats of yours, you could have opened your own yard."

Case found this amusing. "Have you ever thought about having your own boatyard?"

"Of course, I have. It's been a dream to some day have my own place to build wooden boats."

"I've thought of it," Case said, "but I don't know anything about running a boatyard. And I don't have the time or the input to run one."

"I know how a yard should be run, but I don't have the money to open one, John. I only work for a living."

"Well, I have a little money,' Case said quietly. "I can get a small yard."

That evening in Oyster Bay the two launched a partnership. They discussed finding a modest-sized yard, which should be near marinas and boat clubs. Ed knew the North Shore yards, which were expensive.

Case had a yard in mind located at Oxford, Maryland, where his boats had been repaired and painted. "The owner is older," Case said, "and might be ready to retire. I'll contact him."

Ed's dream was almost a reality, but he had an emergency. He was running out of money. On top of that, he had an obligation to tell Grumman he was leaving.

Maggie thought he should wait. "Why not continue as you are doing? Build weekends and evenings, and stay at Grumman," she said.

Ed Cutts had framed the 28' 10" sloop, but now there was no boat money left to continue. He immediately put in a call to Oberlin and asked if he would come and check out the boat. When Maggie walked out to the shed, Ed said Abe would be over in the morning. He casually asked her to buy cold cuts and things for lunch.

Maggie said she not only didn't have any money, but that there was nothing in the bank.

"Oh my gosh! And he's coming tomorrow!" Ed worked late that night getting the boat cleaned up and in better shape.

Abe Oberlin arrived to find Ed and Maggie and their three children lined up outside the boat shed. He examined the hull very slowly going from bow to stern and said, "I'm very pleased with what I see."

Ed said that he would be giving up his Grumman job to build full time. "I'm now out of money, but ready to continue with your boat. There's a good chance I might be getting a small boatyard with a new partner." Oberlin gave him an additional payment, and Maggie produced a light lunch.

For the next few evenings Ed continued building the boat while awaiting word from John Case. He said nothing to Grumman at this point because of the needed paycheck.

While he was working two jobs, Ed thought about the consequential move and about Maggie's objections and family expenses. Everything depended on his partner finding an affordable boatyard in a good location. If John Case found a yard, would they make it a success? In a period of uncertainty, nothing was clear. It was like a wind-driven fog, off shore, erasing buoys and landmarks.

⚓

Chapter Five

New Boatyard and John Case

During winters, John Case berthed his largest yacht on the West Coast. He had once lived in Washington State where some of his yachts were built, but later he made his home in San Bernardino, California. In the spring, his captain would take the current yacht down the Pacific coast, through the Panama Canal, up the Atlantic coast to Norfolk and into Chesapeake Bay. For repairs and sprucing up, it went to a boatyard in Oxford owned by Ralph Wiley.

Chuck Wiley, a boat surveyor, remembered John Case's power yachts coming into his father's Oxford boatyard. "The quality of work in my father's yard was so extraordinarily good that people brought their boats from New York, from Florida, and from around the country."

Each spring, John Case's captain would take his yacht to Long Island where Case used it for New York Yacht Club events and races. In the fall, he went cruising from his house in the American Virgin Islands before the captain took the yacht west again.

John Case always liked Ralph Wiley's scenic unspoiled boatyard on Maryland's Eastern Shore. On a hunch, Case phoned Wiley who had started his yard thirty-six years before. "Ralph, have you thought about selling?" Case asked. There was a pause.

Coming out of the blue, this question startled Wiley, for he had carried this idea in the back of his mind for twenty years since he was fifty-two. He often told his family, "When I get to be sixty-five years old, I'm going to sell the yard and do things like cruising."

Chuck Wiley remembered when his father turned sixty-five. "There wasn't enough given business, as there is now, to sell the yard at what it was worth and for the amount he needed to retire. And now he was seventy-two years old. I had a sail loft in Annapolis and wasn't in a position to take over the yard."

Ralph Wiley knew this was a golden opportunity and that Case could afford to buy it. "I'm getting on in years," Wiley said, "and will probably have to think about selling it. I might sell it for the right price."

"How much would you want?" Wiley gave him a price. Case, who never argued about money, accepted this and said, "I'd like to think it over for a week or so."

Encouraged by this, Case phoned Ed and told him about the yard. "This older guy is going to sell his boatyard soon. Go down and take a look at it."

"I don't want to go down to Maryland and look at mud flats," Ed said. "I like Long Island Sound, and I hope to continue working here."

"There're no mud flats," Case said. "Have you ever been down to the Chesapeake?" Ed admitted he hadn't.

"Well, you're pretty opinionated, aren't you?"

Ed tried a more persuasive tack. "Traditionally, the finest work is done in New England. A location in the South might not attract customers from New England and New York."

"Eddie, it's beautiful down there. I think you ought to go there and look. And take Maggie with you."

Maggie wanted to live in Northport near family and friends. Fully expecting to rule it out, they made the trip south. Driving from Easton, they crossed Peach Blossom Creek, as lovely as its name, and passed the Easton Country Club. Trippe Creek had docks, green-lined coves, and usually some surface ducks or a heron. Before spring migration, one saw flocks of canvasback and teal. Thousands of Canada geese either fed in farm fields or flew overhead in V-formations with their horn-like calls. Ed and Maggie passed winter wheat in fields that had grown tobacco centuries before. Corn would be planted soon. Loblolly pines towered along the quiet road. A small building, formerly a train station for passengers and commercial-seafood shipments, sat by a side road to Trappe, but the tracks had been ripped up. The Oxford Lower School stood at the edge of town, and approaching a Victorian hotel, Maggie and Ed saw a small boatyard on the water to the right.

Oxford was a historical town with narrow tree-lined streets and blocks of white Victorian, Federal, and Colonial Period houses, many with southern columns. In 1965, everything seemed to move at the sedate pace of previous centuries. At the end of the main street, they saw the old Robert Morris Inn, which had been renovated from the original 1710 building. Beyond the Oxford-Belleview Ferry dock, sailboats and some commercial watermen were moving in the Tred Avon, framed by large maple trees in the foreground. The scene recalled when Oxford was once Maryland's second major seaport.

From Tilghman Street, Ed and Maggie turned into Wiley's Boatyard, a large lot that retained its natural beauty on 4.5 acres. The gravel drive ended at the two red building sheds. Red cedar, holly, ash, and white spruce shaded the spacious lot. Tall American chestnut, black locust, and occasional southern pines cast their shadows. The boatyard was facing southeast on a cove of Towne Creek.

"Before I was all the way into the road, I was in love with the place," Ed said. "It was just what a yard should be in my imagination." Maggie and Ed passed a small cottage and saw, nearer the water, a vine-covered house that looked like an old English cottage, but lacked a thatched roof. They parked near a faded red shed with open sides where men were working.

Ralph Wiley showed them the two sheds, the marine railway, and a derrick on tracks. Builders were repairing wooden boats. Then Wiley led them to the ivy-covered house, where he lived, with his office in a weathered addition. He told them the rustic old house, named *Byberry*, appeared in the 1695 town records and was the oldest in Oxford. It had originally stood a quarter of a mile away on Morris Street. That was until he got tired of living on a houseboat, and bought it in 1930, and had it moved to the boatyard. The white houseboat remained on the lawn near the water.

In his autobiography, *Preacher's Son*, Wiley wrote how he had searched to find a contractor who could move it. He made sure the contractor had insurance and then left town on moving day, foreseeing problems. The men removed a shed from the back to get it down the narrow road lined with houses, but the house, rolling on logs, did some damage to buildings and lamp posts. Wiley wrote that the contractor discovered brick and stone under the house's wood exterior, making the move more Herculean than planned.

"It's a post-and-ballast-stone construction," Ed Cutts said later, "with oyster shell mortar covered in wood." He thought the house was built by ship's carpenters and probably earlier than 1695.

Maggie Cutts liked the town, the house, and the scenic boatyard, but she lacked Ed's enthusiasm. "I'll never get used to this place," she said. But, she understood this boatyard was a great career opportunity for Ed.

Back in Northport, Ed told John Case he loved the beautiful boatyard and liked Oxford. It was a commercial-fishing, crabbing, boating, and boat-building community, and a popular vacation spot for boaters. Case said he would negotiate with Wiley.

Over the phone with Case, Wiley sounded dejected at giving up the yard — and his good customers. Seeing that he was having second thoughts, Case suggested that Wiley could be available to consult and also work on designs for his own customers. Both men agreed, and the yard soon changed hands.

On his visit to check out the town and the boatyard, Ed had noticed that Wiley seemed a little depressed about selling. It was true Wiley had mixed feelings, which Chuck Wiley observed at close range. "As much as dad wanted to sell the yard, when it became a reality, it was a heart-wrenching thing for him. He loved the yard tremendously. It was his creation."

Ralph Wiley had a long and successful career at his boatyard, which he sold to Cutts & Case in 1965.

William Hingst

Wiley had trained as an engineer at Stevens Institute in New Jersey. At that time it was the only school in the country teaching naval architecture besides the Naval Academy. After working at a company making artillery-shell casings, he and his wife took their 39' sloop south, searching for a perfect community where they could have a boatyard in a "rural area on the water," as he phrased it. The search ended when they reached Oxford. (Wiley)

After renting space at the Sinclair Yard on the north side of Towne Creek, Wiley built a sports fisherman he had designed for a New York client. On the opposite side of Towne Creek he saw some undeveloped land that looked suitable for a boatyard, so he bought the land for $4,000 in 1929 and hired local men who put up the first shed, some docks, and a railway. "The day of the Stock Market Crash," Chuck Wiley said, "Dad was up in New York City, receiving payment for the first boat."

With the new yard up and running, Ralph Wiley designed and built *Scrappy Cats,* which were 16' cat-rigged boats with 175 square feet of sail. His yard turned out thirty of the racing boats, which at first cost $40.

"They were planked at 1.125" with white cedar over white oak frames, very conventional," said Chuck Wiley. "Dad built a lot of motor-sailers from 34 feet on up, to the largest at 62 feet." These were double-enders, typical of the era, with a ketch rig. They sailed surprising well, he said, as some owners discovered during the war, when gas was rationed.

Wiley's yard turned out the first two of the popular *Comet* class. Number One is on exhibit at the Chesapeake Bay Maritime Museum, where Pete Lesher, chief curator, knew the history of the design. C. Lowndes Johnson of Easton was building *Star* boats, which he and his brother also raced. A founding member of the Tred Avon Yacht Club, Mrs. Maria Martin, later to become Mrs. Wheeler, asked Lowndes to design for her sons a small fast boat,

Lesher said. She wanted it similar to the *Star*, but with a center-board. Wiley built the first of the new design originally named *Crab*, but when the new class was introduced at the 1933 New York Boat Show, it carried the name *Star Junior*.

"The *Star* class was raising the dickens about it," Chuck Wiley said, "because they didn't want that boat to be related by name to the *Star* Boat. So they changed it to the nearest thing where they could be safe, and called it a *Comet*."

As Ed Cutts prepared to move south, he told his boss at Grumman, "I realize this move is a big challenge, and there's a chance it might not work out. If that happens, I would be coming back to ask for my job again." They agreed to this. Ed thanked the men who had given him the opportunity to work on Navy and NASA projects. "I really felt guilty about leaving them," he said many years later, "because they were so good to me."

When Ed and Maggie Cutts sold their Northport home, they paid the mortgage and had $15,000 left to apply to the new yard. They loaded everything, including one motorcycle and tools, into a truck, which Ed and his father drove. Maggie followed with the three children. A boat hauler transported Oberlin's 30' hull.

Arriving at Oxford, Ed, then thirty-eight years old, and his father looked and felt somber. "We were complete strangers. We knew no one, so we felt low," Ed said. They drove into the boatyard and parked. A man with red hair appeared, called some men to begin unloading, and introduced himself as Plink Loscomb.

Vernon took Ed aside and said, "That red head is a good man. Don't let him go." Ed soon developed a good relationship with Plink, his yard supervisor.

A well-dressed man came up to Ed and asked, "Are you the new guy?" Ed admitted he was. "Well, I just came down to welcome you and to wish you luck." Ed began to feel better right away. This thoughtful neighbor was a local businessman named Barclay Trippe.

"I never forgot that," Ed said forty years later. "I have always felt a friendliness toward 'Barky,' who was special."

Ed, Maggie, and their three children settled into the oldest house in Oxford. The office addition, with its low angled ceiling, had a step up to the living room through a low door, which could be hazardous to tall people, as were other doors in the house. The old living room with large stone fireplace and ceiling beam was of fair size with two windows facing the water and docks. The other door opened to the front hall with front and back doors at either end. Continuing into the dining room, facing another large fireplace, once used for cooking, were two windows facing the water and two opposite looking to the front drive area. Beyond was the small kitchen and dining area that led to two bedrooms.

On the right of the front door was a steep and narrow, winding staircase. On the second floor were two bedrooms for the children, where antique floor boards creaked, like night insects, beneath a rug. Some uneven boards encouraged doors to close. Door frames were angled slightly and hazardous for six footers. There were steep ceilings and gable windows facing front and back. Ed thought shipwrights might have built the house, with good reason. From 1694, Oxford was an official port of entry for Maryland, as was Annapolis, which at that time was named Anne Arundel.

Ed saw the boat hull and tools were stowed in the sheds where he took inventory. "I had some nice machinery, such as a big thickness planer, but some tools which I didn't own were already in Oxford," he said. "There was a 36-inch bandsaw that I would need occasionally, and a very large jointer, old but good."

Nevins went out of business in October 1962, and Ed attended the auction where he knew some of the people. Historian Tom Nye saw Ed and said, "He got lots of tools including the large router that he had actually used at Nevins when he was apprenticed there, and I think it's still in use in Maryland."

"I just bought the tools as a remembrance," Ed said, "because I loved the place." He often used the router, but this revealed one facet of his character that would grow. In the future, he would collect motorcycles, boats, cars, and more.

Ed kept the dozen men that were working at Wiley's yard and, after observing their skills and abilities, decided where to use them. "They were good workers, but they were not doing the highest grade of work as at Nevins," he said. "There are different classes of yachts, and those built here were all strip planked — small strips of wood nailed down on top of each other. My own boats were either carvel planked, or they were double planked. But they were all lined off and planked. You have to have a really good builder to properly line off and plank a boat, the traditional way of the great northern yards."

On October 2, 1965, the *New York Times* carried a most unusual notice. In part it read as follows, "Know therefore: Edmund A. Cutts and John M. Case announce they have purchased Ralph Wiley's yard and will maintain his principles and business at the old stand. We respectfully solicit your interest, inquiries & commissions." The letter "S" was printed "F" in the notice — to create a Shakespearian announcement. Ed drew on his printing ability, as he wrote this with John Case. The ad went on to say Ralph Wiley is available in a "design and consulting status." The bottom had their initials, location, and phone.

After the change of ownership, Wiley was at the yard almost every day, talking with customers and people he knew. He wrote, in his book, how he thoroughly enjoyed being there with activity in full swing around him.

Years later, Ed admitted that Ralph Wiley was "sometimes a pain in the rear," but he understood it was difficult for him to say goodbye to the yard he loved. "He was really sad about selling." Ed thought that Wiley not only resented him, but that he also spoke to Case about replacing "that young fellow." It is likely that the change of command to a younger captain, after thirty-six years, bothered Wiley.

Working on Oberlin's sloop, Ed supervised the builders to see they met his exacting standards. On building John Case's boat, they learned, for example, to use a light inside the hull when planking to find any openings. "The men were good workers and willing to improve to new and better ways and methods," Ed said. "Soon we were producing some very nice work indeed."

Eddie, at ten, helped his father from the start at the new boatyard, and even little Ronnie found ways he could join in. "They would hold lumber up at the other end when I was trying to band-saw it," said Ed, "and things like that." Short laughs interrupted his account. "I remember saying to little Ronnie to hold it higher, and all you could see were his hands, which were over his head. He was only a little kid. I put them to work here and there (Northport) very early, and if they weren't helping me, then Maggie was."

Eddie Jr. was alert to anything interesting going on. He saw one builder who often arrived late for work, despite the foreman's orders. Plink, who in many ways was like a sergeant, went to the man's house one morning at 7:10. "He proceeded to pull him out of bed," said Eddie, "pushed him into his truck in his pajamas, and drove him to work. That's the kind of a guy he was." Plink had been there twenty-five years and proved to one and all he could run the yard.

The family loved the historic house on which Ed made improvements. For the steep stairs to the second floor, Ed built railings strong enough to support anyone in trouble with the higher-than-expected risers. In the dining room, Maggie needed a corner cabinet with a glass front, so he built one complete with wooden hinges, as he did with other wall cabinets. She left most of the decorating and placing of pictures to Ed. "She wasn't too interested in that," he said. "She knew I was going to go nautical on the stuff."

When cold weather arrived, the house overlooking Towne Creek cove proved its quality. "This little yard was very well protected because it faces south," said Ed. Oxford people would leave their homes in winter "because it would blow a gale in the front door. But not here. This house, as Maggie often said, was 'snug and warm.'"

Within a year, a man from Grumman arrived at Cutts and Case. "They sent Jimmy King to ask me if I would like to come back," Ed said. The visitor told Ed he would be working on the Engineering staff if he returned. "Thank you for the offer," Ed said, "but you must know I never got an engineering degree." King knew that, but because of the quality of Ed's work on Navy aircraft and other projects, which depended on engineering ability, the offer stood. "No, Jimmy, I put my life here now, and this is it. Things are going well, we're busy, and I'm designing and building." He then took King on a tour of the yard and some favorite boats.

Recalling the visit, Ed said, "That was certainly nice of them. I had no aeronautical engineering training at all, but they knew I had a brain that liked to tackle difficult problems and work them out. I always loved Grumman, a wonderful company to work for. They were nice people." The feeling was apparently mutual.

Ed's wealthy partner, John M. Case, who made the boatyard possible, had helped develop the earliest computers. After earning a business degree at Harvard, Case worked at the New York Stock Exchange, where he had tallied figures and hand-posted sales on a big board. In 1931, Case moved to a fledgling company called International Business Machines to work for the founder Thomas Watson, Sr. Eddie Jr. said. "With his knowledge of banking and business management, Case worked on methods to process and program information that companies wanted, using a solenoid and punch-card system."

Eddie's respect for John Case was apparent. "Watson had sent him to the Pentagon to train computer operators and to help program their IBM computer, which was gigantic in size and used thousands of punch cards daily." They were working to break the Japanese Naval and diplomatic codes using information from cryptographers there and at Pacific receiving posts. This was before December 1941. Case's programmable computer system was used at Pearl Harbor and other key locations, but there was a radio blackout before the attack.

Case entered the army and became a Lt. Colonel with the 18th Armored Division as a tank commander under General Patton in Germany. After the war he returned to IBM where he was promoted to Manager of the New York Metropolitan District and Special Representative for Banks in 1951. He hoped to head the company as he helped train Tom Watson, Jr. When Case realized that Watson was grooming his son to head the company, he looked around and then spoke to the head of Fairchild Camera.

"Sherman Fairchild was getting older," Ed Cutts said, "and mentioned he would like to get someone to run Fairchild. John, thinking it would take forever for him to get to the helm of IBM, went to Fairchild. He became Executive Vice President his second year. Sherman Fairchild kept looking over John's shoulder," Ed said, "and wouldn't let go of the reins." Case left and began a computer consulting company — Case Labs. When Ed first met Case, he was retired.

"If you had to have a partner, it wouldn't be possible to find a better one than John," Ed said. "John Case was a wonderful man, straight as an arrow, decent, considerate, and just a fine fellow in every way."

In this partnership, they each contributed to a successful boatyard, while bringing markedly different talents and skills. John Case arrived in Oxford quarterly to check the finances and

John Case and Ed Cutts at their boatyard in Oxford, Maryland.
William Hingst

the way things were running. He liked to stay in the boatyard at
the guest cottage, which was actually the house boat that arrived
around 1890. It appeared small, cozy, and friendly with an easterly
view of the tranquil cove and the muster of masts. It was a short
walk over a lawn to the 1695 house. The office door opened to
side-by-side desks, office machines, old wood wall cabinets and
bookshelves filled with catalogues of hardware and nautical supplies. Up on a wall was a newspaper printing block used for the
Shakespearian *New York Times* announcement.

"Early on, John Case came here every quarter and went through
the books," Eddie Jr. said. "He would have a meeting with the
accountant and a few business meetings with my father. This was
primarily to see that my dad was actually making the place go

the way a person should, in order to suit his business obligations. When he saw dad was upholding his side of the bargain, he began to be more at ease."

Outside the office window to the south were the weather-faded, red sheds with sun and patches of shade from the nearby trees. On the railway men were either painting boats or were preparing one for launching. Builders and boaters walked past. This was a scenic and tranquil work setting for John Case, accustomed to office-building views of Manhattan.

Case asked Ed how the business was going, but he left the running of the yard in his partner's hands. They discussed what was going on with various boats in stages of repair or completion, and they talked about what was new and intriguing for the future. Case often talked about the importance of continuing research, for he had witnessed the costly development work at IBM, and he knew its importance.

This forward thinking impressed Ed Cutts, who had worked with space-age metals and cutting-edge materials at Grumman. He started to contemplate some research areas, thinking there must be better ways of constructing wooden boats. Perhaps, they could last longer.

Linda Cutts, from seven years old up, remembered her father's business partner. "My mother would always have me clean up the cottage when he was coming, and he always left me a 50-cent piece in a special envelope. It meant something back then. Whenever he came, my parents always went over to the houseboat cottage to have a drink with him, and then they went out to dinner."

She remembered Case looking over records in the cottage and spending time in the office, and it seemed to her that he was a little secretive. "He was an outside presence, and his presence was always known because he was such a huge man. He was taller than most, and a giant to me. He didn't have to say very much.

When he had something to say, it was important. People were intimidated by him just because of his sheer size."

As Eddie grew older, he saw a lot of his father's partner. "John Case, in a lot of ways, was like a big brother to my dad," he said. "He really liked him. As he put it one time, 'Noblesse oblige,' an obligation of the nobility to the non-nobility to help them out." Apparently, this did not imply any conceit or superiority on Case's part, for he was speaking as an experienced business leader guiding a younger partner.

"People don't know much about him, for he was very unassuming," Eddie said, "but he had some very important connections. One time, he and his wife were invited over to a wedding in Scotland, and they were set up in a room of a castle. When the hostess asked him if they could move to another room, he said, 'Certainly, quite all right.' In the course of the move he asked them what was up and learned the King and Queen were due to arrive.

"John Case had a personal audience with the Pope on several occasions. He moved in very elevated circles, but in an unostentatious way. You would never know it, for he was the most honest, straight-forward person," Eddie said. "You just don't find many like him."

The Cutts & Case Boatyard was busy, and Ed Cutts understood that Maggie was adapting to the change of location. "She got interested," he said. "Early on, she certainly knew that's how I was going to make my living, so she helped. She's been a very good wife. Even when she felt I was making wrong choices, she would help me any way she could." He paused a moment, weighing his words. "They weren't wrong choices, and in the end they were correct. And Maggie became a very happy girl." She often shared his enjoyment of relaxing in two lawn chairs, facing the cove, to watch the activity of sail and power craft maneuvering in the cove. In his front hallway, Ed had a print of a similar scene — Claude

Monet's *Jardin à Sainte-Adresse*. In a garden of flowers, the artist and others view an off-shore panorama of steam ships, pleasure boats, and one five-master.

Because the boatyard needed more facilities, Ed made improvements. He put sides on the open sheds and added one building, but he was determined to take his time. Growing up in the Depression teaches many lessons, especially when there is nothing to spare. He knew there was no room for extravagances, as he improved the boatyard gradually. "Go slow," he said, "and don't get yourself in trouble. I don't like borrowing money." Raising his right arm, he pointed to Easton. "Well, you see a bank on every corner," he exclaimed. "I just don't know how all of the money gets into the banks so they can lend it. I try to stay out of debt, I tell you. I don't mind a little, but if you get me into debt, I get very nervous."

Helga Fontanes telephoned Ed Cutts in 1967 to tell him she needed a larger boat than *Cygnet* and had decided to sell the small sloop. Ed replied he wanted to buy it back, and he did. Mrs. Fontanes sailed the 23-footer, with its shallow keel and centerboard, south on a leisurely trip. "I sailed her down to Oxford, with a cousin (who had helped Ed build it) and two others. We had bad weather at times, but I didn't have to worry. We sailed outside in the ocean and also in the Inland Waterway. She's very, very seaworthy, and you can single-hand her." With several overnight stops, she brought the boat south to Cape May, into Delaware Bay, south under the Annapolis Bay Bridge, past Tilghman Island, and into the Tred Avon to Cutts & Case.

Ed's first sailboat, which he designed and built, had returned home. "He liked to have all his boats back," Mrs. Fontanes said years later. "People around him know this, but not exactly why."

Ed said, "We like to keep it at the yard so we can keep an eye on it." Following maintenance and painting he began sailing *Cygnet* when he had the time. Later on, someone wanted to buy the sloop, so with mixed feelings — and hoping she would be properly cared for — Ed said goodbye.

Ed Cutts had long dreamed of owning a famous East Coast boat. This was a 33' classic motor yacht used by famous boating photographer Morris Rosenfeld. Tom Nye remembered that when Ed visited City Island, he was always keenly interested whenever he spotted *Foto*. Ed made a few attempts to buy it, but the price was always too high. Then in 1967, Morris was gone but his son Stanley was using the yacht and photographing races with his two brothers.

The yacht was built in 1929, making her thirty-eight years old and reportedly showing her age. Ed Cutts believed it was important for maritime history to save her. It would be a tragedy if she were destroyed. Ed knew he could restore her to the way she once looked, because his yard had rebuilt yachts in worse condition. He had a feeling that maritime museums would someday want this gallant, classic, unique yacht, which helped document American yacht racing from 1929 thru the mid 1960s.

Ed had loved this boat for many years, from afar, but he sometimes envisioned the thrill of piloting her at high speed, kicking up spray from the flaring bow. But for now, he would keep track of *Foto* — while keeping his dream within.

Chapter Six

EASTERN SHORE, NEW DESIGNS, AND KNOCKDOWN

THE FIRST CHESAPEAKE BAY BRIDGE had opened thirteen years before Ed Cutts and John Case bought their new boatyard. Up until 1952, the ferry ran from Sandy Point, east of Annapolis, to Stevensville on Kent Island, and then over the Kent Island narrows to the Eastern Shore.

Ed Cutts didn't think the Bay Bridge, which was joined later by a second bridge span, improved things for the residents who had been relatively isolated and liked it. "This Eastern Shore was really a place to get away from it all, for many people," he said, with a serious face befitting an earnest opinion. "But the bridge changed a lot of that."

Travelers could take a one or two-car aluminum train, called *the Bullet*, from Wilmington to Easton. It was streamlined but unusually short, with the stubbiness of a bullet, so that one could joke it had lost passenger cars.

Summer visitors to the Eastern Shore before the bridge had an impression of a private, insular and almost secret country — a Maryland Brigadoon. Residents had a pride mixed with love for their area, conversing about crabs, oysters, duck hunting, boating and sailing races. Some chose to ride after foxes on large estates. Here, one finds a culture, outlook, and way of life harkening back to centuries of English rule.

Historians have chronicled the events and famous people of this unique area. Paul Wilstach wrote, "Such regions receive their nicknames because they have character. Character over long periods begets legends, and legends develop a cult. The Eastern Shore has character and legends and a cult of its own. . . . It lies geographically apart, a land of almost unvarying unity of character, of history, of economy and of interest." (Wilstach)

Beginning in the mid 1700s, the boatbuilders of Baltimore and Bay communities on both shores began building fast schooners for carrying trade goods to the Caribbean and France. These designer/builders are believed to have copied features of the fast French merchant ships that came into American ports. The lightweight schooners Marylanders built had a pronounced rake to the masts that could be lengthened with topgallants and topsails. Another opinion exists on who influenced whom. Since a few Baltimore boatbuilders went to France to build ocean going-vessels, others believe French boatyards were really copying new Baltimore schooners. By 1805, American designers and builders had developed this faster schooner design that could not be overtaken. Speed was necessary for three good reasons: to avoid impressments of crew into the British Navy, for shorter round trips, and for financial profit.

American boat building and these fast schooners were more than a good thing for the country when the British blockade started the War of 1812. These schooners saved the country and shortened the war. Builders modified these ships to take a small complement of cannon for privateer duty, officially authorized in writing by Secretary of State James Madison, serving President Thomas Jefferson. These schooners sat lower in the water with most guns amidships — presenting a small target for the large English merchantmen. Privateers were smaller, faster, and more maneuverable. An excellent book called *The Republic's Private Navy* quotes from an old document: "Master carpenters of the entire Chesapeake Bay region were experts in the construction of fast sailing schooners. Such vessels were labeled 'sharp built,' 'pilot boat constructed,' or 'built in privateer fashion.'" (Garitee)

These Baltimore privateers flew a staysail and jibs, topgallant sails, and a tall gaff-rigged mainsail. New York City ranked second for building privateers of various designs, followed by Salem and Boston. Five hundred registered privateers, known also as ships of Marque, searched for the British commercial shipping around the world but especially in the English Channel and the West Indies. "Every one of Baltimore's 122 commissioned vessels was a bona fide oceangoing raider, capable of subduing an armed merchantman. Most of the Baltimore vessels were about 150 tons and only eight were below 100 tons," Jerome Garitee wrote. Elsewhere, smaller boats were used offshore. *The Niles Weekly Register* estimated that the American privateers captured or destroyed 1,750 British ships. These losses speeded the decision of the British — once the leading seapower — to end the war. (Ibid.)

Dorchester County built seven privateers, but the highest Eastern Shore total came from St. Michaels, a small town where shipyards built thirty-one schooners to Baltimore's sixty. This amazing record sheds light on the number of skilled boatbuilders in Talbot County, with most of the boatyards in St. Michaels.

Talbot County continued its rich boat-building tradition when Ed Cutts and John Case took over Ralph Wiley's boatyard in 1965. Descendants of families that had been early arrivals on the Eastern Shore of Maryland were still living and working here. Perry and Richard Spenser, William Harrison, and Noah Richardson were Talbot County builders of ocean-going privateers before and during the war of 1812. Thomas Kemp began building in St. Michaels and then relocated to Baltimore. When the war ended, these fast schooners, with their cannon removed, could resume carrying cargo.

The watermen working the Bay created locally-built boats, especially the unique *skipjacks* that rake the oyster beds under sail. At first these boats were schooners and other types of craft, but they evolved into the familiar single-raked mast and a clipper bow. They carried no on-board motor, but in later years could be powered by a small pusher-boat with an inboard engine to reach oystering grounds.

Work boats called *pungys* were in use around 1840, before the Civil War. They were schooner rigged and almost always gaff rigged, but they differed from schooners, said Pete Lesher, the chief curator of the Chesapeake Bay Maritime Museum. "A schooner of that period had a fore staysail, a jib, and maybe another jib in the fore triangle. For *pungys* there was only one headsail. The *pungy* was lighter rigged — not rigged for heavy weather as was the schooner." These sailed mainly in the Bay, he said. "They weren't really meant to take ocean passages, but some of them did travel coastwise." These were oystering craft, as was another famous workboat.

Bugeyes, which developed later in the 1870s from the double-ended *Chesapeake Bay Canoe*, also carried one jib. "They weren't over-rigged like the modern racing canoes are. Standard *bugeyes* had jib-headed (or sharp-headed) sails on the fore and main masts," Lesher said. The *pungy* had a keel while the *bugeye* had a centerboard.

Builders built *canoes* and these two Bay workboats from logs, Lesher said. "Seven to nine-log boats were common among *bugeyes*, and some had eleven logs." But, the largest *bugeyes*, measuring about 60 feet, were built differently. "These were not log-built," he said, "but were plank and frame."

The shipwrights who built privateers, trading schooners, and workboats passed down their skills, often within their families. John B. Harrison of Tilghman Island, a descendent of *privateer* builder William Harrison, built many workboats including the

Bugeye Edna B. Lockwood in 1889. When taken out of active service in 1967, she was the last oystering fleet *bugeye*. This National Historic Landmark vessel is now at CBMM.

A descendant of Noah Richardson, Captain James B. Richardson, built eighty to one hundred wooden boats and schooners at his Cambridge yard. These were mainly *bugeyes*, *skipjacks*, and smaller workboats. The last boat Richardson built himself was a *bugeye* called *Jenny Norman*. Shortly before he died, he designed a *buyboat*, which his son-in-law, Thomas Howell, built in his honor. CBMM takes visitors for rides on this boat, which is named *Mr. Jim* after James Richardson. *Buyboats* bought shellfish and seafood from workboats on the water and kept them on ice until dock delivery at day's end.

Inland farms and vegetable canneries played a major economic role on the Eastern Shore, along with the harvesting and canning of Chesapeake Bay oysters. From millions of bushels harvested from the late nineteenth century, the numbers have declined precipitously, and tragically.[1]

But non-working craft also appeared on the Chesapeake. With improved gas engines and skilled boatbuilders, boatyards built recreational sail and power boats and birding skiffs. At his boatyard, Ed Cutts was continuing the Eastern Shore boat-building traditions with finely-built wooden sailboats and yachts.

An Easton resident, C. Lowndes Johnson, liked to observe Ed and others builders working on a new boat. Ed took a liking to him, which wasn't always the case with visitors, for he asked many to leave. "Lowndes was an elderly gentleman at the time, small in stature and a pleasant man," Ed said. "He was extremely interested in what I was doing, and he watched constantly as we worked. He wasn't a pain in the ass, and you would hardly know he was there, but he would ask you later on what did you think about this, or why did you do that? I thought he might have been a schoolteacher." Lowndes never told Ed about boats he had built.

For years he had constructed popular *Star* racing sloops on his Miles River property in Easton, before he designed the *Comet* class, mentioned earlier.[2]

Abe Oberlin arrived in Oxford, 1966, for the launching of his new boat, named *Joie de Vivre*, which had specs of: 29' 10" LOA, 7' 7" beam, 4' 9" draft. He test-sailed it in Chesapeake Bay with his wife and family. John Case, waiting for his own boat to be finished, went sailing with Abe who let him take the tiller. John said he liked the way it sailed.

Ed had used his half model to lay down the lines and make the molds for Case's new sloop. Her specs were: LOA 33', LWL 24' 8", beam 7' 7", draft 4' 9" with a white oak keel and framework, cedar strip-planked above the waterline and single carvel below. In choosing wood for a new boat, Ed Cutts had his favorites, which are quite standard. "White cedar is what we like. We use it from the south, but I find there is not a lot of difference with northern white cedar," he said. "Cedar has a resistance to decay, smells nice, and is pleasant to work with. It does a good planking job, is light in weight, and also glues well.

"We like Honduras mahogany best," he said. "There have been small boats planked with mahogany, but I don't like mahogany for planking. There's a much better wood, and it only weighs about half as much. It's Spanish cedar, the same color as mahogany," he said. "It's softer and lighter. It can be twisted and bent, and it holds together and glues very well. It has a beautiful look of mahogany to it." His favorite wood for building spars was Sitka spruce. For cabin work, he usually used mahogany or something with a beautifying effect.

In Spring 1967, the yard launched Case's sloop *Rebellion*. Ed Cutts and Eddie Jr. were aboard when Captain Geeze Loscomb delivered her to Long Island. Eddie remembered him as a respected captain and delivery skipper noted for rope work and sea stories.

Rebellion was moored at the Sewanaaka Yacht Club convenient to John Case's house at Oyster Bay. Not long after this, yacht designer Olin Stephens II spotted *Rebellion* at her mooring. Something about her lines aroused his interest, so he looked her over. Later, Stephens sent a note to John Case saying it was one of the most beautiful boats he had ever seen. John Case appreciated this significant praise from one of yachting's great designers, as did Ed and the builders. Case also owned two motor yachts: *Claymore* at 64'9" and *Ariel* at 42'6".

Rebellion, a Cutts double-ender which Ed built for John Case.
Benjamin Mendlowitz

While Abe Oberlin wasn't interested in organized club racing, he did have one memorable race with his brother, his partner in a large dress-manufacturing company. "When I had *Joie de Vivre*, my brother had purchased a 45' Dutch boat. One day, I was cruising on Long Island Sound with my fourteen-year-old son, when we saw my brother's boat with the captain and mate. It was a light breeze day, so we tied up together.

"My brother is very competitive, and so is my son. They got to discussing which boat was faster," Oberlin said. "We started to race. It was a mistake, because we moved so far ahead my brother's boat was out of sight. The next day he was so disgruntled that he sold his boat."

At Cutts & Case the building of *Rebellion's* sister ship was underway. As it neared completion in 1968, her owner Ken Wilson died suddenly, so his son Steve took over the boat. He asked Roger Vaughan, a friend and maritime writer, for help. A disagreement ensued about the deck hardware. "I had a discussion with Ed Cutts about putting a second set of winches on it because we wanted to run spinnakers," Vaughan said, "and his being very opposed to that."

"You don't need a second set of winches," Ed told him. Vaughan said they did, so it was built with two sets.

Eddie Jr. remembered this. He said that two sets are not needed very much "because you don't often hoist a genoa and a spinnaker together. The single winch set serves both." His father had another reason for his opposition. "Ed didn't like the idea of non-designers suggesting to him how to lay out his boats," Eddie said. "Dad took his yacht design with a degree of seriousness that few achieve." Vaughan didn't think Ed had any sailing experience with a spinnaker, but Eddie confirmed that his father had first raced with a spinnaker on *Cygnet* in winning the Long Island Invitational.

Wilson christened the boat *Grizzly Bear*. "I don't know why they picked that crazy name," Ed said with a wrinkled forehead. One evening as the new sloop sat at its Cutts & Case dock, Wilson invited some friends aboard, including New York songwriters and musicians. Nearby boaters noticed they tracked mud into the boat and that one visitor was wearing cowboy boots.

The next morning word of this boat party reached Ed. He marched out on the dock and told Steve Wilson, "You've got to treat the boat with respect." He spoke with authority, remembering the care put into its building. He may have sounded like an angry schoolteacher talking to a student. According to the story, which could have changed over time, the owner replied, "This is my boat. Where did you get the right to tell me what to do?"

"It's like my daughter," Ed replied. "If you marry her, you're responsible for her, but I'll always be her daddy." Following this exchange, Wilson moved his boat to Annapolis. Then, he asked Ed for the design plans. It had been one of Ed Cutts's principles that he didn't give out his designs. "They don't take the same care in building that we do," he said, "and they do things such as covering the wood with fiberglass."

On that particular boat, Ed stated he had lofted it full size to the loft floor. He explained he didn't have any plans. Wilson said since he had bought the boat that he deserved to have them. This led to disagreements over the phone and a standoff.

After *Grizzly Bear* had another owner, she came back to Cutts & Case. Ed was in good spirits when his "daughter" — named after the nemesis of the Northwestern woods — returned home. Boat owners at Cutts & Case talk of Ed treating his boats like his own children. A later owner of *Grizzly Bear* knew about this. "Even though I owned and sailed the boat, I felt it was really Ed's." He was happy when he returned to Ed Cutts his double-ended sloop, with graceful lines, whose unfortunate Latin name was *Ursus Horribilis*.

A lawyer in Philadelphia became an owner and later sold this sloop to Dr. John Hedger of Salisbury, Maryland. The physician owned a Lippincott *Lightning*, which the yard had repaired. He was undecided about moving up to a 33' sloop until he sailed *Grizzly Bear*, and then he was sold. "It feels like you're in the water — like my Lightning — not over the water," he said. "I wanted a boat for overnighting that could heel over like a Lightning, and this one does."

In 1969, a visitor from Detroit, who told Ed he was looking for a new boat, arrived in Oxford on vacation. Adolph Egli was the director of applied research for the Ford Motor Company and headed the Aerospace and Research Division. Ed described Adolph as having penetrating eyes and a Swiss accent. After examining Ed's boats, he was impressed, but was cautious about ordering one. At this time he was deciding what size boat he wanted, so Ed loaned him *Cygnet* to sail for a few days. Watching from shore, Ed admired Egli's handling of the fast sloop and said, "He knew how to get the best performance from a responsive boat. And he passed other boats."

After three days, Egli made a decision and told Ed, "Eddie, make me a 40-footer that will sail like this boat." Ed sat down with him to find just what he wanted and sketched ideas. Then he began the drawings.

The new client had an analytical brain and was obviously alert for any possible engineering or structural errors. Egli expected perfection, which was not new at Cutts & Case, for Ed Cutts now had a client much like himself. After approving the design, Egli checked Ed's specifications before leaving for Detroit. "Eddie, what do you calculate for the displacement?"

Ed said, "13,400 pounds displacement," and years later he spoke of this. "Egli was not completely trustful of anybody down the line, and this included designers of cars and boats." When Egli asked for a drawing, Ed replied, "Well, as a rule I don't usually give my drawings to anybody."

"Well, Eddie, what the hell? I'm having this boat built, and I would like to look at the lines."

Ed decided to make an exception because his customer was a first-class engineer who would understand them. "So I gave him a little set of the lines, and he took them back to Ford and put his brainy guys on it to see how it met my calculations."

A few weeks later Egli returned. "Well, Eddie, you are pretty good, I have to admit. You were only 37 pounds off."

"Adolph," Ed said, "my work is perfect, so you are 37 pounds off, or whoever took the lines off the boat. It's a very thin line, and you may be on this side of the pencil or that side. You better go back and tell your brainy guys to get with it."

Egli was stunned momentarily, but dropped the subject. "He was shocked," Ed said, "that I would tell the head of Ford Research that he was off. You see, 37 pounds doesn't mean anything as proportioned with 14,000 lbs." He grinned at the memory with a light laugh. "You use a planimeter to find the displacement. It's a gadget you use to go around the lines. You add and subtract, and it tells you what the area of that section is. You do that for all the sections of the boat, and then you add those sections up and figure the boat's displacement. If I took the dimensions around a boat twice, there is no way I would get within 37 pounds of my first measurements. It would have been impossible because the shake of the hand would change. Thirty-seven pounds was a joke!" Ed paused to let this sink in. "After that, he had more confidence in me. Perhaps he thought he'd better check up on me.

"He was the finest engineer, and this he had to be as head of research," Ed said. "If Ford wanted to know something about anything, they would ask Adolph Egli, who had a whole group under him. He was a brilliant man and a great pain in the ass in the beginning, but later on we became closest friends." Ed would sometimes do a funny, but good-natured, imitation of Egli's Swiss accent with friends like Abe Oberlin.

In 1969, while Cutts & Case was building *La Mouette* for Egli, a future customer walked into the yard. "I was in search of a boatyard that would put up with a man with an old wooden boat and no money," he said. His name was Tom Morris. He had bought a vintage 30' sloop in Georgetown that he sailed to Annapolis. After checking the yards there, he went over to Oxford to look over boatyards. "I went around the corner, and there was this boatyard. First of all, I thought I was in Maine. It looked like a boatyard ought to look. It wasn't too fancy, and they liked wooden boats there. And that's where I stayed."

To save money on the dock fee, Tom Morris tied up to a piling off Cutts & Case, using a plank to reach the dock. "I probably spent three-quarters of weekends for the next two years working on the boat," he said. "Then, I was a novice and really didn't know what I was doing." He commuted from Philadelphia in a Volkswagen Beetle.

Morris put down a new deck by himself. At times he was stumped and not sure what to do. But he developed a strategy to find out. "I'd sort of keep my eye out when Ed was walking around the yard and plan my path so I could intercept him." Morris would ask Ed for a minute of his time. "In about three minutes Ed would have broken the ice jam, and I'd be off and running. I always said Ed could give you, in a three-minute conversation, three months worth of work. Ed is a man of few words," he said. Tom Morris moved in 1972 to Maine where he began Morris Yachts, which grew and expanded.

In 1970, Cutts & Case launched Egli's ketch, christened *La Mouette*. "The name means *little gull*," Ed said brightening up at the image. "Isn't that a pretty name?" She measured 37' 4" on deck

Cutts family group photo, with (left to right): Eddie Jr.; Marguerite (Maggie); Ed Sr.; Ronnie; and Linda in a 1969 photograph.
Cutts Family

plus the bowsprit. Egli put his new boat through its paces and found she was a swift flyer. "He went out and had improvised races with other boats," Ed said, "and passed them."

Ed's sailboats have performed well since *Cygnet*, for he is interested in the subject of speed, although he was never interested in designing a racing class. "If I were going to design a boat — whether you said it was for racing or for cruising around wherever you wanted — it was going to be as fast as I could make it."

Egli began an unconventional sailing method that befuddled other boaters, and Ed, laughing, described what happened. "He would sometimes sit high up on the main spreader holding the joy-stick remote for the auto pilot. He did this sometimes if he wanted to watch a race. People would come back and report they were mystified because they saw the boat sailing with no one at the wheel."

Egli and his wife bought a house and settled in Oxford where he continued sailing *La Mouette*. He and Ed liked to get together and discuss engineering concepts. "We both had a driving interest in knowing things that weren't apparent," Ed said, "so we paid close attention to each other's thoughts and opinions."

Abe Oberlin was sailing *Joie de Vivre* out of Oxford on weekends, staying either on the boat or the houseboat cabin. He was considering moving up in size, so he spoke with Ed. "I've decided I want a larger boat built with the same care for cruising. Would you design a 46-footer for me?"

In conferences with Ed, who drew some ketches, Oberlin explained features he wanted for comfortable cruising. He planned to single-hand the boat, so he needed a self-trimming jib to avoid fouled foresails. After Oberlin approved Ed's drawings, Cutts & Case began work on the new boat to be named *Spellbound*. It measured 47' LOA with bowsprit, 36' LWL, 10'8" beam, and 3'9" draft.

"The topsides were strip-planked because the crew had been using this method and understood it," Ed said. "Strips were nailed vertically, with bronze nails, into each other. Possibly you could pre-drill — we used to if the nail was a large enough size. And always use glue. In those days before epoxies we used waterproof glue. Above the garboard hollow the planking is fastened to lead ballast. The bottom is carvel planked." Ed has always used carvel on his boats, never lapstrake.

This ketch had an interesting innovation — a horizontal wheel that Oberlin credited to Ed Cutts. "I didn't design the boat with a horizontal wheel just to be different," Ed said. "But I designed it that way so people could sit all around the wheel and not interfere with the helmsman, no matter where they sat."

Ed Cutts came up with a wheel design which had a centerboard control, which he had neither seen nor read about previously. It could be another Cutts invention. "The shaft was hollow, and a second shaft went through it to a specially-made reduction gear and hoisting winch," he said. "A worm gear allowed that no brake was necessary so that the board stayed secure in any position. A crank handle, fitting the middle of the steering wheel, was at hand, so easy adjustments could be made."

The ship's wheel also served a social purpose at the end of a day's sail. "If you pull the crank handle out," Ed said, "you could put a folding cocktail table on top when you were sitting in port, and everybody had a table under which they could stick their legs." When the sun was over the yardarm, and the boat anchored, tired sailors had a social place.

After the Cutts & Case yard completed *Spellbound*, Ed Cutts and Eddie, who was then fifteen, accompanied Oberlin on a shakedown cruise down the Chesapeake to Cape Henry and out to the ocean. "Something happened to the diesel engine," Oberlin said,

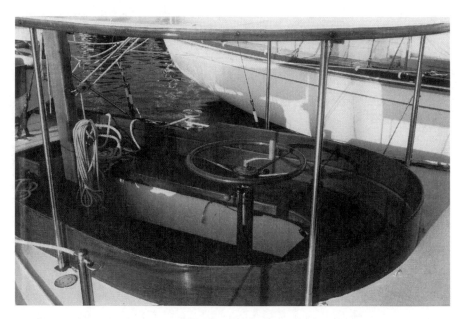

Spellbound's cockpit with the crank handle for centerboard control in the wheel. *Spellbound* is the graceful, spirited ketch on the cover.
Wayne Brown

"so we had to shut it down." They came about and returned under sail, and *Spellbound* handled beautifully, he said. "The boat drew 4 feet with the centerboard up and about 7½ feet with the board down, and the great thing was that when sailing in the Chesapeake with the board up, you're a lot better off." At the boatyard they discovered a simple alternator problem. That year, Abe Oberlin sailed *Spellbound* out of Cutts & Case.

In May 1971, Oberlin asked Ed to help him sail it to his place on Long Island. Ed brought along fifteen-year-old Eddie, and nine-year-old Ronnie, because he thought a cruise would help them learn more about boats and piloting. The pleasant voyage, however, would evolve unexpectedly into a dramatic learning experience.

Spellbound under sail.
Michael Moore

Early one morning they left Oxford, passed under the Bay Bridge going north, entered the Elk River and the Chesapeake and Delaware Canal. They were motor sailing when they left the Canal and headed south in Delaware Bay. When they passed Artificial Island, the breeze picked up, so they cut the motor.

Oberlin described what happened next that early afternoon. "We were going to Cape May, and it started getting very dark. I was at the helm, and we had full sail — genoa, mainsail, mizzen sail, but not the staysail. It became darker and darker, and there were no marinas. It can get pretty rough in the middle of Delaware Bay because it's so shallow."

Oberlin called to Ed who was working below, "Eddie, we better take some sail in."

"Nah," Ed's voice came up the hatchway, "this boat can handle it. We don't have to." He continued organizing supplies and luggage.

The following wind, about three points off the port beam, was now at gale force and increasing with the main and mizzen sails well out to starboard, and the genoa out and straining for all it was worth. Eddie Jr. was perched on the cabin hatch, looking ahead and occasionally checking the sails. Young Ronnie sat in the cockpit, thrilled at the increasing howl of the wind.

"OK, Eddie,'" said Oberlin, firmly gripping the horizontal wheel. At that time he was an aircraft pilot. "I had a lot of experience with that kind of weather, but Ed had a lot more sailing experience than I had." The ketch speeded on its course.

The wind strengthened as Ed climbed slowly up the hatchway ladder, grasping it firmly. He stopped, squinted into the wind for a second, and yelled, "Squall line! Squall line!" A higher velocity gust suddenly hit them. Eddie Jr. rocketed into the main mast, which he grabbed and held.

"Bring her into the wind," Ed yelled from a cockpit corner. He began hauling in the self-furling jib. Eddie cautiously worked his way aft to join Ed. After they uncleated the main and mizzen halyards in the powerful gale, they tried to wrestle down the main. The wind speed seemed more than sixty knots. It held the sail tight against the shrouds. They couldn't move it at first, but it began to lower slowly.

"As they started to get the sail down, I tried to turn into the wind," said Oberlin. "But, with all my strength, I could not turn that wheel. We had a very powerful commercial autopilot on the boat, and I thought I had turned it off. In my haste, I didn't push it all the way in." The wind howled, the main and mizzen were still up, and Ed yelled, "Bring the boat about!"

Oberlin struggled, not knowing why the helm wouldn't move. "I thought that was my end and that Ed and Little Eddie would get blown overboard. Do you know how you get superhuman strength when you think that's the last moment you're going to have on earth? I overrode and broke the autopilot." He was strong from health-club workouts.

Spellbound started to come about, under the screeching of the rigging and the flapping sails, and struggled with the wind nearing the port quarter. Although the halyards had been let off, the slightly lowered sails were held in place by the gale. The genoa clew ripped, as they struggled to lower the main and mizzen. The high velocity wind moving abeam pushed the vessel into a knockdown — and sails with booms out hit the water. The experienced crew reacted in a gymnastic and acrobatic challenge that many sailors have experienced. At the hatchway, Ronnie saw loose gear, charts and galley items sliding to the cabin sole. Some spray came in the ports. "We should have had them locked, but we weren't ready," he said. "We were down maybe ten seconds, it's hard to tell."

Spellbound righted herself and gained a little headway to continue coming about. Ronnie saw the jib blow out. Fortunately, no one was overboard. The boat was pointing higher with sails rapidly flapping and stays like screeching banshees.

"The blast was so hard," Ed said, "it drove the battens right through the pockets." Eddie Jr. saw the main and mizzen battens "go straight up and out of sight, never to be seen again. The wind was blowing so hard," Eddie said, "you had to shut your eyes." They pulled the sails down, slowly. In addition to the ripped pockets, they had a torn genoa leech.

Abe Oberlin, as an airplane pilot, knew something of wind speed and its effects. "I'll tell you how bad it was," he said: "The Glen Martin Aircraft plant was in that area, and that squall pulled a roof off the aircraft factory! We had a wind indicator, and it hit the stop, which was about 80 knots!" They found out later the air speed had hit 83 mph and that Martin Marietta had evacuated their control tower. When the wind dropped, the boat was all right except for the autopilot and sails. Oberlin looked over at Ed when they took a break. "Ed Cutts, you build a hell of a boat." Ed just laughed in reply. Later they had a Scotch to toast the valiant boat.

Continuing down Delaware Bay under power, they came upon some life preservers, overturned dinghies, and a Coast Guard patrol-rescue boat. Over the radio came: "Yacht *Spellbound*. Please be on the lookout for any damaged boats or survivors." They acknowledged but found nothing. At Cape May, people said a 60' boat had overturned.

The following morning they motored up the Atlantic coast. In Port Washington, Ed ordered a new autopilot clutch, left the sails for repair, and ordered a new genoa.

"I believe we were hit with a white waterspout that day," Ronnie said. "It came right up the stern. Suddenly all hell broke loose, but the boat held up very well. She's a strong boat." *Spellbound*, with a good ballast-to-weight ratio, had proved her mettle.

Chapter Seven
CYCLING, FLYING, AND SAILING

THE CHOICE OF A SPORT may be for competition, health, or for the stimulating, sheer joy of the endeavor. In addition to sailing and power-boating, Ed had another favorite sport which he began to enjoy in younger years. He loved riding motorcycles. A rumbling increase in pitch to a trumpeting hum, the road rushing by, and a gale-force wind brought this thrill to Ed Cutts.

Ronnie called his father "a daredevil" and wasn't exaggerating. On one occasion, when living in Northport, Ed had a motorcycle race with an old friend which he discussed. "Bob Hannon had a Ducati and considered it the fastest thing on two wheels," Ed said. "We were on the Cross Island Parkway, and he goaded me on to go faster. We finally pushed them as fast as they could go, and my little BMW beat him at 83 miles per hour. He was so disgusted he gave me the Ducati." This cycle is still in the Cutts & Case collection, which became larger with many unusual cycles after Ed moved to Oxford.

The whole family liked riding motorcycles, and Ed said, "This included Maggie who learned that I didn't just putter when driving someplace." Since Northport, Ronnie had loved taking short motorcycle rides with his father on the BMW R27 250cc, and he began to experience his own love of speed.

Ed took him for rides on the Easton-Oxford Road on his Velocette 500 Clubman. "It was his favorite machine of all and mine too," Ronnie said. "The sound of that thumper was music to our ears. Dad always had a rope with him and used to tie me to him. They worried I would fall off, because I sometimes fell asleep while riding." Ronnie was about ten years old and wore a helmet, as did Ed who started wearing one when he married.

On a straightaway with no traffic in sight and going about 50 mph, Ed sometimes stood on foot pegs so Ronnie could hold the handlebars. "I would sweep under his legs and be driving the Velo," Ronnie said. He would turn the throttle up as he became more experienced. "I can still remember rolling the throttle up to 100 mph and then slowly bring her back to highway speed. We were real daredevils, and I really loved motorcycles." When he was fourteen, Ronnie had his own small motorcycle to drive around the boatyard at a suitable rate.

Eddie and Ronnie, as they grew, helped out at Cutts & Case. "I always remember working here, when I was eight, nine, or ten years old," Ronnie said. Eddie and Ronnie both attended Saints Peter & Paul High School in Easton. At the boatyard in the summer, they worked on wood preparation and finishes. During the winters, they each worked in restaurants. "We had to work to make money, because this wasn't handed to us," Ronnie said.

While working at Seaman Seacraft, Ed had designed a 33' cabin cruiser, a slightly larger version of the 31-footer built for Boris Lauer-Leonardi. In a 2004 interview, Ed said he remembered Seaman had built three of these. "I think they had flying bridges," he said, appearing somewhat unsure for a moment. His confusion appeared out of character for a man who had designed the boat.

"It was long ago," he added, "and I didn't work on building them." At that time, he was building *Lightnings*.

If it weren't for the popularity of fiberglass, which was taking over the boat shows, Seaman Bros. might have turned out more of Ed's cruiser design. Ed said he designed the 33-footer with a V-8 engine of about 200-hp or more. He said Cutts & Case had one of these cruisers for a time.

In 1965, Seaman Bros. boatyard was getting ready to close, when the yard delivered one completed cruiser to a New York customer and another to Ed Cutts. This had a partially-built cabin and no engine. Charterboat captain Michael Keene of Easton wanted a sports-fisherman, so he bought this unfinished cruiser from Ed in 1968. "I took it into my backyard and finished it there," he said. "It had a cabin started, and we cut the end of it off." This change permitted a suitable cockpit for the small fishing parties he would take out of Ocean City. The cruiser did not have a flying bridge, Keene said.

A check of Leonardi's 31'6" yacht, built in 1963, sitting on its cradle in Cutts & Case's large shed, revealed a smart little cruiser with a round bottom and attractive cabin but without a flying bridge. A week after the earlier conversation on the cruisers, Ed asked if it had a flying bridge, and was told it didn't. Once again, acting uncertain and speaking softly, he said, "Oh, I forgot." It appeared that Ed, at 77 years of age, had embellished a little and got tripped up. He then said a round bottom is an advantage in offshore cruising.

Sometimes Ed was annoyed for not remembering all the details surrounding an event. "Ask me what happened yesterday, and I won't remember," Ed said a few times at eighty with a big grin. He was joking, for his mind was still sharp. What he often did, however, was to condense an event and skip important details. Fortunately, family members, friends, or clients, who were there, could add information he had forgotten.

In the spring of 1972, *Spellbound* again sailed to New York, taking advantage of a favorable wind. "We really flew," Oberlin said. Her classic lines, custom features, and bright work were a magnet for admiring boaters. "Wherever we'd go into port, we got attention," he said. "People would ask if it was an old boat."

When asked for an opinion of Ed Cutts as a designer/builder of wooden boats, Abe Oberlin said, "I think he's at the top of his class. There's nothing on a wooden boat that Ed can't do personally. He cast the keel and made the centerboard on *Spellbound*. I think it has 11,000 pounds of keel out of 21,000 pounds. He also made a lot of the castings. He figured out everything. He designed the sails just as he designed everything," Oberlin said. "Ed's an all-around boatbuilder. I have no experience with any other, but his boats were beautiful and fast. They're all fast."

Spar-building was something Ed learned from the LaBlanc Brothers at Nevins, and since then he had designed and built spars for all his boats. "If you were going to build a wooden spar, you would never use epoxy," he said. "But then everybody does it, but it's not the right stuff to use. Because if you go too fast, you don't have an opportunity to keep tightening the clamps all day long, until there is no seam you can find with your eye.

"The other thing is epoxy doesn't like sunlight. If you're going to varnish a spar, you have a mast out in the sunlight all the time, and it's not right," he said. "So there are selections of materials that also have much to do with it. There's a whole line of studies. You have spars that are fifty years old or more that are perfect — perfect," he said hitting a joyful, approving tenor. This pitch contrasted with his usual baritone range.

"And you ask yourself what the hell kind of glue is this they were using? Herreshoff's hollow spars were easier to make. The round spar is terrible to make. And also they had varying thicknesses, but the box spar was exact all the time. And so it was more dependable."

Ed Cutts used Sitka spruce for spars and, like most builders, usually selected white cedar for planking. Asked about fir, he said, "Fir you may use for a clamp. Decks are pretty much the same material as the hull in our boats. Some builders use plywood decks, but I never liked plywood because the weight is very heavy. But it has certain advantages," he said. "We don't use pine. It doesn't have the longevity expectations that cedar does."

Ed learned from experience where to find suppliers for any type of wood. "If we need spar quality, they would know what we are talking about. We don't use much oak anymore, but white oak would be the only oak you would use." Historian Joseph Goldenberg wrote that early boatbuilders who arrived in Massachusetts from England used red oak at first with disastrous results. Their boats didn't hold up, and so the master builders were blamed. They were experienced with English oaks but unfamiliar with New England varieties. (Goldenberg)

In 1974, Joe Ruddy, who was a DuPont salesman-engineer, ordered main and mizzen masts for a 42' motorsailer. For winter layup, he had his boat in another Oxford yard, where a fire had destroyed a shed with his masts. Asking around Oxford and St. Michaels, he learned Ed Cutts could build wooden masts in the age of aluminum. Cutts & Case built them of spruce to original specifications. "From then on," Ruddy said, "I kept my boat in Ed's place, and we got to be friends." He and his wife spent weekends on the boat and vacationed on Chesapeake Bay.

In the early 70s, Ed Cutts took up flying. His Navy experience with fighter plane ordnance and flying in PBYs led to this goal. He cycled over to the Easton airport to talk with instructor Bill Newnam, who had flown fighters in WWII. During lessons, Ed quickly learned that he had one recurring problem. Newnam would ask, "Eddie, what the hell are you leaning into the turns for?"

"I leaned as if I were on a motorcycle," Ed said. "Of course, you don't do that in an airplane. You just sit there because the centripetal force holds you straight. The instructor got a kick out of it because I would go to the airport on my motorcycle."

Once Ed earned a pilot's license, he bought a Cessna 172. "It was a wonderful little plane, and Maggie loved it because we could go to New York and see her relatives in 1¾ hours. You would be worn out if you tried that in a car and returned in one day." They flew between Easton airport and Long Island airport, for a one-day round trip. The plane could go 125 mph, he said, but flight speed was about 110. "It was a safe plane to fly. It had 40-degree flaps, so you could float down without power if you wanted." He flew over the New Jersey coast on these trips. "Returning," he said, "it would be black on the Atlantic side and lighted along the shore on the right."

As a pilot with engineering experience, he felt comfortable with the sound of the six-cylinder engine. "It was almost a purr and smooth as silk," he said. One time Ed became aware the purr had a strange clicking sound. He was flying south at night with Maggie and her mother, who didn't like flying, seated behind him. He checked the gauges, the fuel level, and the radio. Everything was normal. He looked over his chart to determine his position and the nearest airport. Wanting to check on his passengers before saying anything, he turned around. The noise increased. Maggie smiled and seemed fine. He turned further and had his answer. The emergency was over. His mother-in-law, with eyes shut, was counting her rosary beads.

During these trips, Ed missed the convenience of transportation when he arrived at small airports. He decided a motorcycle could be the answer, so he re-engineered a Honda cycle, a CL 100 circa 1971. "I cut the frame and shortened the bike to fit," he said. "It came apart in two pieces with a regular locking mechanism I made, so tools weren't needed. It was handy, and two people would have transportation."

Ed's father Vernon had lived a long life, but in 1972, he died at the age of 91. Ed knew, all his life, that the two sides of the family were distant and mostly out of touch because of Vernon's marriage to Adelaide. When Vernon died, however, Ed saw the families come together, because of their mutual love for this exceptional man.

Three years later, Ed learned that Buddy's health was failing. Ed hadn't seen very much of his half-brother, who was twenty-three years older. After retiring from the Borden Company, Buddy Cutts lived in St. Petersburg, Florida, where he drove a school bus. One day his son Bob Cutts was visiting Buddy with his own wife Pam and their two boys, Robert and Michael.

"The family was sitting on the front porch," Bob Cutts said, "when up came Ed and Maggie on a motorcycle. We didn't know they were arriving until they drove up, and we couldn't believe our eyes." He and the others thought they had driven all the way down from Maryland on the small bike, before they learned Ed had unloaded it from his plane and assembled it. "It was amazing," Bob said.

When Ed sold his Cessna after twenty-five years, he gave the special Honda cycle to the buyer. He had never thought of patenting his take-apart motorcycle, which could have proven popular with small-plane owners or cruising boaters. "Why, I'm doing this stuff all the time and with many different things," Ed said. "Patents are a bother and very expensive. But, once in a while I get one." He thought for a spell. "That was an old-model motorcycle, and there's open gas in a pan involved. So it's a little dangerous to take on a plane."

In 1977, Ed and Maggie Cutts began to take a special interest in a 15-year-old Oxford boy, Seth Hetherington. "Ed would have me at his dinner table two or three nights a week," Seth said. "I was sitting there because I had a dysfunctional family." After his father had moved out of their Oxford home, Seth's mother began concentrating on his two younger sisters.

"Ed was my surrogate father. When I was having trouble or any issues, that man would do anything for me. And he did it all."

Seth was at the boatyard or the house much of the time during a formative period from fourteen to eighteen years of age, and Ronnie was his best friend then as in the future. "We would sit with Ed at night for hours and talk about yacht design, life, sailing, his experience with Herreshoff," Seth said in 2007. "I don't think he would be the yacht designer and builder he is today if it wasn't for Herreshoff. I often stayed there two or three days, and he would give me gourmet food. I sat at his dinner table as a family member many a meal, and the round table now in the kitchen is the same table I sat at thirty years ago. He would take a pencil and on a piece of laminate of the dinner table draw more things than you can imagine. When we were together with him, it wasn't only boats but also motorcycles and airplanes." Ed sometimes took his boys and Seth flying.

"During the years I lived in Oxford, I spent more time at their dinner table than I did at home. It was an exceptional part of my life," Seth said, "the years I had with Ed, the teenage years, which are the toughest ones."

"Our dad was always sketching and cartooning boats," Eddie Jr. said, in 2010. "He would sketch them on the table top while having a cup of coffee. We have many of his inspirational sketches that were done on paper place settings in diners . . . while in a discussion of the characteristics of what the boat he was drawing would be. Those drawings were often grabbed by us, sometimes left on the table. Truth is he knew in his head he could always draw it better in his studio and produce it."

Ed's boys worked together on summer vacations for a number of years. "We handled all the antique boats — we cleaned, varnished, sanded, and planked," Eddie said. "Ronnie and I got into so much trouble, but it was funny, and Ed would come to our defense. The important part was he would always ground us in a

John Case watches Ed drawing a new design.
William Hingst

very philosophical way. He'd say, 'When I was growing up, here's what my father would tell me about the importance of life.'"

When the last boats were coming out of the water for storage, November 1977, Ed Cutts began drawing a new boat for customer, Tom Wellman, who ordered a 42' 4" sloop. In the construction drawings and building, Ed emulated techniques he had learned from his mentor. "If you were going to build a boat that was going to be sectionally wide in the garboards," Ed said, "the very wide keel would swell too much, and you had a problem. If you put in an exceptionally wide piece of wood, its shrinkage and swelling would give you some trouble after a while.

"Francis Herreshoff considered a wide keel would be a good thing," he said, "but he knew of the swelling problems. Francis asked, 'Why have a keel at all?' What he did was to bring the top of the ballast up into the boat. And he put a rabbet into the side of the lead. Then he had the builders plank right into that rabbet. It was a wonderful way to do it, and this would avoid all future problems. Some of his boats have not moved at all, so they are just as solid as the day they were built."

Ed designed Wellman's sloop with the Cutts horizontal wheel. And he specified self-adjusting ports, invented by Ralph Wiley, which opened automatically to windward and closed to leeward. The yacht, to be named *Jeanne,* had a special feature not usually seen on smaller yachts — bookshelves and an armchair. Reading was important to Wellman while cruising or weekending on a boat, so he and Ed worked out plans to include a comfortable armchair. The client knew the very armchair he wanted — a buttoned, red-leather chair identical to the one once owned by Governor Thomas E. Dewey of New York State. Wellman ordered this. "The chair was cut and made to fit the hull contours," Ed said. As a result it is fixed, permanent, and an integral part of the design, forward in the main cabin at a slight angle to keep feet clear of the companionway, and next to a reading lamp and built-in bookshelves.

After the yard completed the boat, Wellman presented a duplicate "Governor Dewey" chair to Ed. Now in the living room between the door and a water-facing window, it became Ed's favorite chair.

Seth Hetherington, who had worked on *Jeanne's* garboard planks, said, "I watched *Jeanne* go from a keel to a boat in the water." He helped the crew, including Downes Curtis, with the launch and then witnessed an interesting scene. "Ed Cutts wouldn't let the customer go for sea trials on the boat," Seth said. "He told Mr. Wellman, if I remember correctly, 'This boat is mine until I give her to you.'" He was checking for anything that might have to be modified or changed.

As a tribute to the battleship *Iowa* from his Navy Yard days, Ed designed an out-curving bow for *Jeanne.* "It's not clipper bowed," Ed said, "for it has the same curves as the *Iowa.* I just liked it. I

Jeanne, completed in 1979, measured 44' LOA. The cabin has a built-in Gov. Dewey armchair for the owner who liked to read on cruises.
Benjamin Mendlowitz

made the deck wider forward so you could handle anchors." It's interesting that he added this information rather pointedly. A month before, he had been told that an article on *Jeanne's* launching, while favorable to the boat, had quoted a knowledgeable observer who saw neither an anchor nor a hawse pipe. Ed countered this criticism firmly. "The boat didn't need a hawse pipe. And when she was fitted out, she carried two anchors with the rode in the forepeak."

When the yard made wood hardware patterns from Ed's designs, a foundry made the bronze castings. "We made sand castings and cast right here for large ballasts, because they were hard to transport," Ed said. An example was *Spellbound's* ballast of 11,000 pounds.

Ed's interest in all components of a boat included engines. In 1977, he had an idea for a new kind of piston engine, so he drew up engineering plans and built it. This was unlike other steam engines, because this one didn't have a separate boiler. "It had a heat maze on top that collected heat as it was turned by a burner-type heat source, which heated up almost cherry red," he said. "There was a timed water injection, which burst into steam immediately and drove the pistons down. That was an interesting engine, unlike any other steam engine," he said, "so I thought I could patent it, and I did. But, it didn't pan out as well as I'd hoped on bench tests." Soaring gas prices in 2007 motivated Ed to say he was thinking about working on the engine again. His machine shop was on the second floor, so he said he would need help climbing. He was seventy-nine at that time and didn't follow through on this engine.

After 33' *Rebellion* returned to the yard in 1977, Ed loved sailing her. Eddie Jr. and Ronnie raced her at the Tred Avon Yacht Club, and Ed occasionally joined them for the longer races. Judging by the trophies on shelves in Byberry House's living room, *Rebellion* achieved recognition with the competitive Cutts as skippers. In the Family Racing Invitational of spring 1978, they placed first, and in 1979 Family Spring Series they were first again. They garnered another first in the 1980 Family Invitational and won a plate trophy for second place in the Choptank Cup Performance Handicap Racing Fleet (PHRF) Spinnaker Race. Also in 1980 they were second in the Hammond Memorial Race, third in the Oxford Regatta race to Oxford, second for Chesapeake Bay Yacht Racing Association week, and first for the Family Racing Fall Series — all Club events.

Seth Hetherington often raced on *Rebellion*, mostly with Eddie and a few times with Ed. "Ed would always watch us from the shore," Seth recalled, "to see how we trimmed the boat. He was very critical of how his boat was sailing. I was surprised the few times I was caught sailing the boat light sheeted. He always commented if you didn't draft the boat properly."

Ed sailed in a few Annapolis-Oxford races. "He wasn't as keen for it as Eddie and I were," Seth said. "He had gotten us into racing, which is what he wanted to do." Ed often said he had no interest in creating a racing class. That is too bad, for when his sailboats raced, they did quite well.

When talking to a customer who wanted a boat built, Ed had a modus operandi that served him well. For one thing he moved slowly. He always tried to learn as much relevant information as possible before starting sketches. He wanted to know the basics: the client's ability at the helm, special wants and interests, whether single-handing or using an experienced crew, the size and ages of the family, and where they planned to cruise.

Ed would discuss cost boundaries and options with a client. He gave an example. "For instance, a diesel engine costs twice as much as a gas engine of the same horsepower. Diesel engines are very heavy things. Recently they've been trying to make them lightweight, but they seem to be having their problems. Diesel fuel does weigh more than gasoline, and the battery load is considerably more. It takes more cranking power to push the pistons with a compression ratio of approximately 15-1 compared to gas engines at about 8-1." With weight an important consideration, Ed preferred gas engines, which he termed "very safe with modern fuel injection."

Besides his recommendations, he would listen carefully to each client. "I would sit down with the client until I was pretty sure of what he wanted. When we saw that his head was on straight, we went ahead." At this point, he would sketch the boat and refine the design until the client was satisfied. Then he did a scale construction drawing and carved a half model. In the tradition of the great boatbuilders he used these models to loft the lines, but for this step he invented a completely unique system, discussed in a later chapter.

Among the experienced men regularly working for Ed Cutts was a skilled African-American sailmaker named Downes Curtis. He had learned the arts of canvas and cotton from an English sailmaker in Maryland. He had worked at Ratsey and Lapthorn, the well-known firm which had made sails for America's Cup yachts for a hundred years. Ronnie Cutts had good memories of Downes, as well as the famous sail company that began in England in 1790 and spread to the US. "They were good, and there's no question about it. People today don't know just how good they were. Sails today are probably 100 percent better than they were forty years ago, but you've got to look at how a Ratsey clew was sewn. People don't know how to hand-rope like that anymore, but Downes Curtis knew."

Downes Curtis, a fine canvas worker and sailmaker, with Ed on *Spellbound.*
Cutts Family

Sitting in his small, neat cottage where his nautical carpentry was evident in the cabinets, Ronnie looked up at a framed picture of Downes. "He was a very good friend of mine." In his Oxford loft, his brother Albert worked with him.

"Downes made sails for Scrappy Cats and things like that," Ed Cutts said. "He did all of our canvas work, such as sail covers and sun awnings for many years. He was a very personable fellow, much liked by everyone. In every function of this yard, he was included as one of us, and we always had a lot of fun together."

During summers and after school, Downes sometimes hired local kids and taught them sail making and canvas work. "Some of them are very successful," Eddie Jr. said. "They all have a deep abiding respect and pleasant memories of Downes Curtis, and so do we." His photograph sat on the fireplace mantle of Ed's living room.

At sixteen, Seth Hetherington left Saints Peter and Paul School because he wanted to work for Downes to learn about canvas and sail work. Ed Cutts spoke to Jack Streeton, Seth's uncle who was the Commodore of the Tred Avon YC. The two persuaded Downes Curtis to hire Seth because of his enthusiasm for canvas, and Downes gave him a job at $90 a week. Seth bicycled to the loft, where he learned canvas work from one of the best.

"If Ed needed a sail repaired, he would pick up the phone and call Downes, and we would be there in a few minutes," Seth said. "Downes was the oldest sailmaker who ever lived and was trained by an Englishman. Downes taught me the trade of what I am doing today." Seth runs the Mobile Marine Canvas Company in Harpswell, Maine.

Seth took a deep breath over the phone before he told how Downes Curtis, returning home at 4 a.m. one night, had a head-on auto collision. He was taken to the Easton hospital where he was examined and released. "They sent him home, and he died of a brain aneurism that night. He had a bleeding in his head, but they didn't know. But he had a peaceful . . . ," and here Seth stopped a moment for a quick audible breath. "Don't you know the guy touched my life the most?" He took a steadying breath. "Now it hurts." He told how Downes Curtis had died before the airing on PBS of a TV documentary on him.

From 1987, Seth lived in Bethesda attending college in Washington for four years, but he kept returning to the Eastern Shore. "I spent every weekend somewhere in Oxford, but most of the time it was at Byberry," he said. "Ed cooked up amazing meals and had a dinner-time rule in the household: 'Take the phone off the hook and hang it until we're done.'"

As fiberglass sailboats became popular, some owners of small wooden boats coated the bottoms to cover defects or to preserve the boat. At City Island, they coated *Blue Jays*, *Snipes*, and *Lawley 110's*, and at Easton sailors heard someone had applied fiberglass to a *Comet*. Boaters around the US did the same. Coating sounded like a solution to prolong the life of a wooden boat. But not to Ed Cutts. "Well, that can be," he said, "but they have to up the hull strength required. For one thing fiberglass is very heavy, so they have increased this [weight] seriously in a racing boat like a *Comet*. People who put glass on wooden boats horrify us. We don't see any need for it."

Sometimes people called Ed Cutts to ask for his advice. One caller in 2005 was Judge North, who owned three Chesapeake Bay sailing canoes. North asked Ed about one of his canoes that had a lot of water in the hull.

"You can put a dehumidifier inside and then cover everything with sheeting," Ed said. "Do you have a scale? We have one that takes up to 5,000 pounds. The weight difference would show water was being removed."

North then asked him about putting fiberglass over a hull to protect it, as some people had suggested. "You'll trap the moisture,"

Ed said, "if it's coming from the inside." Then, he went on to compare fiberglass and cedar. "Fiberglass is heavy stuff. It weighs 100 pounds a cubic foot, while white cedar weighs 22 or 23 pounds." North decided to think it over. Ed never found out what happened.

Whenever the subject of fiberglass came up, Ed often seemed to be lecturing to students. He would go into great detail comparing fiberglass and wood. "Any designer with a bit of brain knows what he can do with that savings in weight. If you build two boats exactly the same, one a wooden boat and one a glass boat, you would find the wooden boat has a much better ballast-to-weight ratio. If it were a power boat, it would sit higher on its lines and have a better power-to-weight ratio. Since the engine now doesn't have as much to drive, the boat will go faster." He paused to let this sink in.

"Fiberglass is even heavier than cement. Look it up in an engineering book because I don't like to give out wrong information. Putting glass on a boat also changes the structure badly," he said. "A good designer should know what direction he wants to put the strength and should put the strength in that direction. Of course, you can do that with wood because wood is a uni-directional material. But fiberglass is not. Fiberglass is a two-directional material, so if you need the strength that way, you must also take it the other way. This is adding an awful amount of unnecessary weight for someone who really understands the requirements of the materials he's using."

In comparing boats of fiberglass and wood, there is a difference in the cost of major renovations and maintenance. When asked about this, Ed avoided cost comparisons, but a metaphor rolled off his tongue. "If you like to dress well, it will be more expensive than if you are content with overalls. But if you are sartorially interested, you must dress well. If you marry a beautiful woman, you try to give her everything you can. And when a man marries a beautiful boat, he should feel that way. He should do the best he can for her, because he admires her and so does everyone else."

While yachts are sometimes constructed of steel or aluminum, Cutts & Case had a boat in their yard that used another material. It was back in 1966 when a large blue yacht tied up at the outside slip for painting above the water line. This was Maryland Governor Spiro Agnew's official state yacht, which carried the name of the previous governor, *Millard B. Tawes*.

Eleven-year-old Eddie Cutts had his cousin Jeff Durstewitz visiting for a week. They had secured two air rifles and a supply of BB pellets. "We were gunning everything in sight," Eddie said. "Boys will be boys."

A scaffold was hanging over the state yacht's port bow where painters were prepping the hull. "One of the painters began to chip away at a rust-flaking spot," Eddie said, "and a piece of fairing fell off the bow into the water — about half the size of a Volkswagen. The yacht groaned a bit and listed a few degrees to starboard. The painters were shaken and horrified. My dad and the foreman Plink were very upset."

Then, Plink went over and explained the strange occurrence to the yacht's captain. "Oh, that happens all the time," said the captain. "Don't worry about it." He checked where the concrete section had broken away and made a phone call. A truck would deliver fairing-cement bags, he said, and after application, the yacht would look fine.

After the chunk of the hull vanished into the water, Ed and Plink marched the two sharpshooters out to the ship. "Before the now-missing port bow and amongst stern faces, we were asked to explain," Eddie said. "The accusation was that we had BB-gunned the port bow off the Governor of Maryland's yacht. We were horrified that we could have done such damage. We were told our BBs had ricocheted as we were gunning along the shoreline on yesterday's low tide. That night we slept in the anxious discomfort of cold sweat, with no BB guns."

The boys learned more the next morning. "The consensus was that rust or vibration might have caused the damage," Eddie said. "We discovered the men had enjoyed a good laugh at our expense, because we couldn't have done it."

⚓

Chapter Eight

RESEARCH AND DEVELOPMENT

IN 1978, John Case moved fulltime to California, but he still returned to Cutts & Case for quarterly visits to monitor the operation of the boatyard. He wanted to hear from Ed about everything going on, including plans for the future. Sixteen-year-old Ronnie Cutts had heard Case talking about research, and he remembered this years later.

"John Case encouraged Dad to do experiments for improvements in wooden-boat construction," Ronnie said, "and for a greater degree of protection from rot and water damage." Ed didn't need persuading to make the wooden boats he loved even better, but Case set him on course.

Seeing that fiberglass boats were popular and less costly, John Case wanted to advance wooden-boat building. "He had a great interest in technical matters," Eddie Jr. said, "and he had a long-distance vision." Case had been at IBM during the development of the computer process and helped develop programs for banks and business. Without a doubt, Case's far-sightedness resulted in Ed's fitting research into a busy schedule.

"John was always looking forward to the cutting edge of things in technology and in companies," Eddie said. "He knew things had to change, but he always looked to be sure that the change would be profitable — sometimes in money, sometimes in technology, sometimes in research and development. It had to be profitable in something, or in his opinion it should be dumped."

In 1979, Ed embarked on a course that was challenging and maybe impossible. He planned to analyze, in detail, the standard methods of boat building. This research would include everything from framing and planking to the use of metal. He was looking for an improvement in the areas of strength, weight, and wood protection. He wanted to increase a wooden boat's lifespan, as well. "Boats," he often said, "should last longer than we do."

Ed spoke of a technical advancement that his favorite designer had made. "Nat Herreshoff introduced screws. He would have the screws made of bronze, and then he could fasten planking without having two men. Before that, if you riveted a boat, you had to have a man on the inside to peen the copper rivet over a washer. Notice the difference in labor," he said. "But screws had another effect in that they didn't go fully through the frame. They weren't affected by swelling or shrinking like the fully penetrating rivet was." He paused briefly, his eyes looking bright and alert.

"Nat Herreshoff was scientific in figuring out the scantlings of all the parts in a boat and their relationship to each other. So his boats not only came in lighter but also with material economy," he said. "Of course, the Herreshoff boats were beautifully made. He used the most modern things he could find. But he didn't have what we have now."

Ed wondered where and how he should start his research, despite a background in metal engineering and boat building. "I thought there was a great science in wooden-boat building, but that it had never fully been considered," he said. "I decided to put the toolbox away and to work with a microscope. I would try to find if something was going on here that nobody knew about.

"I examined the structure of wood. I decided early on that I would like to know more about the material and how it was working." He found a graphic example. "The pendulum of a clock doesn't change lengths. If it did, the clock would be changing its time also. It swings with absolutely perfect timing to the other end of the swing, but if you should increase its length, it would change. And if you should decrease its length, it would change also. But, sideways the wood was changing all the time, which didn't affect the timing of the clock."

Standard construction with bronze screws going through the outside of the hull bothered Ed. "This is the same as putting perforations in a piece of paper," he said. "It weakens it, and of course, the paper will tear easily. Perforating the outside of the hull with countersinks and bronze fastenings weakens the lineal strength of the boat. Now, the boats I've seen have always been strong enough to withstand that. But if it wasn't done that way, then the boats could be slightly lighter and just as strong." He paused a moment. "That would translate to speed."

Ed desperately wanted to find some technique to eliminate holes outside the hull. And secondly, he wanted to reduce the amount of metals. "You can't avoid the metal," he said. "You've got the engine, the shaft, struts, and propeller, so you're going to have some electrolysis. The idea is to reduce it, especially in the hull structure. The total mass can make a difference, so the object is to avoid metal as much as possible. Then the whole hull becomes inert with minimum electrolysis reactions from the salt, copper, and water," he said. "But, of course, a hull had those things that could not be avoided: the bronze and the fastenings, the cellulose carrying it in the wood, and any acids that were introduced. They will give trouble to the wood. That's what I was trying hard to avoid and to discover if it were possible to avoid it."

At this time, Eddie was helping his father when he was reviewing the function and task of the frames in his boats. Recalling this, Eddie said, "When the planking tries to change its width — its shape due to moisture and other reasons — the frames will actually hold the lumber from moving. That's their job. The actual shape of the boat is determined from the molds and the varying widths of the planking. The job of the framing is a tensile load to keep those planks from moving."

After hearing Eddie's comment, Ed added his observations about plank-on-frame construction. "In order to hold the planking in place, you had to cantilever loads across the frame. That meant you had to put a hole in the outside of the plank in order to put the screw in, and then that screw carried the load in a cantilever fashion across to some other place. That's not good because it shouldn't have to do that. It should be able to carry its load directly, where the load is put on it.

"So, the only way to do that," he said, "would be if the lumber could be arrested from swelling, as the frame is trying to do. Arresting it, in the center of the planking substrate, would be direct, would carry the load better, and it would do something else. If you could do it this way, it would avoid puncturing of the outside of the hull for the screws. A constant puncturing."

Ed was just warming up as he summarized his research work and his thinking. He sat in his red-leather, Governor Dewey chair gesturing now and then, speaking logically like a professor of physics.

"Now, the diameter that was cut for a plug in the outside of the hull was quite large. If using a #12 screw and calculating the sectional area of that plug and that screw, it equals a small groove across the plank. I decided to groove the lumber and to put chords inside." He stressed key words like "groove" and watched to be sure his description was clear.

"When we first came out with this idea, we did it with stainless-steel wire. We put it right in the center [of the two planks] where the load was going to be exerted. It avoided putting a hole in the outside of the planking, which was not a good thing to do."

In 1981, Ed Cutts had turned to available epoxies that had impressed him in his earlier experiment for a roller-furling head-sail system. Eddie, who had worked with his father, described this process. "He took three chain links and fastened one-foot tubes to the outer links, alternating for a light and very strong luff. We designed and made a block that would hold the stainless-steel roller chain in teeth, so the head stay was held fixed and aloft. The difficulty was that we had to get a rope somehow onto a piece of chain."

Ed Cutts tried different methods without success, but he remembered epoxies from his work at Grumman. He tried soaking the rope in an epoxy.

"When it was hard, we could machine the rope and drill it," Eddie said. "You could actually cut threads into the ends. It was very interesting." This process rotated the jib for any amount of reef.

"Still," Ed said, "you could let the sail down. It worked fine, but it didn't sell. When you patent things, you don't know if they'll take off or not. Most of them don't, but still you have hopes." He discarded the roller-reefing system. In a way this experiment was profitable, because Ed saw the great potential in epoxy. And he wanted to apply this strength to hulls.

In an experiment, Ed put braided wire in a groove cut into a piece of wood and filled the groove with epoxy. He then discovered the epoxy accomplished more than he had expected. "The epoxy transported into the end grain on each adjacent side of that groove, and that prevented linear migration of moisture down the planking."

Using a simile, he said, "If it rains, the top of the tree gets moisture, same as the root, because of capillary structure, which the Lord made. It's just like a pump but there's nothing running." Ed's religious beliefs often appear casually in his conversation. "When you plank a boat and water gets to the end grain of the lumber, it begins to travel linearly," he said, "because that's how it was designed by the Big Designer. This process stops it by putting a groove in there and waterproof epoxy. With its low surface tension, the epoxy liked capillaries, and it went in, hardened and sealed. So it was fastened to them by thousands of spikes into the capillaries," he said. "Other glues were more surface oriented, but the epoxy went any place there was an opportunity."

Ed's customers, associates, and friends know about his goal to extend wooden-boat life far beyond expectations. When he heard reports that some epoxies were good for hundreds of years, he began running tests to compare the products. "I soaked them in salt water and did whatever I could to see what the results would be. And I checked them with a microscope and continued to do this for quite a while. We noticed no deterioration, although we looked for it." He discovered when using epoxy as a fastener, water didn't migrate in the wood. "And if water can't migrate, you won't have a problem," he said. "You couldn't prevent it the way things were built before because every screw hole was a possible migration spot — one of many hundreds. And there was electrolysis too."

Ed thought that stainless-steel rigging wire might be suitable to use with epoxy, but as before he had to run adequate tests. Stainless steel in 1981 was the strongest material easily available, he said.

The summer of 1981, Adolph Egli, the Ford research director, was vacationing in Oxford, and sailing *La Mouette*, the 37' 4" sloop. After watching Ed experiment with epoxy, Egli started working with him. To run a test for strength, they took small pieces of wood with 3/32nds rigging wire epoxied in a groove inside and ran a loop outside the block. While the bond appeared to be strong in shop tests, they needed to know exactly how strong.

At the Maryland State Roads Testing Division in Easton, Ed told the test-machine operator. "We would like you to pull the wires from the wooden blocks."

"Sure, no problem," said the operator. He set up the test on the small blocks with external wire loops.

"And then can you tell us what the yield is when they come out?"

"Sure, no problem," the operator said with a smile, as if he expected the wires to come right out. Ed and Adolph watched this critical test of the theory. The apparently-simple test of pulling out the looped wire took much longer than expected.

The mood became an intense competition of sorts, and tension was increasing, Eddie said. "In the end, all the engineers in the place were standing around. The machine was moaning and groaning until it pulled the wire out." They repeated the test a second time with another epoxied steel wire. It took 1,232 and 1,240 pounds of pull. The test was a success. Now Ed Cutts, Adolph Egli, Eddie, and Ronnie knew how well the epoxied wire would hold. Putting the technique into his construction plans, Ed designed an experimental, round-bottom, mahogany, rowing skiff, and planned to build it.

Mrs. Peter Black, of Royal Oak, saw Ed's drawing and ordered the skiff, to be built with the new Cutts Methods, for her husband. Ed with his son Eddie began on the construction.

They build it with epoxy packed around 7 x 19 stainless-steel braided wire, roughly ⅛ inch, in grooves between the double layers of carvel planking. They launched the attractive rowing skiff called *Ocean Gem* that year. Its specifications are: 13' 6" LOA, 8' LWL, 4' beam, and 3' 6" draft.

With the help of an attorney, Ed Cutts applied for a patent for what he called the "Cutts Method." In 1982, the US Patent

Office granted this to him. In 2005, at seventy-eight, Ed agreed that the patent had probably driven other builders away from the new technique. But, he had feared that his "Method" might be used incorrectly and be unsafe, so that he could be blamed for any injury. This was a strong fear, perhaps irrational, he carried through the years. His refusal to release construction drawings for publication followed this scenario. He could be adamant and even act rude when requests came in for plans, but he was always cautious on the side of safety.

"The test dinghy had metallics in it," Ed said, "which I was hoping somehow to avoid. My desire was to build a boat without metal or with an absolute minimum of metal. I felt if I could make the wire of an inert mode that it would have tremendous lasting power." Nevertheless, he was proud of the little boat. Twenty-five years later he would tell people to look at it in the water at the foot of the dock. "It was experimental," he said, "and still it's in perfect condition."

In 1982, Ed learned about a new product called Kevlar from his customer and friend, Joe Reddy, an industrial salesman at DuPont. In the Wilmington laboratories, a chemical scientist was experimenting with different formulas of cord materials. Stephanie Kwolek had first developed, in 1965, a new polymer solution from para-aminobenzoic acid and had then wanted to make it into fibers.

David Tanner, director of DuPont's Pioneering Research Laboratories, wrote about the ten years of research and development behind Kevlar. "Experienced fiber technicians advised against trying to spin it. Stephanie went against conventional wisdom and insisted on extruding it through the spinneret anyway. Surprisingly, it spun well," Tanner wrote and then gave the results. "The stress-strain on this fiber was startling. The physical test lab had to run it several times before anyone would believe the results. The fiber was *very* different, had the desired extreme stiffness and heat resistance and breaking strength many folds higher than existing fibers." The article said that co-worker Herb Blades also deserved credit. (Tanner)

"With the sheer tensile strength of Kevlar, if it was the wrong kind, it could be pulled through the epoxy," Ed said. He conducted experiments of his own in 1982–3 with various Kevlars. Then, DuPont developed a form of Kevlar that was very tenacious in epoxies, which held it to breaking strength — this was called K49. "I heard what DuPont was saying about the material's characteristics," Ed said. "They were astonished and so was I. Kevlar, as they named it, could not be stripped out of the epoxies without destruction. Therefore, I could get close to achieving the strength of the Kevlar itself. I said, 'Man! That's exactly what I've been looking for!'

"I felt it had to be braided so it would interlock with the capillaries in the wood. I went to a company that could braid the material for us, the way we wanted it. The results were tremendous." Speaking with excitement and joy, he said. "It was five times the strength of steel and not biodegradable." A triumphant "Ha-Ha" followed. "It was light as a feather, it was unreal, it was unbelievable. When I found it had greater tenacity in the wood than the stainless steel, I knew I was onto another product.

"You have to have proofs of these things, because you can't tell someone to put his money into something of which you have no proof," Ed said. "Of course, when you do anything like that, you run risks." He knew of some problems and tested for evidence of others. "Epoxy weakened," he said, "if exposed to bright light, but between two layers of planking and paint, this was never an issue." His experiments proved that Kevlar cord neither stretched nor moved once it was set in epoxy. Ed invented more tests to ascertain its long-term reliability.

About a year and a half after completing the experimental skiff, Ed was convinced this new technique was dependable and would last. Therefore, he started using Kevlar-49 cord with epoxy on a major job. They were rebuilding the lower futtocks and hull of a 48' yacht from the 1930s, owned by Joe Murray of the Classic Yacht Club. The results turned out to be excellent.

The original "Cutts Method" brochure went to over a thousand people who requested it over a three-year period, starting in 1987. After the boatyard's successful renovations with braided Kevlar-49 from the mid-eighties, he modified the groove layout. "The loop was at the sheer and then went down and under the boat and up the other side and looped again. It was a continuous cord," he said. "But we found there was a better way, because it didn't have to be continuous at all." The cord is cut at the top of the planking, where it would be covered by the decking or sheer plank.

Aside from Ed's background in metal-machining and boatbuilding, one might wonder what additional studies led to his research achievement. After tenth-grade high-school studies at the Navy Yard, he studied engines, was a machinist, and then did ordnance work for the Navy.

Books, of course, carry tremendous impact. The reading that people choose can produce a major influence on their lives, defining who they are, what they know, and how they solve problems. Ed's books, piled on shelves around the house, illuminate much about the man. In his small and private design den are books from the Society of Naval Architects and Engineers, to which he belonged for years. In 1985, he became commodore of the Classic Boat Club of America, so books from this club are on the shelves. In the front hall bookcase under the stairs, are: *The Encyclopedia Britannica*, issues of *Nautical Quarterly*, and copies of the New York Yacht Club's Members' Handbook.

In a second-floor bedroom of Byberry House was a green shaded lamp on a large desk. A large bookcase spoke of Ed Cutts's self education and research. In 2005, the collection included *Traditions and Memories of American Yachting* by Olin Stephens, *The Yachtsman's Guide to the Racing Rule*, and *The Way Things Work*. Next to some fiction classics, possibly belonging to his children, were technical volumes: *A History of Mechanical Inventions, Properties of Glass and Refractories*, and a thick reference work, *The Practical and Technical Encyclopedia*.

When reminded about his technical volumes, Ed smiled, nodding as he recognized the book titles. He began to talk about schooling in general. "I don't put too much stock in formal education." His family and friends have all heard this. "The designer of the microwave oven had three years of schooling," he continued. "Nat Herreshoff studied yacht design informally. A lot of the greats weren't formally educated. Edison got through the fourth grade; that's all, and look at what he did. They had their own minds and they did very well." He was informed that Thomas Edison had home schooling. "Of course," Ed said, "it's all basically home schooling."

Ed studied required high school subjects at the Metropolitan Maritime High School and at the Brooklyn Navy Yard. Although he had mechanical drawing at the school, he had been drawing since he was a boy. He had learned freehand drawing by practice.

Francis Herreshoff, who liked Ed's early designs, considered drawing a most important skill. In *Sensible Cruising Designs*, the Publisher's Preface by Roger Taylor quoted a letter from the designer: "As for the training — if you want to become a yacht designer later, I think if you can draw as much as possible [particularly freehand drawing] it will give you a sense of proportion better than any other kind of training . . . you should draw a great many things from your own imagination, for after all the designer must draw things before they exist. Sometimes I think the training in freehand drawing is more important than training in mechanical drawing, and if you really love freehand drawing this is a good indication of your later ability as a designer. Of course later on I think it is very necessary to serve your time in a boat shop, where boats are really built, as this is the only practical way to learn construction." As we have seen, Herreshoff gave Ed this sound advice, which he followed.

"I found my master teachers," Ed said. "Herreshoff answered my questions, and Nils Halvorsen and Nevins answered the boat building things I wanted to know. That was education for me. I went to the finest people, such as the head of a yachting magazine, and a great designer. That's much better than sitting in a class of fifty people who don't want to learn."

From his Navy and Grumman experience, Ed learned the need for precision when lives were at stake. But, he also studied engineering and marine architecture on his own. His private studies of technical books and scientific papers surely gave him the equivalent of a technical-college degree. Educators may have different opinions, but not everyone is invited to join the engineering staff at Grumman Aviation. It was an honor he appreciated.

After using Kevlar with epoxy in successful repairs, Ed Cutts wanted to use this new technique in a larger boat to prove its value to others. Ongoing experiments were proving that the Kevlar neither stretched nor moved once it was set in epoxy.

In 1983, Ed's yard received a flattering mention in *Nautical Quarterly* magazine in an article about another boatyard. "Concordia Company is one of a handful of yards — among them Paul Luke of E. Boothbay, Maine; Joel White in Brooklin, Maine; and Cutts and Case in Oxford, Maryland — that can legitimately be considered latter-day versions of Nevins, Herreshoff, Quincy Adams and the like." When this article was read to Ed Cutts, he was silent and thought for a moment. "I've seen some Concordia boats, and they were excellent." He admitted it was good to be included with the top yards. (Meyer)

John Case owned large cruising boats, such as his 52' yacht *Tonya*, from 1970 through 1974, when he bought his 64½' yacht *Claymore*. On a visit from California in 1983, he told Ed he was thinking about another boat. "I always liked J. P. Morgan's *Navette*, which was 65 feet." They discussed how Morgan had used the motor-yacht as a commuter from his Hudson River estate to Wall Street or to the New York Yacht Club's mid-town dock. Morgan avoided driving in rush-hour traffic, as did other wealthy yachtsmen.

Case said that Morgan had let him look over his yacht. "It had many features I liked, such as a narrow beam."

"I do too, John, because it means a faster boat," Ed said. "Of course, his boat ran on steam."

"She could go 16 to 18 knots," Case said.

"Well, after all, Nat Herreshoff designed her. It seemed to me, John, she was sort of austere. Our boat would be more modern but with classic lines."

"I liked her looks, especially that long after-cabin, which was a beauty. Can you draw and build something like it — 65 feet overall?"

Ed produced a drawing, featuring a long cabin with a row of windows. They both agreed on the drawing. "I like to name a boat when I begin on it," Ed told him, "so I can be emotionally connected to it. I think *Americana* would be a good name."

John Case digested this. "I don't really care for that name, but I don't have an alternative." As a result, they gave the future motor yacht a second name — *John's Boat*.

"The boat was designed to go 21 knots," Eddie Jr. said, "and for a good reason. It could go from Oxford to New York City in one daylight day, and this was the intention." He also said the yacht would become "a good calling card for the business and type of work this company is capable of doing."

Ed's design had two engines, a large gasoline-powered engine, with a high power-to-weight ratio, and also a small diesel engine. "The idea was to run her on gas to go from here to New York in one day," Eddie explained. "Then you could shift to diesel-fuel power and cruise Long Island Sound at approximately 10 or 11 knots, and only burn gallons an hour instead of the higher consumption rate.

"It's very unusual to have two engines of such different horse-power and sizes," Eddie said. The diesel was 65 or 70 hp, and the gas engine was 280 to 300 hp. "It had a phenomenal amount of torque at 2100 rpm, so you needed about a 3-inch diameter shaft."

After Ed completed the construction designs, the project sat in a back file for awhile. In 1983, Cutts & Case milled wainscoted pine for cabin tops and pine for the station molds. Expert marine joiner Emory Balderson, who had built yachts for John Trumpy in Annapolis before going to work for Wiley, remained when the yard changed hands. He built the cabin superstructure and the molds for the hull. But, again the work stopped, and all this was hoisted overhead to free space in the shed. Ed decided to suspend building the hull because of the work backup.

Ed's brothers and sisters had all owned boats, so their children had experience on the water when growing up. Michael Cutts, son of Ed's nephew Bob, enjoyed boating on visits to Cutts & Case as a boy. In 1982, he entered the US Naval Academy. Forced to drop out for health reasons, he later attended the US Maritime College. After he went to sea for ten years, he worked for a Florida shipping company in charge of oceangoing ships.

In 1985, when Ed's daughter Linda married in Oxford, festive music and dancing filled the boatyard. Ed surprised everyone by doing the *Lindy Hop*, a 1930s dance named for Charles Lindberg, the first man to fly the Atlantic.

When John Case was ready to retire to California in 1985, Ed paid off one loan from his partner. John generously dropped a smaller loan. They were a solid team to the end.

After an article and editorial about Ed Cutts, the boatyard, and his building method appeared in a 1987 *WoodenBoat* issue, a visitor from Norfolk arrived to talk with Ed. Dr. Crile Crisler was a heart surgeon who loved boat building. He had built wooden boats for many years in his home shed. "We hit it off very well," Crisler said. "I think he's the smartest person about boats that

I've ever met. Whatever I asked him, it seemed he had already thought it through and had an insightful answer. I guess that is typical of Ed.

"I asked him if, when using the Cutts Method, the Kevlar cord might not crawl or shift in the grooves after some time," Crisler said. "To show this wasn't the case, Ed showed me what he had done. Some years previously, he had cut a groove into each of two separate blocks of wood and epoxied the ends of a length of his Kevlar cord into those grooves, leaving a length of cord free between the blocks. He then forced the blocks part, thereby placing tension on the Kevlar cord, like the string of a musical instrument, until plucking the cord produced a middle C." Ed had then securely fastened the blocks to a single plank, which he put aside to see if the Kevlar slipped over time.

"The preparation had been there many years," Crisler said, "and still produced a middle C when plucked. I thought that was not only a test of his method, but I was impressed with what an elegant and simple way it was to demonstrate that."

Eddie Jr. recalled his father had set up this test in the middle 1980s, about 28 years earlier. In a 2013 test, the Kevlar cord still resonated middle C.

Dr. Crisler had come up to Oxford to look for miniature *skipjacks*, which the Applegarth Boatyard had built there. He wanted a cruising sloop that could tow a small outboard skiff for fishing the seaside of Virginia's Eastern Shore. He needed simple cabin accommodations with four berths. He and Ed agreed on the dimensions.

Now the doctor got to the reason for his visit. "Can you sell me a design for the little sloop, which I could build in my home shed? I want a boat derived from the *skipjack* heritage."

Since Ed had left the Long Island boatyards, he had never sold his designs to be built elsewhere. And he wasn't about to change.

"Sorry, but I never sell my drawings. After I designed it, anybody doing a poor job of building it would reflect badly on me."

After the doctor heard this, he told Ed about boats he had built, including a hydrofoil sailboat, which he had modified to achieve 35 mph. Ed began to take an interest in his visitor. "I'll consider it," he said. "If you would go home and send me pictures of some of the boats you built, then I can get an idea of what you can do."

The doctor followed through. Ed evaluated the boat photographs, recognized the doctor's ability, and agreed to give him construction plans. With a sketch from his file, he developed construction drawings for a sloop design he called a *Hummingbird*. It had a *skipjack* bow and bowsprit with a raked mast for its low-aspect-ratio rig.

Crisler was the first "outsider" granted permission to build an original Ed Cutts design, and he understood Ed's attitude. "Ed only produces and licenses a design if he has confidence that the person requesting it will have the capability and honesty to see that the boat is built exactly as designed. He worries about providing a design which results in an inferior boat, because it was not built to specs but still has the Cutts name on it," Crisler said. "I think he probably wouldn't do a custom design for someone he didn't like. In other words, having Ed design a boat for you is a very personal thing — I would say a privilege — not just a commercial matter."

Dr. Crisler had been building boats as a hobby starting in the mid-70s and had completed thirteen. He called it "something between a hobby and a business." Because of his busy medical practice as a heart surgeon, he expected *Hummingbird* would take a while.

⚓

Chapter Nine

OLD YACHTS AND THE *FOTO* ODYSSEY

SOUTH OF MAINE, one finds fewer boatyards with builders experienced in wooden-boat repair. This is true for private boats and for commercial boats as well. Norman Bloom of Norwalk, Connecticut, has sixteen oyster boats from 20' to almost 100', based from Southern Connecticut north to Guilford. Eight of these are wood and date from 1924. "They are a ten-times-better workboat than any of fiberglass or steel," he said, "by the way they carry a load. Put a hundred bushels on them, and they really lose no speed."

Bloom's company hauls the boats once a year, does minor repairs in Norwalk, and brings up boatbuilders from New Jersey for caulking and bottom work. For major rebuilding, they run down the coast to Port Norris on Delaware Bay to Steve Fleetwood's boatyard, which also did repair work on Bloom's father's 25 boats.

Norman Bloom said he is worried for the future, for he sees the experienced wooden builders are getting older, with "not many young guys coming in. We are probably one of the last industries using wooden boats." In New Jersey, he co-owns five oyster boats with his brothers.

Ed Cutts, with his years of experience, spoke about rebuilding. "If the old girl needs a complete rebuild, it's often a lot more work than building a boat from scratch." He discussed one problem. "Frames break because the lumber that the boat is planked with swells sideways. Not the long ways, because it's absolutely dependable — you can make a clock pendulum out of it. But crosswise it swells and shrinks," he said. "People who are designing don't realize that the species of wood they are using has much to do with it, and they had planked a boat with a species that warranted a bigger frame.

"The trouble with framing a boat is that one half of the frame is working. When you bend a piece of wood, half from the middle is compressing . . . and only the outside is trying to come apart. People don't realize that. It should make a big difference in the engineering thinking behind this. So when you put a larger frame in, you must realize that you are not getting the full strength of that timber, because half the frame is going into compression. If you bend anything with a whole bunch of laminates, which wood is made of, by God, half of it from its neutral center will be a stretch, and the inner will be a squash."

Cutts & Case continued restoring older motor yachts and sailboats to their former beauty and condition. In 1984, Joseph Murray, who belonged to the Classic Yacht Club, brought in *Widgeon*, a 48' 6" motor-yacht built by Dawn Shipbuilding in the 1930s. The men found extensive water damage, and had to redo all the bottom of the hull to the waterline. "We repaired the aft frames and installed futtocks at the turn of her bilges," Eddie Cutts said. "We used the Cutts Method in the whole lower hull for strength." This was the first use of Ed's epoxy and Kevlar method for rebuilding since its development, and it worked fine.

Another rebuilding job was a 40' trunk-cabin sedan yacht built by Consolidated Ship Builders on City Island, which came into the yard in 1995. The original owner's son, Bill Bunting, inherited the 60-year-old boat, named *Trouper II,* and discovered she was loosening up and taking in water. Soon, he found the cause. "The double-planked boat was riveted every inch on the inch on the ribs," Bunting said. "Consolidated didn't have real, wide frames but narrow ones. Rather than stagger their rivets, they did them in a straight line, which caused a split."

With the water getting in, Bunting knew it was time to do something. After unsatisfactory experiences with two boatyards, he phoned Ed, "who I knew could certainly do the work. But, I know he's always busy." Ed told him to bring *Trouper* over. Bunting had known Ed for twenty years from the Classic Yacht Club. In 1985, Ed was commodore of the Chesapeake-based club. Impressed with the results from the Cutts Method using Kevlar chord and epoxy, Bunting wanted this technique used on his yacht. After he told Ed and his sons what he wanted to accomplish, the yard went to work.

"From the waterline down she was completely replanked with cedar from North Carolina," he said. "Cutts put a new stem in the boat, getting the timber from a dismantled warehouse in Philadelphia. That was a big, heavy piece of oak that was probably over a hundred years old." Maryland Public Television filmed this.

Bunting asked Ed about a problem resulting from the higher-powered replacement engines he had installed. "If I push her, the water comes up past her sides, so you're just running through a tunnel, because she throws so much spray up and over the deck. I want a rail or something that will help to turn that water down.

"I didn't want a spray rail," he said later, "because that's not her vintage. I wanted a rail in her copper-paint line — under water." After their discussion Ed thought over the problem and came up with two rounded rails about 18 feet long. "It was an idea I had," Bunting said, "but truly it was something that Ed designed and put on her." The owner didn't think this design had been done before, but boatyards and builders may know the answer.

When asked what he thought of the deflectors, Ed explained how a designer faces choices. "With each benefit there is a side effect. If you want to trade one thing for another, you want to make sure you're getting the one that gives the most benefits."

When Bunting's yacht was completed, he took her into the Bay to see how the new under-water spray rail performed. "Cruising at 22 knots, you still don't see it," he said, "because when she comes up on a plane, she lays flat on top of the water. Her bottom is fully Kevlar corded with Ed's patented process. It's a fantastic process. I've never been happier with anything, and it plain does not leak, period. The only way water gets in her is through the shaft log. She'll get a drip in there every now and then."

Ten years before, a vintage 1928 cabin cruiser had come into Ed's life — a boat he had admired since the day he first saw it at City Island. This was *Foto*, owned by the great yachting photographer Morris Rosenfeld, and later by his son Stanley, who had been his father's skipper.

After WWII, on trips to City Island, Ed would sometimes spot the 33' 6" motor yacht sitting at a dock with its wide flaring bow and look of a 1930s cruiser. When out on the water sailing, he occasionally saw the distinctive yacht cutting through Long Island Sound throwing out spray. *Foto* was familiar to racing sailors since it covered important East Coast races.

"It went like a rocket," Ed said. "It was the best damn boat around, better than many of the boats Rosenfeld was shooting." Ed had made up his mind years before that he would like to own the classic yacht.

Morris Rosenfeld had owned two earlier boats carrying the same name. His grandson Richard Rosenfeld of Elkton, Maryland, looked these up in *Lloyds Register of American Yachts* at the G. L. Blunt White Library of Mystic Seaport. The first *Foto* was a 32' Red Bank dory formerly owned by the Police Department, Richard Rosenfeld said. The second was a 26' Hacker, but a 1929 hurricane wrecked it. Naval Architect Frederick Lord designed the third *Foto* to meet Morris's requirements for a chase boat that could more than keep up with America's Cup contenders. In 1929, Kanno Brothers of City Island, New York, built the soon-to-be-famous working yacht. Richard said his grandfather never used a numeral after the name.

Foto could circle around to capture shots of the racing boats of all sizes from ocean racers and 12 meters to smaller classes — and speed ahead, leaving them behind. Rosenfeld was able to photograph competition high points — rounding buoys, retrieving loose spinnakers, tacking duels, and close finishes. He loved to catch two or more yachts together with a play of shadows and lines. His use of filters and special lab work contributed greatly to his magnificent photos.

Foto was the moving camera platform for many of the 1.2 million photos of East Coast racing and boating that Rosenfeld took during his career. His great black-and-white photographs in yachting magazines and now in the Mystic Seaport collection illustrated his mastery of composition, timing for the key moment, and use of sun and shade. The magnificent clouds in his photos were sometimes part of the natural scene, but at other times were air brushed or double printed using cloud negatives, as his son Stanley wrote in *A Century Under Sail*. (Rosenfeld)

Wherever important East Coast races were held, *Foto* was sure to be present, which entailed a lot of traveling for Morris Rosenfeld. "I know he went north as far as Bar Harbor, and maybe further, and south as far as Miami," said Richard Rosenfeld. "I don't know if he got to Key West, but he did work in Florida, spending many winters there when he was young. He had a hotel room with a darkroom."

When Ed was sailing on Long Island Sound, either with friends or in his *West Coast Mercury*, he would sometimes see *Foto*. On one occasion when he was sailing with Maggie, he set his course toward a paddle-wheel steamer slapping the water astern.

Tourists lined the deck. *Foto* was maneuvering near the steamer, and with binoculars Ed could see Rosenfeld peering out, holding his camera. His son Stanley was at the helm.

As they approached, Ed told Maggie that boaters every-where hope to have their picture immortalized in a publication. "Therefore, they do their best when Rosenfeld is around." Maggie listened, not knowing what he planned. At twenty-seven, Ed was no different, so he decided to pull a maneuver Rosenfeld would snap. With sails set, he headed toward the steam paddler's power-ful wake with increasing engine hum, splashing of paddles, and churning up choppy waves. "She was going at a good clip, and there was a stiff breeze," Ed said. "We decided to sail through the wake of that cruise boat." This was hardly a mutual decision, for Maggie looked uneasy and then alarmed. Ed held his course. The plywood sloop collided with a wall of turbulent water. "It threw us straight up into the air," Ed said. "We were surprised at the amount of force. Our boat almost came out of the water. After assembling ourselves, we turned around. Morris was right there on *Foto*, camera in hand, and I knew he had photographed us."

Ed and Maggie and their boat survived the risky stunt. But, he had learned first hand about the power of a large vessel's wake. In the following weeks and months he often checked *Life* magazine and leading boating publications at the library. But the picture never appeared. He wrote to the photographer. "I was after Morris to send me that photo, but I never got it," Ed said. Years later, Stanley visited him in Oxford and told him the reason. "Morris decided it was too dangerous a stunt to release as a picture because others might try to copy it."

Foto's measurements were 33' 6" LOA, 32' LWL, 8' beam, and 2' draft. The narrow beam was for greater speed, and the bow had a wide flare that deflected spray, as did the lesser flare of the hull. The design was utilitarian because bow spray could ruin photographs, and salt water can damage cameras and lenses. The cabin gave the photographer shelter to store cameras or reload film, and they lived aboard.

In a heavy beam sea, *Foto* had a sharp roll, which Stanley wrote about. "This motion could be considered a virtue since it brought us back to even keel very quickly, but on rare occasions cameras flew up and off their perch on the engine hatch, and if those aboard weren't quick in their nautical two-step, they too would take off." (Rosenfeld)

Stanley piloted the yacht to the spot his father wanted for composition and lighting. His uncles also helped. "Both my father's brothers were involved in all aspects of the family business," Richard Rosenfeld said. "David and William, at various times, took turns piloting, photographing, developing, and printing, mounting, etc."

Ed Cutts liked this boat for its functional abilities and its speed. "She was a great boat and maneuverable, but not perfect. Well, what boat's perfect?" This was Ed the perfectionist speaking of a widely-admired yacht.

As designed by Frederick Lord, *Foto* featured a large propeller and an oversized rudder, giving it great ability to maneuver. Roger Vaughan and Jack Sherwood quoted Stanley Rosenfeld speaking of this. "In a seaway, going slowly, a wave would pick the boat up, and [it] would start to broach. But a shot of throttle would control the stern, no matter how big the waves. It was a good boat upwind and down." (Sherwood)

Stanley kept the boat when his father died in 1968 and con-tinued his work. Many of the photos with a "Rosenfeld Studio" credit were his. When Ed began to ask Stanley about selling the yacht, the price was always too high.

After more years of demanding high performance use, the famous boat began to show its age. Then, Stanley wouldn't sell Ed the yacht because he didn't think Ed would want *Foto* in such poor condition. In 1978 at the New York Yacht Club, Stanley talked to Gordon Colley, a former captain of a NYYC flagship. Colley told Stanley he would like to buy the yacht for use at his own marina near Atlanta. Stanley agreed to this, but said, "I might want to get it back in the future."

Ed Cutts occasionally phoned Colley about wanting the boat, but the answer was always not now. Then, Colley moved away. No one at the NYYC knew where he moved, but everyone remembered the swift yacht.

For Ed it was a mystery, but he kept asking around. He learned that Colley had moved to Florida and then to New Mexico, so he phoned him there. Colley said he'd sold the yacht, which he thought had a few years remaining, to an old friend named Larry B. Smalley in Georgia. "I'm certain," he told Ed, "that you wouldn't want a boat in such poor condition." Ed said he still wanted it and thanked him. Determination, perseverance, and patience were Ed's lifelong friends.

The yacht was registered to Colley in 1979 and 1980, and then to Smalley. Ed discovered Larry Smalley wasn't in the Atlanta phone book. The phone operator found the name in a town near Augusta. Over the phone, Smalley said he still had the boat, and added, "Some of the wood is getting frail, and it needs work." This was not encouraging, but Ed still wanted to buy it. "I plan to keep it," the owner said.

In 1984, Eddie Cutts Jr. went to visit Florida friends at Hobe Sound. His friend's parents belonged to the Jupiter Island Yacht Club, where Eddie hoped to interest somebody in a custom boat or in rebuilding work. For this he had brought along a small portfolio of Cutts & Case boats.

At the Club cookout, Eddie ran into Donald Kipp, a past commodore of the NYYC, and a Cutts & Case client, who told Eddie some surprising news. A group of yachtsmen had purchased the entire Rosenfeld photo collection, estimated at 1.2 million images. They planned to donate the collection to Mystic Seaport Museum and also to construct a building to house and archive them.

That evening, Eddie phoned his father with the news, and they agreed they should try again to purchase *Foto*. They thought others would be searching for the old yacht.

In Oxford, Ed immediately phoned Smalley to set up a meeting. "The boat's not for sale," Smalley said, "but you're welcome to come and look at it if you really want to. However, its condition is in rough shape."

Eddie told his Florida host that something important had come up and caught a plane to Augusta. There he met Ed at the airport. After being mistaken for tournament golfers, they stayed in town overnight and drove a rental car to Clarks Hill Lake.

They met Captain Smalley, who led them to *Foto* sitting in the lake. Its slip was under a shed roof intended for a smaller boat. Ed and Eddie immediately saw that the bow was exposed to the elements, including the drip line. *Foto's* profile was familiar, but she looked dispirited and tragic like a famous actor in clown makeup. She was white with a light blue trim, heavily applied. "Everything on the boat had been painted with house paint from top to bottom," Eddie said. "The paint also covered the cabin wood work."

Smalley started the engine, which caught right away. He had used the boat, he said, to fish on the lake, occasionally. The cabin contained a strange cargo of household items, appliances and mechanical parts, with little space for a person to move. "We saw lawn chairs, air conditioners, parts for his Chris Craft, and all kinds of strange stuff piled up as if in storage," Eddie said.

The bow was in the worst shape because of exposure. Eddie walked forward topsides to check the condition near the bow, and without warning one foot broke through the deck with a splintering sound. This answered questions about rain damage.

The owner said he would only sell on condition that *Foto* would be properly rebuilt. The question was: Could it be restored to what it had been?

Father and son consulted quietly a little ways off and agreed that it could. They walked back to Captain Smalley, standing by the boat. "We want to buy it anyway," Ed said to the surprised owner.

Then they had to convince him they could rebuild it, so the two showed him pictures of yachts Cutts & Case had built or restored. Smalley looked these over and then agreed. "He saw we had the capability to put it back into excellent condition," Eddie said. "And the owner was aware of the historical element — the importance of restoring this famous boat known to so many yachtsmen over the years.

"He finally agreed," Ed said, "to sell the yacht for a ridiculous price — $2,000." He would have paid far more, in spite of the condition. They looked around for any piece of paper handy and wrote out the contract terms in long hand.

Moving did more damage. On the yacht trucker's trip to Cutts & Case, a poppet on the flat-bed trailer punctured two white cedar planks of the hull. Ed and Eddie Jr. felt it was the trucker's fault and not the boat's. But, the boatyard didn't ask the trucking company to pay for the damage. "I never sued anyone in my life," Ed said. "I don't believe in it. We can all make a mistake and have something go wrong." Ed carried this attitude his whole career.

As they examined every inch of the boat, the news was not all bad. They discovered most of her problems were above the deck. In checking the truck damage and later in drilling holes for the drain and a transducer, they found that the cedar was sound. "The planking," Eddie said, "was like new, in excellent condition. We replaced a couple of planks, cutting out the stove-in area, but the quality of the planking was fine.

"When we repair a boat, we like to target what's wrong with it structurally," he said. "Then we fix this, so it won't happen again. With *Foto* we added to the structure of the transom and back by the rudder." They also cleaned out the seams and packed them with epoxy.

"It was mostly work from the deck up, and also in the interior," Eddie continued. "The general tone of the interior is the same, but it is slightly different around the galley. You have to understand it was a workboat, kept like a workboat. We upgraded it." This meant moving the head from an unfortunate galley location to a forward closet, which was necessary for any future cruising. It is inconceivable that another boatyard would have left the head out in the open.

Just how bad was her condition? "*Foto* didn't have any rot," Ed said. "Just tremendous weather depreciation and complete lack of care, with exposure to the elements like rain and snow. The Rosenfelds used the boat as a tool. When they needed it, they grabbed it and took off with it and expected it to perform well. But they didn't repay it much with care and love. So the boat was in a very depreciated condition after many, many years."

Ed had overlooked both the severe weather damage and the neglect that came following the Rosenfeld's forty-six years of use. Morris Rosenfeld had lived on City Island and had his own dock. City Island Historian Tom Nye knew where the Rosenfelds had the yacht maintained. "For the most part they hauled at four different yards: Kanno, where the boat was built, Consolidated, Minneford, and Nevins. He had it worked on all over." Nye thought the boat was probably overused. "It did take a lot of beating."

Eddie Jr. remembered that when they found the boat her bilge was dry. The cabinets, unfortunately, were beyond repair, so Cutts & Case built new cabinets, taking specs from the damaged ones. They were guided also by 1929 photos of the boat's interior.

In Oxford, work on *Foto* continued over four years between regular work for customers. "We had a business, so the idea of a business is you should make a profit," Ed explained. "We had a crew of fifteen but we only used certain men on *Foto*. Mostly, it was Dennis Risher, my two boys and I. When you have to take something apart and rebuild it, that's more difficult than building a yacht. But we used whatever we could and rebuilt her exactly as she was."

The cabin needed new veneer, for one thing. They stripped off the old stuff and glued an overlay of mahogany. "This was 5/16ths thick on the cabin sides," Eddie said. "You end up with basically a new cabin side."

"In resurfacing, everything is different as to the depth needed," Ed said. "We veneered the cabin with the same kind of mahogany it was built with." To repair the major bow damage they used the Cutts Method for greatest strength.

The General Motors V-8 replacement engine, put in by Morris Rosenfeld, needed work, so it was sent out. "They re-bored the cylinders, put in slightly bigger pistons, and added new engine rings," Ed said. "It's the same engine."

When a newspaper interviewed Ed after the rebuilding was completed, he angrily blamed the original owners for the boat's previous condition. For some inexplicable reason, he said, "The Rosenfelds were all slobs."

Robert Rosenfeld read the article when it came out. Years later he said in words worthy of a diplomat, "I was unhappy with the tone of the article. It was unfair." He also didn't like the cover of the Easton weekend magazine, that "hinted at an exposure of my family."

Ed Cutts wasn't apologetic when he heard Rosenfeld's response. He became incensed, which might have been defensive anger. "People have got to be discreet," he said loudly with emphasis. He added that reporters should tone things down — even something that he had said.

In the interview, Ed had greatly exaggerated the sorry state of the *Foto* when discovered on the lake. Originally, Eddie's shoe had broken through the deck. But he didn't fall through the hole, as reported in the article that quoted Ed. It was one shoe and one small hole. Neither was the boat full of water, as described, for they had found it floating and dry. The article went on to say the cedar planks were so loose on the frame that the hull "looked like Venetian blinds." (Vojtech)

Why did Ed exaggerate the boat's bad condition with water-soaked hyperbole? Ed answered, "I don't remember." He had been known to embellish a story; some fishermen have done this according to reports.

Exactly what did the journalist see? Ed, at seventy-nine, had a possible explanation. "The reporter may have seen the boat in an earlier stage." This is possible, because when being restored, the hull had plank sections removed, veneer removed from the topsides, and an open section of foredeck and bow. This state was not, however, what Ed and Eddie found in Georgia, or the boat couldn't have been useable for fishing — or even floated.

In July 1989, Cutts & Case launched *Foto*, rebuilt with infinite care. Stanley Rosenfeld and Gordon Smalley travelled to Oxford to be there for a trial cruise. Writer Jack Sherwood and photographer Bill Hingst were also aboard.

Ed, wearing a Classic Yacht Club cap, piloted the yacht for a run off Tilghman Island. Stanley Rosenfeld was shorter than Ed, with impressive, graying hair and dark eyebrows. Reaching open water, Ed gave him the helm. Stanley, who had spent so much of his life piloting *Foto*, pushed up the throttle. As the yacht accelerated, he registered surprise. "With this new more powerful engine, she goes faster than ever before."

"No, that's your old engine but rebuilt." Ed remembered Stanley's amazement.

Surveyor Chuck Wiley did the insurance survey on *Foto*. "When they finished with her, she looked exactly like she did when I first knew her many, many years ago when I was racing on Long Island Sound. She was a lovely boat then, and that's what she is now. If she's taken care of, she'll be around for many, many years because of the way Ed fixed her."

The 1989 Classic Wooden Boat Show in Newport was coming up. Ed invited Joe Reddy to cruise up on *Foto*. The two left Oxford a week before the show. After the C & D Canal they encountered a thick, murky Delaware Bay fog.

Ed Cutts talks with Stanley Rosenfeld on *Foto* after a cruise and speed trial on Chesapeake Bay.

William Hingst

Foto churning through the water, after the rebuilding, is a spectacular yacht — now as in earlier times at *America's Cup* races.
Stark Jett

"Ed was at the wheel, and the fog didn't seem to bother him," Ruddy remembered. "I was the navigator, and we were flying along in this fog. Suddenly we would pass fishing boats that were anchored there. You could see the mouths drop on all the guys who were fishing, as they watched this speed boat pass them in the fog."

Foto, able to make 32 knots, was then cutting through the water at about 20 knots in visibility estimated at 125 feet. "I'm concerned," Ruddy told Ed, "that we won't see these guys soon enough to zip around them. We might run into one of the boats." Ed adjusted the throttle and told Ruddy he was slowing "to make him happy. Joe was used to a boat that went 8 or 9 knots all his life. To him we were speeding."

They fueled up in Cape May and then went into the ocean heading north, planning to make Sandy Point in northern New Jersey in the afternoon. The weather was nice as they made good time off shore. They spotted Atlantic City and her beaches off to the port. Then without warning, the engine stopped.

They worked on the motor, searching for the reason, and after an hour they made a discovery. "We found the fuel filter was plugged up with all kinds of debris that we presumed was from the tank," Ruddy said. "Fortunately, we had a spare filter aboard, so we put it on and continued." This delay put them behind schedule, so it was dark when they entered Sandy Point to anchor near a marina.

The next morning they weighed anchor and continued north. All was well as they entered New York Harbor. They were by the Verrazano Bridge when the engine died again. They were drifting in the center of a busy shipping channel. "In New York Harbor there were always freighters and every other damn thing going back and forth," Ed said. "If you don't get out of the way, they'll sound their horns. They don't realize your engine is out. It was an anxious moment, but we dealt with the problem fast."

"We thought for sure it was the fuel cartridge," Joe Ruddy said, "so we took it apart, and lo and behold it was jammed full of stuff. We didn't have another cartridge, so we did our best to clean it out." Buffeted by wind and tidal current, they worked fast. They kept an eye on all approaching ships. It took about 15 minutes to finish. "The motor started, we crossed our fingers and made it to City Island," Ruddy said.

"I'm sure we can get the gas tank cleaned," Ed said. They asked all over, but couldn't find a mechanic to do this. They did buy a carton of new cartridge filters before leaving. As they reached Long Island Sound, the engine predictably stopped, only to be resuscitated with a new filter, applied with the swiftness of an Indianapolis pit crew. They continued to Connecticut's Essex River and tied up at a marina.

Ed had an old friend from City Island, Doug Soper, who showed up the next morning, towed them to his yard, and found another mechanical problem. "Running lean on fuel had burned the valves," said Ruddy, "so Soper took the head off and fixed the valves. And he took us round Essex and to his home for dinner and drinks. He was a wonderful guy." The gas-tank and valve work took several days.

According to the plans, Mary Lou Ruddy and Maggie Cutts were to fly up to Newport and reserve a bread and breakfast. Ed phoned Oxford daily to inform Maggie of the situation. "I was standing there," Ruddy said with a laugh, "and I always heard him say, 'Maggie, send money, we're getting short,' and that became our key phrase for the entire trip."

With the boat show starting the following day, they left Essex. Off the Rhode Island coast, Ed said, "Let's have a drink. After all we've been through we need one." They enjoyed some sort of grog while Ed kept an eye out. When Ruddy expressed surprise at seeing lobster pots going past, Ed said, "Don't worry about it. The boat is built so that if any get to the bow they'll move aside, and never get near our prop." Sure enough, many floated by on both sides, much to Ruddy's relief. Lobstermen do not take lightly to cut trap lines.

It had become pitch black as they looked for the Newport harbor entrance. Around midnight, they tied up to a vacant slip at Fort Adams, where the show was being held. In the early morning they polished brightwork and brass.

When the show opened, the wives arrived with a car and reservations. People at the boat show came aboard *Foto* to admire her. Many had questions that Ed enjoyed answering. He told them of the noted yacht's history covering America's Cup races and about maritime photographer Morris Rosenfeld.

Ginger Marshall Martus, who published a quarterly on antique-boat restorations, attended the show dinner. In the past, she and her father had known Ed. "We had a marine hardware business in Manhasset Bay on the waterfront called A. & R. Marshal," she said. As a girl, she sometimes worked in the store, which was Ed's favorite place for marine supplies. Ed enjoyed seeing friends and meeting new people. He motored Jon Johansen, publisher of *Maine Coastal News,* around the harbor on *Foto* so he could take pictures of various yachts for his paper.

After the show, there was a catered dinner in a big tent. Because of the time Ed and his sons had spent skillfully rebuilding *Foto* to her former beauty, Ed hoped for an award. But, he said nothing. They did give him an award. At the dinner they gave him a case of beer. One might wonder what the judges were thinking. Ginger Martus thought this was for making the longest trip, and added, "I think he was a little upset. He should have gotten more recognition, I guess." She took a photo of the restored yacht.

The dinner festivities back in Newport ended in an unforeseen but highly memorable fashion. "These guys came in dressed in Continental uniforms with what looked like muskets," Joe Ruddy said. Others had fife and drums, and they all stood in a row. "They played a song, and at the end of it they put their muskets up in the air and fired, shooting holes in the top of the tent." Nothing could really follow that act, so the celebration ended.

Ed and Joe Ruddy tied up the yacht at the New York Yacht Club station in Newport. Someone told Ed he would have to move, because the boat length was too short. This comment didn't sit well with Ed, a club member since 1980, so he left a message for the Commodore: "This is the boat that made your grandfathers and fathers famous. This boat is tying up here because it deserves to." The Commodore's reply is not known, but he probably agreed.

On the way home, *Foto* stopped at Mystic Seaport. Ed said, of the enthusiastic reception, "They made an awful fuss over the boat."

Chapter Ten

LATER DESIGNS AND BUILDERS AWEIGH

"I DON'T KNOW when I became president of Cutts & Case," Eddie Jr. said. "It was probably around the late 80s or 1990. Actually, in a family business like this, the presidency is a title. It's all shared." That said it all. Ronnie continued as Vice-President and Head of Construction. Owner Ed Cutts remained CEO, had final say on decisions, and drew designs.

Ed sometimes said that he and Abe Oberlin, friend and client, thought alike. When Oberlin heard this, he laughed, and said, "Yeah, I do. I let him do whatever he wants. We get along very well." Oberlin remembered disagreements when *Spellbound* was under construction. "I wanted electronics, and Ed wanted as little as he could get on the boat. Basically, he was a pure sailor from way back, you know."

Now, Oberlin told Ed that he wanted to order a larger boat — a ketch of about 60 feet. "I made preliminary sketches," Ed said, "which Abe approved. Of course, he would have had a professional crew aboard it, a deckhand and maybe someone else to help. He didn't use a crew on *Spellbound*. Still, he wanted me to make the boat self-tending."

Ed began the design work but then learned that his friend was facing a marriage breakup. "His plans for the future were changing," Ed said. "I thought the new boat would be wrong because he was the kind of man who, once he told you to do something, would have gone on with it. I felt it would have been unfair to him at that time." So, the design work and planning for this 60-footer stopped. Ed said that he and Oberlin had never talked this over.

When Oberlin decided to discontinue sailing in the early 90s, Ed bought back *Spellbound*, the 46' ketch. He was being true to form. His boats, built with infinite care, are indeed his children. It allowed him to maintain them properly, to sail them, and to approve new owners.

Ed and Maggie Cutts enjoyed the tranquility of their boatyard, the water view, and the landscaping with old and ornamental trees.
Cutts Family

Ed loved to sail *Spellbound*. "Many people wouldn't believe the speed she has. She'll sail at 8 to 10 knots all day long, hitting 11 knots at times," he said. "It's unheard of for a boat of this type and size to go like that." The sails, he pointed out, were originals that had lost some shape, with the exception of the new jib. "New main and mizzen sails should increase the performance," he said. "She's an amazing boat. That's why, when Abe planned to sell her, we got her back."

One winter, Chesapeake Bay was covered over by ice that became so thick it eventually tilted the Sharp's Island Lighthouse to resemble Pisa's famous tower. Bill Hingst, the photographer who later photographed the lighthouse for *Newsweek*, was out on a dock with his camera. "Suddenly, somebody zoomed by me at 40 mph," he said. It was Ed Cutts ice-boating.

Ed came up to the dock, his 18' ice boat luffing into the wind, and shouted, "Do you want a ride?"

Hingst climbed into a seat behind Ed, in a jacket unsuitable for the wind-chill factor. "We went zooming out, but the ice was too bumpy for pictures," he said. "There was nothing to hold on to. If something happened, we would be at the mercy of the ice."

Large flocks of Canadian Geese took off when the careening iceboat headed at them. "Ed was at the controls, and there is no one better at driving a contraption like that," Hingst said. "It was a hell of an ice boat."

Ed had fashioned his contraption inexpensively. "I didn't look at any designs. I made it out of what I had: the fuselage was out of an old boat boom, I had a truck steering wheel, and a seat for two people." It had a solid wind-break, some side support, and 110 sq. ft. of sail. "I made the blades. I knew what to do," he said, "and it would go 50 mph." He speeded up and down the Tred Avon River as far as Easton about nine miles away. "It pointed well, and it gives you a cold wind in your face." As for dangerous, thin ice, he said, "You can sense it. If you put weight down, it's like bending a piece of glass." In this major freeze, he saw other ice boaters enjoying the sport.

In 1994, it was an unprecedented occurrence to have an Ed Cutts's design taking shape away from his boatyard. This was happening in Norfolk where Dr. Crile Crisler was building the *Hummingbird* sloop at his home boatshed on weekends. Construction problems led Crisler to drive up to Oxford for advice. Ed answered the questions and drew sketches to show details of the building process. "It was remarkable to me how much he had drawn into those simple plans," Crisler said. "Everything was really there if you had eyes to see it. I think he had almost sailed the boat in his mind, as he designed it. The transom was curved and raked. The bottom still had some 'V' in it, so that was a complex area."

Although Crisler completed *Hummingbird* nine years after Ed gave him the plans, the actual building time was two and one half years. "It was the design that was difficult and not the Cutts Method," Crisler said. *Hummingbird's* LOA on deck was 29', beam was 8' 6", the draft 1' 4" with the centerboard up, and weighed 6,700 lbs. "There was a self-tending jib to facilitate single-handing and a genoa," Crisler said. "Inside were enough facilities to get by for cruising." These included: four berths, a stove, and a small navigating table. Passengers would find a cedar bucket fitted with a toilet seat under the V-bunk cushions. "Ed's design showed a generic trailboard on the bow as found on all *skipjacks*," the doctor said, "but I designed the details of the board and built it."

In 1996, Ed and Maggie received a boat-launching invitation that pictured a large hummingbird and a mysterious crow in the lower corner. Ed said he would try to be there. At his house on the Lafayette River in Norfolk, Crisler was ready to launch *Hummingbird*, which he called "an elegant little sloop." On the launch day, people started arriving at his place on the water. Dr. Crisler was then sporting a lightly trimmed beard that made him look like a schoolteacher or sports coach. He came across as intelligent, friendly, casual, and reserved, with a quiet humor.

"Thirty minutes before launch time, there were a couple of hundred people in the yard," he said. "I heard a boat horn and looked up. There was *Foto* coming up the river at full throttle with celebratory flags strung all over." Ed and Maggie had arrived.

The stern of the sloop displayed the name *Sally Hubbard*. Visitors asked if she was a famous historical person. "She was an old maiden aunt who lived in Mississippi and who drank a lot of Old Crow whiskey," Crisler said. This accounted for the crow on the invitation. After he christened the sloop with a fifth of this bourbon, and when the much-admired boat sat in the water, he said, "They all toasted Aunt Sally with more of the same."

Crisler berthed his sloop at the Norfolk Yacht and Country Club. "It attracted attention and was recognized as an unusual boat," he said. "I did race it a couple of times. We won second or third prize once. I'm not a skillful sailor in regard to racing, but it certainly performed remarkably well. The low-aspect-ratio rig wasn't designed for speed. It was designed for power to pull a small boat." Working *skipjacks* pulled a dredge for oysters. Watermen call this "drudging."

Ed Cutts and Crile Crisler discussed another boat that he could use for fishing in the shallow water on the "sea" side of Virginia's Eastern Shore. Crisler was interested in a *garvey* configuration. "This is a scow-type power boat," he said, "with a rounded bow, open cockpit and center console, associated with New Jersey. We talked about the possibility of a tunnel to reduce draft. Ed was initially working on a small inboard with the prop inside the tunnel. We finally decided to keep it simple and use an outboard." Ed made a scale model and drew the construction plans.

Because his medical work kept him busy, Dr. Crisler began on the new boat in 2002 after he retired. Since he was working alone practically all the time, he had to be resourceful. "Most all my help

Dr. Crile Crisler built this Ed Cutts sloop in Norfolk, VA, naming her *Sally Hubbard* after a maiden aunt. Years later she went back to the original name Ed had given her — *Hummingbird.*

Crile Crisler

with heavy items came from chain falls, leverage, and jacks," he said. His wife occasionally helped on this two-year project.

The scow was another unusual and challenging design for him. "Remember," Crisler said, "that the *garvey* Ed designed has some very complex aspects because of the uniquely shaped tunnel." He explained that most recreational tunnel boats have a scooped-out tunnel that causes turbulence in the water emerging from the tunnel going to the prop. "Ed designed the bottom shape to feed water smoothly to the tunnel entry, along with a streamlined shape for the tunnel. This provided an undisturbed flow of water to the prop. That combination is unique as far as I know and was very effective."

Specifications for this *garvey* are: 24' 6" LOA, 7' 6" beam, and 1,500 lbs. total weight. It had a Honda 4-stroke, 130-hp outboard "mounted on a jack plate so that once on a plane, the motor could be raised, so that the boat would run in about 8 inches of water." After about five years, Crisler donated the *garvey* to the Chesapeake Bay Foundation.

Ed decided to see the Miami Boat Show and drove Maggie down to the Ruddy's in Northern Florida. Then they all continued to the boat show on the Ruddy's boat. Ed, feeling unusual pain in his big toe, said, "You know, I've got to have it looked at." It worsened. One night after dinner, they went to a hospital where a doctor cut an ingrown toenail. When they were back home again, Ed's Easton doctor told him it was diabetes.

The second largest shed at Cutts & Case with its front wall of windows revealed Ed's Museum. At this time, *Foto* was on display through the windows. Drivers and pedestrians on Tilghman Street appreciated this, and many walked up to peer in, or ask permission to look inside.

Boatbuilders at Cutts & Case have arrived with different backgrounds. Dennis Risher, with floor-finishing experience, wanted to learn boat building when he began there in 1978. "One early job was on a three-cockpit Hacker speedboat, which I varnished," he said. "In time I was helping out with everything." He worked under Emory Balderson during the training process. "Mr. Cutts expected us to learn by a kind of osmosis. Some guys expected an instructor-type approach. Mr. Cutts wanted you to figure out things for yourself from the guys working around you, like on sport teams. Then it's a matter of style, learning his particular style and way to do things. He knows what works and what doesn't. A lot of it is formula, like a recipe for cooking."

After many years Dennis became Lead Builder. When a new man is hired, Ronnie often puts him under Dennis's watchful eye. "It's been neat," Dennis said, "because Mr. Cutts has always given me the ability to do the best job I can do. We're never hurried up because of expense. Ed told me, 'It's all about the boats. They might fuss about the bill, but be sure it's the very best you can do.'"

Dennis had worked on rebuilding Bunting's boat *Trouper II*, but still remembered the yacht's prior condition. "Everywhere he went, the boat would be sinking. It was an old traditional boat — with a life span probably exceeded. It was repaired with Mr. Cutts's method." Asked about this, Dennis said, "I can do things traditionally or with his method. He's come up with this new method, and I've seen a lot of neat work. For many guys in traditional building this seems kind of foreign to them."

Walking through the red shed nearest the driveway, Dennis pointed out a small tender in its mold being planked. At the far end, illuminated by a large window and overhead lights, was a beautiful new spruce mast, complete with hardware fittings and ready for wiring, shrouds, stays, and crosstree. "That is 55 feet long, and it's for a steel-hulled boat," he said.

Ed Cutts had not forgotten his situation when he first began at Nevins, so the boatyard sometimes hired a man who needed training. "We guide, steer, help, and show them how to do the work, so it will be beautiful," he said. "There is a main core of people in the yard that have been with us for a long time whom we try to keep happy. Some people stayed involved with us long after they retired. One man, Donald Wilson, was here thirty-five years or more. He worked for Wiley before. I could never pay him as much as I knew he deserved — I mean he was that good. Completely dependable. He could do any kind of work, and he did beautiful stuff."

In 2007, Don Wilson remembered Ed supervising construction and training new builders by demonstrating. "If Ed had a job to do, he told you about it and left you alone. And he would come and check it, and if anything was wrong, he'd let you know." Wilson paused a moment. "But I never had that problem. He was a nice guy to work for."

Don did a number of different building jobs from *Rebellion* through *Spellbound*. "I installed engines and did carpenter work and electrical work." He had fond memories of young Ronnie riding his first motorcycle around the yard. Don said his favorite fishing, years earlier, was catching crabs. "We used to wade out in the water and run them down with a crab net. But now you can't do that." With pollution problems the Bay is not as productive.

"Most customers," Ed said, "come here from New York, Pennsylvania, Maryland, Virginia, and Ohio, and we have had California and West Coast rebuilding work. Requests for boats and repairs have come from Europe and Saudi Arabia."

Sometimes a boat came in for re-rigging. This was the case when a man brought in a 44' sloop, built by Ralph Wiley in 1944, which he wanted rigged as a ketch. Ed determined the sail footage and mast placement suitable for the ballast weight and boat length. He learned how her owner planned to use her and where, because as he said, "Ocean sailing is far different from Chesapeake Bay sailing."

A Philadelphia couple, who knew about Ed Cutts's fine reputation as a designer, bought a vacation house in Oxford. Mr. and Mrs. Edward Parker looked over Ed's boats before they chose him, in 1989, to build a motor boat with a small cabin. After Ed made some sketches, they looked them over and agreed on a trunk cabin boat with clean lines suitable for day cruising. It was similar to a classic 1930s lake boat or afternoon launch.

Cutts & Case began on this boat in 1997. That same year they did some construction on 65' *Americana*, which started after a representative from another country visited the boatyard in 1995. The story of *Americana*, or *John's Boat*, will be told shortly. (Chapter eleven)

In 1997, Cutts & Case were building the Parkers' trunk cabin cruiser using the Cutts Method. It measured 27' LOA, 8' beam, and 2' draft. Builders were planking this boat, to be named *Curio*, when another Philadelphian arrived in Oxford. Lee Casper had read about Ed and his new construction technique about ten years before in *WoodenBoat* magazine. Although he was an architect who built homes, Casper enjoyed boating and building boats in his free time. His first project was a 25' Wittholz-designed sloop, which he sailed out of Rock Hall, Maryland.

"I was hankering to build another boat," Casper said. After meeting Ed and his sons, he closely observed the planking work on *Curio*, with Kevlar braided cord and epoxy packed into grooves in the first planking layer. "I thought the Method looked extraordinary, and that if this works the way it's described, it should make a remarkable boat."

Although Casper loved sailing, he decided when he saw the boat and the design that he wanted to build a similar cabin cruiser in Philadelphia. Ed was very cordial and showed him everything in the yard. At the end of the tour, Casper said, "Ed, I would like to build the boat, and I would like to buy a set of plans from you."

Ed had heard similar requests and answered automatically. "Oh. No, I couldn't do that. I'm sorry."

"Well, why not? You're in the business. Don't you want to?"

"Well, there's a reason I don't want to do it. You seem like a nice fellow, but suppose you don't build it correctly and the boat fails? I don't want to have a boat built with my system deemed a failure."

Lee Casper laughed. "How about if I sailed my sailboat down here, and you take a look at the job that I did? You'll see whether you think I'm capable of it?"

Ed didn't want him to do that and led him to the living room in his old house to show him photos of his other boats. Amid the collection of half hulls, pictures and photos, Casper spotted a framed photograph of Ed as a young sailor. It was curious because it was exactly like his own Navy picture that sat on his mother's mantelpiece.

Casper knew they had both been in the Navy at the same place and time. He decided to take a chance. "You know, Ed, somehow you look familiar. I think I ran into you at Samson, New York."

Ed's jaw dropped. "I was at Samson. Really?"

The visitor kept up the pretense for a while, then got embarrassed and laughed. "I saw that picture, and I have the same picture, so I just took a guess."

Ed got a great kick out of this and laughed with Casper. For a while they talked about their training, duties, and assigned locations in the US Navy. Then Ed surprised his visitor. "You know what? I'm going to sell you a set of the plans. And I'll give you the patterns and molds for the boat, so the hull will be the correct shape."

In Philadelphia, Casper worked in his warehouse. He discovered, before long, that the plans were "rudimentary," because Ed said he explained to his builders what he wanted. Therefore, Casper made visits and took photographs of *Curio* under construction.

Calling the plans "rudimentary" sounded as though Ed's later construction drawings were not complete. He had some intricate areas worked out in his head, but not completely on paper.

The day cruiser was not an easy boat to build, Casper said. "I had to call every now and then about some detail, and Ed would always take time to tell me what to do." For bigger problems Casper would drive to Oxford where Ed drew rough sketches of problem areas, as he had for Dr. Crisler.

Although Ed guided the two experienced private builders one on one, he admitted that he might have been difficult. "I am a stickler for form," he said, "so I forced them to do everything in the very finest way. And they can get weary of that, you know. Because I'm a pain in the rear, and I know it. For every little detail, I made them accomplish it the way we build it." There were, however, no complaints from Casper and Crisler.

Ed Cutts's *Curio* is a beautifully-built, 1930's style yacht. It is often in the glass-fronted museum facing Tilghman Road at the Cutts & Case boatyard.
Wayne Brown

Cutts & Case launched and christened *Curio* in 1998. "Ned Parker just wanted a boat that would do about 8 knots," Eddie said. "Dad did like to surprise, so he designed a boat that would cruise at 16 knots with a top end of 21 knots. The intention was for a light, strong, extremely efficient little boat. At 27 feet she weighed 2,200 pounds." Using the 87-hp 4-cylinder Chevrolet block to achieve 21 knots, he said, "was really quite a tremendous performance."

At this time, Ed bought back *Halcyon*, the 31' cabin cruiser that he had designed and built for Lauer-Leonardi thirty-six years before. "It was dilapidated when it came in," Ed said, "but it still was solid and everything was A-1." They stored the yacht in the large shed.

Although often 100 percent absorbed in his work, Ed got along well with children. In 1995, his nephew Jeff Durstewitz had brought his wife and two young children on their first visit. "Uncle Ed took David and Emily when they were seven and six on his fastest motorcycle," Durstewitz said. "He took them for a spin, and when they came back, their eyes were as big as saucepans. My wife was a nervous wreck, as my mother had been when he used to take me out."

Ed wanted to share with young relatives the spine-tingling thrills he experienced while growing up and taking chances. Four years later, he took Jeff and his son David out on *Foto* and allowed the boy to steer the high-performance yacht at high speed. "The kids get a thrill out of it," Ed said. "I still do."

A new customer, Tony Davis, with a vacation home in Easton, asked Ed Cutts to design and build him a custom power boat. He was impressed with *Curio* but wanted more of an open cabin-cockpit layout like *Foto*. And he wanted to go faster than *Curio*. Since the customer liked *Foto's* 32-mph speed, this became a performance requirement that would determine design choices. After sketches and conferences, Ed Cutts drew the construction plans for a 29' yacht that would take a powerful engine. "It was," he said, "for day cruising or for Spartan overnighting."

Work began on the boat in 1999 with a completion forecast for 2000, so the client chose the name *Millennia*. Eddie Jr. said that the weight and size of the engine was a consideration for the expected performance. "We put a 385-hp engine in there, which was a standard, moderately-tuned 454 GM block, marinized by Crusader. The boat was planked with white cedar using Kevlar-49 cord."

This boat, built with the Cutts Method and without frames, was light in weight as was *Curio*. "The weight," Eddie said, "is in the engine/transmission, batteries, shaft, struts, and propeller. You start adding it up and it's 25 or 30 percent of the boat weight." He added that in some boats the percentage of total weight is even higher. "In Curio it would be 50 percent."

One couple Nick and Michele Grasberger looked in on the building of *Curio* and *Millennia*. Besides their old summer house in Oxford, this family lived in a stone farm house in Lancaster, Pennsylvania. They also had an old farm house in Pittsburg, because they fixed up old houses as a hobby, which led to their appreciation of wooden boats and Ed Cutts's designs.

"I love things that are simple, classic, and very functional," Nick Grasberger said. "I've always appreciated good craftsmanship and beautiful things that are simple, and, of course, that's what jumps out when you look at Mr. Cutts's boats. His boats are graceful, and they sail better than any boat I've ever sailed on." Grasberger had sailed *Spellbound* and *Grizzly Bear* and taken a ride on *Foto*. After frequent visits to the boatyard to observe construction, he liked what he saw. He called Ronnie's boat-building work "exquisite."

At the 2000 Annapolis Boat Show, Nick saw a fiberglass reproduction of a classic sloop, which he considered buying. At his next meeting with Ed, he told him, "It's a gorgeous little 24' sailboat called *Alerion*."

"I know the *Alerion*," said Ed. "Nat Herreshoff designed it."

"It's the same design as the old wooden boat from Herreshoff," Nick said, "but built by Nat Herreshoff's grandson." Ed soon fathomed it was built of fiberglass.

"Why would you buy a plastic boat like that? I can build you one that's much better for the same price." The price of the high-end *Alerion* at that time was over $70 thousand.

Nick had always admired wooden boats. "I looked around the boatyard in every nook and cranny and asked a lot of questions about the history of certain boats." He also checked out leading boat-building yards in Massachusetts. "Their philosophy on building boats," he said, "could not be more different than Mr. Cutts. They believe the heavier the boat, the stronger the boat, the better the boat would sail."

After talking at length with Ed and his sons about the new building technique, Nick said, "I became convinced that a sailboat made with the Cutts Method would last many generations. I envisioned my grandchildren and great-grandchildren sailing the boat someday." He knew that Ed Cutts told people his boats should last a hundred years with good care, and he believed him.

Nick asked Ed to design and build him a sloop for five people and with a small cabin. Ed began on the drawings, and late in 2001 they were in agreement on his design for a boat — 23' 10" LOA, 7' 6" beam, and 3' draft. When Nick talked about his future sloop in Oxford boating circles, they told him it would never get done on schedule. They knew the last boat *Millennia*, expected to be ready in 2000, had taken about a year longer than promised.

As seen earlier, Ed likes to give people more than they expect in a boat. On trials *Millennia* was coming in at 55-mph, because the owner wanted speed. "She had a steering difficulty early on," Eddie Jr. said. "We were having a problem with the rudder. The boat was going so fast, she was developing an actual bubble around the rudder. It was taking the efficiency of the rudder away, partly due to prop wash. We figured it out and rearranged her a little bit, and purposely reduced her rpm's," he said. "We ended up with a nice handling, extremely fast, light, very efficient boat. With some tweaking and fine tuning, she was giving us about 56 knots."

Sitting in his red-leather Governor Dewey chair, Ed gestured with his left hand to a framed photo on the wall next to him. It had caught *Millennia* planing at high speed. "The owner couldn't believe the performance of the boat," Ed said. "He was jumping up and down. You would wish a boat would run that way, and this one does. That's the most perfectly running boat I've seen," he said, with youthful enthusiasm and obvious pride of accomplishment. "With another boat, the amount of water being kicked up would be very different. Just look at some pictures of others." *Millennia* was skiing along on the surface with a tiny wake. Three generations of Cutts were aboard.

Speed — going like the wind on water and on land — had always fascinated Ed Cutts since he was a teenager. One time, the conversation was of speedy catamarans. "We all look for thrills, and it's a thrilling thing to go 20 knots in a boat in a good stiff breeze. You go past power boats, which you're not going to do in a sailboat." But he had more to say about multihulls. "They are capsizeable and not so good in a heavy seaway. They can make high speeds, if you get one hull out of the water and can take off, but they also become more treacherous."

Drawing on boating lore, Ed said, "*Atlantic*, built in 1903, still holds the record for sailing across the Atlantic Ocean. A three-masted schooner, a hundred and some feet long, she was sailed by Captain Charlie Barr who was hired to break the record. The owner, at the last minute, decided to go with him. After a few days at sea, he came up out of the cabin when the boat was driving hard. 'Forget it, I don't want to continue this,' he said. 'Take her back.' Barr said, 'I was hired to sail this boat across the Atlantic as fast as I could take her, and I am going to do exactly that.' And he called some men over and said, 'Take this man below.' That was the owner!" Ed smiled, enjoying the story with his audience. "Charlie Barr was the best sailor on record."

Sometimes, Ed discussed power boats. "Shorter water lines go fastest right away. If you want to go 200 mph, you do it in *Slo-Motion* — that's the boat's name, and her water line is a couple of feet when she's making speed. She's only 26 to 28 feet, but the bottom that is in the water is only this big." He demonstrated with strong hands. "So that's saying something about concept," he said.

"Someone will say, 'Yes, but that's planing.' Well, every boat planes," he said. "You can't pull something through the water without it rising. So the trick is to keep the weight down so it can rise easily and to reduce its other resistances as much as possible. Which is something I have tried to do all my life. Therefore, I wound up patenting this new method of boat building, which does that exactly."

In his construction design, Ed had shaped *Millennia* to allow it to rise into a plane. "Getting on top of the water is a horsepower-to-weight-ratio problem. Nat Herreshoff couldn't get on top of the water. His boats had to go through the water because the steam-power plants were very heavy. He had a boat 117 feet long, and she could go 16 knots — even 18 knots if he pushed hard to do it. She was considered fast at that time," Ed said.

"The boilers, the engine, and the coal bunkers were very heavy, and all the auxiliaries were heavy. Even though he built comparatively light-weight stuff, still it was ponderous. With steam, years ago, you would have enormous amounts of water, which weighs 60 lbs. per cubic foot. Coal was very heavy, and the engines, boilers, and condensers were heavy iron, so to produce 500 hp in steam, you had to have a good-sized plant," he said. "But today you can put two 500-hp engines in there, and they each wouldn't be much bigger than a small filing cabinet. Now, you can get engines with a lot of aluminum in them, so the weight reduction is tremendous."

At Nevins, Ed did deck work on sailing designs from Sparkman & Stevens, who have a fine reputation for designing boats that win races. In a shed, not open to the public, builders were working on these boats, which had been slightly modified from a successful racing design of a 40' ketch, *Finisterre*. Carlton Mitchell, the owner, had won many races on this boat, Ed said. "He asked the firm to keep the design secret." But, after seeing how this boat performed, boaters started asking S & S for a duplicate ketch. The firm made some design changes and placed an order at Nevins. Ed remembered hearing Mitchell was furious. "It was like a war. Sparkman & Stephens reduced the boat length slightly. They did pretty well racing, but they were not as successful as the original boat," Ed said and added, "*Finisterre* had a really good skipper, which meant an awful lot." Mitchell won the Newport-to-Bermuda race three times. "*Finisterre* means, 'I'm done with the earth'— a beautiful name for a boat," he said.

"Those boats rated well, for they were designed inside the racing rule," he said. "If you were to race an older boat, she would be encumbered by higher numbers. But if designed exactly just for the rule, which *Finisterre* and those fourteen boats were, they had an advantage. The water-line length is very important. That's why the bow and stern came out of the water with well-proportioned ends, so they weren't taxed as high. Once a boat heeled over, it became longer, so it had, according to them, a better speed potential. I don't exactly believe that. I believe that shorter boats can be just as fast or even faster if the designer knows what he is doing."

At Nevins, Ed saw many excellent yachts being built or repaired. "I got ideas on methods of construction from Nils Halverson and the crews at Nevins," he said, "but not the designers. My thoughts were how ridiculous it was to do this in such a way. What a waste of weight and materials. The designers almost never were builders, so they didn't understand." He was quick to add that whatever was drawn was made perfectly at Nevins. "A designer drew it, and that's how it was built. I didn't get into the design side when I worked there.

"I found out early on that it was not necessarily the lines of a boat that made for a fast boat," he continued, "but instead it was the way the boat was put together. The construction of a boat was important to the speed. It is ballast-to-weight ratios in a sailboat, and power-to-weight ratios in a powerboat."

The subject gravitated to the small Bermuda dinghy, which carries more sail than any boat of its size. "Think of the ballast-to-sail ratio," he said. "A 200-pound guy and maybe somebody else, both athletes, can be far outboard. You have to produce stability in a sailboat."

Olin Stephens II had said that he liked to achieve the greatest stability in a racing boat with a minimum wetted area. Hearing this, Ed had a comment.

"But the trick is how you do it. There are so many other factors. Beam increases the shape resistance, and it also increases the surface, so you've got to know where the hell to go and when to stop. A good designer has proportional limits in his head, and no one was much better than Nat Herreshoff. Although I believe that today some designers may know more, I don't think they have a better knowledge of beauty or form."

There were designers that Ed Cutts respected, but, during the years of interviews, the only one he mentioned besides the Herreshoffs was Olin Stephens II. Sometimes Ed would rename his design firm: "Sparkplug and Stephens." He would enjoy this fossilized joke and grin like a kid.

Chapter Eleven
FINLAND AND *AMERICANA*

LOOKING FOR WAYS TO PROFIT from the country's huge forests, Finland's Secretary of Forestry held meetings with leaders of that nation. An official in charge of border security, among other titles, he suggested wooden boats could be a profitable export for Finland. This was Leo Skogstrom, who owned and used some wooden boats of his own. As a result, the Finnish government gave approval for him to make a special visit to the United States. Eddie Jr. said Skogstrom toured different boatyards along the northern and southern Atlantic Coast and the West Coast "to determine the kind of boats with which they might get involved."

In 1995, Skogstrom arrived at Cutts & Case where he checked the wooden boats and observed work in progress. "Leo really liked the type of boats my father was doing," Eddie said, "which are very spartan, light in scantlings, and high tech. They are clean in their finished results and clean in performance. Out of all the boatbuilders he interviewed and spent time with, Leo invited us to Finland to speak to a trade school about our methods of boat building."

Ed Cutts understood the thinking behind the invitation. "They wanted to find a way to use wood to build modern boats — a newer design than the lapstrake hulls, their traditional construction, which they have been doing for many hundreds of years."

In 1996, Skogstrom brought Ed Cutts and Eddie Cutts to Finland. They spoke about their methods of boat building at a wooden-boat trade school in Kotka and also at the University in Hammina. Students in Finland can attend trade schools only after graduating from secondary or high school, Eddie said. "Before college, they begin training you in a field where you show interest and can work well, at schools for various trades and industries. In this way they end up with extremely skilled people."

The Maryland boatbuilders also spoke at a wooden-boat show. The audience of Finnish naval architects and boatbuilders numbered about a hundred. "We met the President of Finland," Ed said, with raised inflections indicating the surprise and honor. "They treated us like kings, because they recognized our yard does very good work and that we had invented a new way of boat building, which they liked."

On returning to Oxford, Ed sent to Finland a set of plans from his 14' rowing skiff. A boatbuilder named Jarno took the designs and built this skiff as an experiment, using epoxy and braided Kevlar, supplied by Cutts & Case. In 1997, second-year Finnish students wrote asking if they could work at Cutts & Case, because they were required to work eight months at a boatyard as part of their training. The yard accepted two students.

A former building project had been halted in the early stages. At this time, Ronnie felt strongly that the yard should continue work on the 65' *Americana*, which was often-called, *John's Boat* in conversation. Ed and his sons discussed whether they would scrap the project, getting rid of the molds and cabin tops, or whether they would build the boat. "We agreed to begin on the hull, with some help from the Finns who were due to arrive," Eddie said.

In the spring of 1997, Hanno Savolainen and Iiro Vanamo from Hammina arrived at Cutts & Case and fortunately had a good knowledge of English. Their first names were conveniently anglicized to Allan and Ike. "We wanted to show the Finnish men how we do it," Ronnie said, "so as we set up the molds and cut the keel, they helped with it. Clint Ray, one of the yard's experienced builders, and I fastened the white cedar planking and put in Kevlar cords." And they used the special Gougeon epoxy that had proved itself in strength tests.

"The Finns were a great pair, a lot of fun, and hard workers with a keen sense of correct woodworking," Eddie said. They helped with fastening the keel and also planking the inner layer, getting "good hands-on experience."

"Sometimes it takes everybody working," Ronnie said, "when you're fitting floor timbers with Kevlar cord, and also when you're doing the entire hull." Out on the water, Allan and Ike proved to be excellent sailors.

Standing in the molds of *Americana* (*John's Boat*) are (*l to r*): Hanno Savolanien, a Finnish builder; a representative from the Finland embassy in Washington, DC; Ed Cutts; and Iiro Vannamo, a second Finnish builder.
Cutts Family

After a two-and-a-half-year period, when *Curio* and *Millennia* were built, two new Finnish men, Oili Oinonen and Jussi Lawa, arrived in April 2000. "These fellows were also hard workers and knowledgeable with the woodwork," Eddie said. "They did a lot of planking under Ronnie's direction and were very good. They observed how the bottom planking was at first fastened to the molds with double-headed nails and later with bronze fastenings into the bulkheads and sealed with epoxy."

Ed said they only get about 16 to 20 feet of length from top-notch lumber. "All the planking has to be scarfed together. We don't like butt-blocks so we scarf. Scarfing is far more tedious to do but it makes a beautiful and much stronger job."

The visiting shipbuilders learned how Ed Cutts designed bulkheads. "In my boats I put in a bulkhead and then at 3½ feet a hanging knee, and after another 3½ feet there's a bulkhead," Ed said. "These are positioned to hold hull shape with the knees also arranged as in any fiberglass boat. No room is lost." Speaking of the 7-foot spacing of bulkheads, he said, "It's big enough for a tall person to sleep and enough space for a state room. A lot of staterooms are 8 feet, but I closed it slightly for higher strength."

Ed described how he arrived at the narrow beam for the 65' hull. "John liked boats of that type, and so did I. Her beam is about the same as an idealized destroyer, with 6 foot of length to one foot of beam. I wasn't thinking of a destroyer at the time. I was just thinking of the dimensions that I thought best for her." Asked about the bow, he said, "That's a classic bow with a little flare. I don't like too much flare for my boats, because they're very light and therefore they don't plunge. Heavy boats plunge their bows down, you know, but my boats don't do that."

When the Finnish builders left in July of 2000, *John's Boat* was now a beautiful 65' seamless hull. It was time for an engine installation and interior work, but building came to a halt. The hull became an object of interest, admiration, and curiosity for visitors, as it sat in the center of a shed. In his heart, Ed Cutts carried a dream of taking the completed yacht up to New England some day. "I would like to show people what a nice yacht we build," he said. Sitting quietly in his kitchen, he had a far-away look on his face.

The expense of completing this yacht was a factor in stopping any further building, and another was the need for the yard to concentrate on rebuilding work. Orders continued to come in because of the Cutts & Case reputation. A 73-year-old cabin cruiser was due to arrive at Cutts & Case. During its lifetime it had been well maintained, but now it needed a refit. This was to be with the Chesapeake Bay Maritime Museum.

In the early 1970s, Thomas and Eleanor Requard had acquired from her father a 38' *Matthews*, built in 1926. The couple used this yacht, named *Isabel*, on Chesapeake Bay. In 1995, they donated the then 69-year-old boat to CBMM. Richard Scofield was in charge of the Museum boat shop, which maintained and repaired their impressive collection. This included recreational sail and power craft, early duck-hunting boats, and workboats, such as a *buyboat*, a *skipjack*, and *crab skiffs*.

Isabel sat at a dock for awhile before being hauled out, but the Museum was concerned about her condition. On her arrival, Scofield saw that that she had a lot of varnish and was getting older. He said it was difficult to find time for this work "with the crew we have and with the number of boats we have to maintain."

For four years they did nothing major on the yacht. Scofield determined that the rebuilding didn't have to be done at CBMM because *Isabel* was from Ohio and not a "collection boat"— built in the Chesapeake Bay area. The Museum had accepted her as a gift from the Requards, he said, because she had cruised in the Bay during a long life. And because she was a fine example of a popular 1920s yacht.

The Requards agreed to pay for renovations, and they went to three or four boatyards for estimates. "They chose Cutts & Case," Scofield said, "because they believe Ed Cutts's Method is the best way to build boats and that it would stand up, and it has. His yard has a small group of builders, and the work is controlled."

In 2002, the yacht went from St. Michaels to Oxford by water, and work began. The renovation was divided up so that the boatyard did all the work below the water line, while the Museum did everything above, including the cabin. Two or three boatbuilders from CBMM worked on it, and Scofield drove over every day to check on their work.

Ed Cutts also became involved checking the progress on the boat. Because his left foot was causing great pain whenever he walked or stood, he began at that time to use a golf cart to get from the house to the boat sheds. "He was interested in everything going on," Scofield said, "and he sometimes gave them tips."

"I would go out and sketch for them," Ed said, "or I'd draw a little picture of what I wanted. Always I was supervising them, and I'm doing that yet with our building." This revealed Ed's established system to get everything perfect, at 75 years of age when he was not doing hands-on building.

Ed spoke to a question boatbuilders and boat owners might ask: How to use Ed's Kevlar-and-epoxy technique when rebuilding a boat with frames? "If you use the Cutts Method, you don't screw to the frames anymore, so you could throw the frames out. But, with the frames connected to the cabinetry and everything, we can't go in there and remove them. If the boat has a good framing system in it already, then maybe you can space the cords differently," he said. "You can handle it according to the problem facing you.

"When you take an old boat apart, after sixty or seventy years," Ed said, "you don't know what you are going to find. When building from scratch, you do exactly what you want to do, but when repairing, you're working with what somebody else wanted to do. And you're not quite sure what it was, until you take it apart."

During this rebuilding, one CBMM builder rode a motorcycle to work, where he saw many Cutts family motorcycles parked in the yard. He talked with Ed, who invited him to look over his large collection. Later, the builder returned to the shed where he shouted to one and all, "Ed's got thirty-two motorcycles!"

Ed heard about the visiting builder, flabbergasted by the size of the collection. Smiling at this, Ed had a laconic, low-key reply, worthy of actor Jimmy Stewart, "Oh, we have more than that." Over his lifetime, he kept almost all his bikes, except for his take-apart Honda and his first customized Indian Scout. But, whenever one bike developed a problem, he sometimes bought another. Consequently, many in his collection needed repairs.

Some arrived as gifts. "People would know that I was enthusiastic about old motorcycles," Ed said, "so if they had an old one sitting in their garage and taking up room, they would ask me, 'How would you like to have this cycle?' and I'd say, 'Sure bring it over.' One time, a man gave me two he had in his garage. They were Hitler's courier motorcycles — DKWs from Berlin. I still have them." Hollywood property departments might take note.

If Ed were to take a ride, and he thought about it at seventy-nine, he said it would be on his little 4-cylinder Suzuki that has over 7,000 miles on it. "I used to really ride my bikes, and I put many thousands of miles on them. I was riding since I was thirteen years old," he said, recalling his Maytag-powered bike.

The present collection, owned by Ed and his sons, boasts some unusual names that motorcycle enthusiasts may recognize such as: Vincent Lightning, Velocette Venom Clubman, and Scott Flying Squirrel. "My favorite," Ed said, "is a BMW Single R27, which I used quite a bit for commuting back and forth to Grumman." Ed knew some of his motorcycles had gone up in value. Was he interested in selling them? Ed smiled, pondering the question, and then for a moment had a far-away look. "I like them, and the boys sometimes use them."

A remark that most of them were not being used drew a rapid reaction. "You're not using the pictures you've got hanging on the wall, but you like them — right?"

His sons take after their dad, with Eddie riding a Norton 500 (Manx type) motorcycle from his father's collection. Ronnie had acquired five or six himself and often rode a Moto Guzzi from Italy. From early years in Northport to the boatyard, Ronnie grew up seeing his dad's love of motorcycles. "Dad thought of riders as daredevils, and he was a daredevil too, in a way. He bought them all the time because he loves them and not to make money from them. Dad loved the way the machinery was built."

Ed Cutts admired good engineering where he found it, whether in motorcycles or in cars like his 1932 Studebaker with a Le Baron body, a Triumph TR3, and a recent green Jaguar, which Maggie used. "Well, some of the engineering I question," Ed said. "But, it might have had a beautiful look to it. The aesthetics are also as important as engineering to the human mind." This emphasis on aesthetics, beauty pleasing to the senses, is a key to his philosophy and to his life's work in naval architecture and building.

In his Museum area near *Foto* and other Cutts boats, Ed has an Indian Scout motorcycle suspended overhead, similar to his first real motorcycle. And there's another reason it is there. "The DuPonts owned Indian Motorcycles," he said. "As they always were good customers of the yard, I decided to put it up." In the evening, the whole tableau with interior lighting behind oversized windows becomes, from Tilghman Street, a colossal painting in a barn-red frame. After a snowfall this view is even more striking.

Ed's collections in this earliest Oxford house reveal much of him and his family. In the dining room the beautiful oak dining table is short and beautifully shined. "It's over a hundred years old," Ed said. Extra leaves are stored next to a glass-fronted gun cabinet with ten-pump and double-barreled shotguns, and a 22-caliber rifle. "I don't like to kill stuff," he said, "but I like things that are beautifully made."

Mementos linking Ed to the past exuded a warm atmosphere. These sometimes changed locations at the whim of Ed's housekeeper. Above dining room windows were a wind-up metal racing car from the 1930s, a carved captain in a yellow mackintosh, a model plane propeller, a metal trolley car, and a photo of champion *Man O' War*. All these held memories for Ed as did a wooden Borden Milk truck from his first Christmas.

On the opposite wall was a weathered payment receipt for a sloop *Robert Emmet* at $100 made out, in 1909, to V. V. Cutts from Fred Groggins Boat Repair, New Rochelle. Next to this is a blue half-hull of a 1987 12-meter yacht. A framed photo of Ed's parents hangs by their funeral prayer cards and one for his sister Adelaide.

Ed's father and mother lived to be ninety-one and ninety-two, but Ed liked to add a year. Soon after his seventy-eighth birthday he said, "Well, I'm working on my seventy-ninth now."

Family pictures pop up, such as Eddie Jr. and his own daughters. Because of a divorce and distant schools, the three girls seldom visited the boatyard. Eddie didn't see them as often as he would like. Probably, this caused a mood of sadness, concealed but recognizable, under his professional appearance. He impresses observers as a gentleman and ethical businessman, communicating in a relaxed manner and right to the point. He often dresses well, but he is also a builder/designer in less fancy attire.

Photos on the dining room mantle included Ed's daughter Linda with her husband, and another of Maggie as a girl with her brother. A card caption reads: "There is no friend like a sister in calm or stormy weather; to cheer one on the tedious way, to fetch one if one goes astray, to lift one if one totters down, to strengthen while one stands." This unsigned poem also spoke of Ed's feeling. "Dad really liked Gladys," Eddie said, "and spoke of her often when we were growing up. I do not think he got along with his sister Adelaide nearly as well."

Ed's love of boats is evident on any wall or corner of his house. When people enter the front door of 300-year-old Byberry House, they can see in the front hall Dutch tiles of square-rigged ships, framed sketches of America's Cup contenders, a large barometer, and a Claude Monet print with boats. There's a painting of the side-wheeler *Nantucket*, a reminder of his father's East River trip at age six, and a photo of *Rebellion*. Stuck in the framed photo of aircraft carrier *US Cowpens* is a picture of Ordnance Technician Cutts on the wing of a plane. "I'm certain that's a Navy Dauntless Dive Bomber," Ed said as he passed through the hall. "I had probably just worked on the bomb racks."

"The whole place is a museum," Ed Cutts liked to say. But it's also a montage of his life and family and accomplishments, especially the photographs and the half hulls he carved over a lifetime so evident on the living room walls and ceiling beam.

In 2004, an emergency phone call came in regarding a boat they had rebuilt in 1990. The owner called to say that his 40' cruiser had been rammed, but survived the blow. *Trouper II* needed to be hauled as soon as possible.

Owner Bill Bunting told what happened on the opening day of rockfish season. The yacht was returning from Sharp's Island Light, south of Tilghman and Kent Islands. "We entered Eastern Bay and had the boat on a plane. We went by a boat at a distance, and I didn't see anybody aboard but a dog. It was a 20' center console boat, and the Labrador retriever was barking." He had a gut feeling something was wrong, circled back, and there was only the dog on board.

"I called the Coast Guard and pressed my Man Overboard button. They asked me to conduct a search. Using my GPS and taking into account the tide and wind, we started the search." After Bunting had searched forty minutes, the Coast Guard asked

In 2003, Ed Cutts joins his sons Ronnie and Eddie who were restoring an early-1900 launch from the Thousand Islands area. Eddie believed it had been a lawn ornament for many years. The Lozier Boat Co. built this power boat named *Nixee*.

Wayne Brown

him to remain at the location until two helicopters and a rescue boat arrived.

The commercial rescue boat backed toward Bunting's yacht to take the dog that he had on board. "You know how people back up like they're trying to make a 100-mile run," Bunting said, "and then slam it into neutral and try to stop in the water? That wave and well of water just pushed her right into me. We couldn't stop her! It bumped my boat at the starboard corner of the transom, a foot above the water line. About the worst place to hit a boat! I can tell you this, if it wasn't for Ed's process, she'd have probably sunk right there."

After examining the damage, Ed Cutts agreed. "It caved in and was like a net inside. It stopped right at the cords." Cutts & Case went to work and rebuilt the damaged, aft section on *Trouper II*.

Bunting, wanting more power, sent two 454's to the boatyard for installation. How fine she looked, after a major repair, was soon evident.

Bunting entered *Trouper II* in the Antique & Classic Boat Show held at the CBMM in St. Michaels. "Very much to our surprise," he said, "she won Best Cruiser, Participant's Choice, and the Judges' Choice. There was now a contest for Best of Fleet between her and a smaller boat, which finally won the award."

After the announcement, a judge walked over to Bunting. "You know you caused quite an argument in our judging contest." The judge leaned closer and said, "Take those damn engines out of the boat."

In the CBMM's Recreational Boating Building, there is an exhibit of materials used in building boats. Richard Scofield said visitors can pick them up to examine them. "There's a piece of mahogany, and a piece of cedar, and a piece of aluminum with a rib down the middle, and a piece of plywood with fiberglass on it. And there is a piece of cedar, with Kevlar cord running through it that Cutts did and gave to us for this display. You couldn't break it if you tried."

Although he had used an earlier Kevlar initially, Ed repeatedly emphasized that Kevlar-49 was the only kind to use with his Method. "It was particularly suited to epoxy use." But, the size of the braided Kevlar-49 may change, he said. "The larger the boat, you would use a heavier cord. There are other things you can do. You can change the spacing of the cords. We generally use 4-inch spacing on the cords and a ¼-inch cord, for boats in the 25, 30 to 35-foot size," he said. "But if you were concerned over the ballasted area, you can change the spacing to 3 inches, or you can put the cord between the other cords. It doesn't weaken the hull any to put more cords in it," he said. "Once you make that groove, then the boat's longitudinal strength is dependent on the lumber that's left. So it doesn't matter if you want to put more cords in it."

Speaking on the application and result, he said, "You just saturate the cord and put it in with your finger as fast as you could do it. And it was beautiful. And its tensile strength was greater by far than a frame. And it was light as a feather. Kevlar is light in weight."

Looking back in his late seventies, Ed Cutts couldn't recall if many people contacted Cutts & Case when the design was published in *WoodenBoat*. "Nobody knew how to do it, you see, so they were in a quandary. So it was something that was talked about, but nobody understood."

Eddie said his father didn't remember. "People were sending in their $3 for a Cutts Method brochure." He estimated two to three thousand requests. He thought his mother, as office manager, probably handled more of this mail than anyone else. "There were requests for a manual to describe its use," Eddie said, "but the manual was never written. It should have been. Maybe I'll get to write it some day."

Personal recognition, as Ed said in his mid-seventies, was something he never cared for. "I never wanted any aggrandizement," Ed said, "so I never sent my stuff in to the periodicals." He was following a precedent of the designer whom he admired most. "Nat Herreshoff didn't want any designs of his printed either." After Captain Nat's death this policy still continued in force.

Ed Cutts never allowed his full-size construction plans to be sold to magazines or builders. "It could be unsafe and someone could get hurt," he said. This genuine fear also dovetailed with his perfectionist approach to boat building.

"Dad's fears of un-safeness," Eddie said, "came from years of fixing others' 'Fixes.' Only a few boatbuilders consider *why* a particular problem is occurring, and then correct it for good. We have been very careful in our work, but it is not possible to monitor others' work.

"Dad's boats were always high strength and lightweight, like a plane," he said. "So, you just can't change things or add to it as you build — without repercussions or considerations."

Ed had consistently ignored any requests from *WoodenBoat* or other publications for boat designs. When asked if he wrote back and thanked them, he looked away. "I'm not sure, but I probably didn't." He didn't remember whether or not Maggie responded to the requests.

Ed quietly admitted that the patent itself might have deterred builders from his building method. Perhaps it appeared as a watertight-door that prohibited anyone from using the technique. Ed had made a decision, however, to protect the invention when it was established and proved; he was following recommendations from his family and from John Case. Builders might not follow the Cutts Method correctly and might even use the wrong Kevlar. People could be injured, blaming Cutts & Case.

The Cutts Method patent, like all patents, expired after seventeen years, which was in 2000. "A patent should continue for the lifetime of the inventor," Ed said. "Other inventors would agree."

Evaluating the Cutts Method, Richard Scofield at CBMM chose his words carefully. "I myself don't know. From start to finish it's interesting. It's a certain method, and I'm not sure everyone wants to do it that way." Changing the topic to the inventor himself, Scofield said, "Ed is definitely a self promoter. He says, 'This is the greatest boat-building method in the world, there's just no question.' You can't argue with the man."

Ed Cutts could get impatient with people who didn't agree with him. If he came across as a salesman, it could be because he relied on his boatyard's reputation and on word-of-mouth recommendations. "My dad said, 'If you don't advertise, then at least you'd better advertise your place for sale.'" He considered this in silence. "I believed the 'Build a Better Mousetrap' adage," Ed said. "If I build the finest boats, people will tell each other. People have come here, so it's happened — but not in high numbers. Even with Francis Herreshoff, not many people came to him until Leonardi published his articles in *The Rudder*, and also his books."

Ed Cutts was sometimes a non-conformist and a rebel. "We are a people that want to be told stories, whether they are true or false," he said almost defiantly. "The world loves B.S. It took me a long time to realize this, and I will probably not touch advertising at this late stage."

Long ago Maggie Cutts started a block ad in *WoodenBoat*, their only advertising. Ed, who read the magazine regularly, said he presumed Maggie placed the advertising. He felt it took money that should be used for boat expenses.

Did he want boaters to know he was designing and building? This question hit a nerve. "I don't give a damn about my name recognition. They can come and see me if they want," he said with firmness. "They hear of me by word of mouth."

When told other builders were running larger ads, he remained a critic of Madison Avenue. "I don't look at competition. I do the most beautiful work that I know how, and that I can get my crew to do," he said. "I don't have to advertise if I'm busy." Did it bother him that many boat owners didn't know he was in Oxford, Maryland? "No, if not a single one knew I was here, it would be OK," he said gruffly. "I'm going to be eighty years old."

Ed occasionally hinted that Jon Wilson got his idea for a publication on wooden boats when visiting Cutts & Case, but his sons saw it differently. Ronnie said, "We were building *Spellbound*, and Jon Wilson came here to watch us building, because he loved wooden boats."

Eddie recalled an earlier event that led to the visit. The yacht *Magic Carpet* was outfitted at Cutts & Case in 1971, Eddie said. She headed north and then lightning stuck her. "She sustained masthead instrument damage and her anchor chain had welded together." After returning to Cutts & Case for repairs, the delivery crew returned to Maine, except for one who elected to remain on board. "This man was Lance Lee, who saw *La Mouette* christened and launched. Lance was moved to see the waterfront scene he had witnessed in his youth, of a small shop moving a newly-built boat out and onto the ways for launching," Eddie said. "It marked a remnant of his past — a disappearing one in the then-present world of fiberglass boat building."

When Lance Lee returned to Maine, he prepared to begin a Boat-building Apprentice Program at the Maine Maritime Museum in Bath. He recommended to a friend, boatbuilder Jon Wilson, that he include Cutts & Case in his many boatyard visits, which was why Jon came by in 1972. "Jon Wilson was in the first two-year class at the school," Eddie said. "After graduating, he began a newsletter to keep in touch with graduates and industry. This later became *WoodenBoat*."

In the October 1987 *WoodenBoat* editorial, Jon Wilson wrote, "In an industry full of businesses trying to distance themselves from wooden boats, here was a man inventing new ways of putting wood together, developing systems for which he would be awarded patents."

Jon Wilson finished the editorial, "I like to believe that Ed Cutts is one of the individuals who, by his example, caused *WoodenBoat* to be born. His commitment to wood's potential seems to be without limit; he continues to be challenged by it. For all of us who care about traditional wood construction brought forward into the future, his work is an inspiration."

This appraisal of Ed Cutts and his boatyard was a sincere tribute from Publisher Jon Wilson, an acknowledged wooden-boat authority, highly respected by wooden-boat owners and builders the world over.

There is a coda. Ed Cutts quietly appreciated the complimentary words for himself and his boatyard in Wilson's editorial and in Groom's article, but for years there appeared to be a falling out and a lack of communication. Ed had ignored all requests to write an article or to submit boat plans for the magazine, as other designers did. Of course, at the root of this were his fears. Over the intervening years, he had obviously been rude for not writing or keeping in touch, but this was bad manners — thoughtless behavior, not arrogance.

In his late-seventies, Ed said he believed that *WoodenBoat* was ignoring him and his boatyard for some reason. He spoke strangely, in a high, far-away, pinched voice. "I don't know why. I wish I knew." He stared ahead in silence.

Communication had stopped between the two men who loved wooden boats as much as anyone; however, Ed always kept that issue of *WoodenBoat* on his living room table for customers and visitors to see. It was still there in 2013.

Chapter Twelve

BOATBUILDING
AND MAINE CUTTS

A DOWN EAST RESIDENT from Upper Penobscot Bay said large Maine boatyards in places like Rockport and Brooklin were building cold-molded boats. These were not traditional wood, but he was glad that his ketch was. He had met Ed Cutts and looked over his boatyard, so he knew Cutts & Case were using Kevlar and epoxy. He said that in the Maine traditionalist sect that's not a wooden boat, which is about plank-on-frame construction. He spoke of the three-to-five-thousand years of tradition.

Methods of boat construction, however, have a history of changing and keeping pace with technical developments. Civilizations the world over once used log canoes. In Virginia, Jamestown colonists found a Native American Powhatan civilization that depended on *quintans,* their version of the log canoe. For these, the native Americans preferred to use the cypress that were prevalent. A Mariners' Museum publication stated, "To help cut the hard wood, a fire would be set in the log. The burned areas would be chipped out with a shell or stone scraper." The tree size determined the canoe length, which could reach about 50 feet, capable of carrying up to forty individuals. When hostilities broke out, their boat handling saved lives. "The Powhatans were able to paddle or pole their quintans faster than the English could maneuver their barges." (Mariners' Museum)

At the end of the twentieth century, Third-World builders occasionally used this traditional and primitive boat-building method. On the Caribbean Island of Dominica, some Carib Indians, called Karaphuna, still occasionally built using fire and a metal adz. Originally they had used a sharp stone. A documentary film shot there in 1979 showed a Carib man scraping a boat of about 15 feet that he was constructing with a friend. Later, freeboards and a removable mast and rigging would be added. In addition to fishing, they can also use the canoes for inter-island smuggling. (Karaphuna)

"You can take traditions back as far as you want to the point of dugout canoes or trunneled planks," Eddie Cutts Jr. said. "A peg was driven into a ship's plank and opened with a wedge, but no one would do it that way today."

The Vikings had used an ingenious method to fasten the planking to the frames as discovered from a well-preserved *skuta* dug up at Gogstad, Sweden, in 1880. Marine architect Frederick Lord, who described this Viking ship, said that experts praised its workmanship and beauty of lines. Estimated length was 79', extreme breadth was 16' 8", and extreme draft 3' 6". The ship with the owner had been buried in blue clay facing the ocean.

Lord wrote, "The planking of the boat is of the lap-strake type. There are sixteen strakes to a side, and they vary in thickness . . . The planks run about 9½ inches wide with one-inch laps. They are riveted about every 6 to 8 inches along the lap and caulked with cow's hair spun into a cord . . . The planks were worked out so as to leave a raised cleat where it touched a frame. Holes were bored in the cleat and in the lower edge of the frame, through these were passed a tough root ¼ inch thick and formed the only connection between frame and planking. The frames were shaped in section and were very light compared with the other scantling. There can be little doubt that the boat must have worked considerably in a seaway." (Lord)

Eddie, noting how the Vikings lapstraked their double-enders, said, "That's tradition too, but we don't do everything that way now. I prefer to double plank because with Kevlar you get all the framing strength."

In 2006, Ed saw scientist Stephanie Kwolek, the discoverer of Kevlar, interviewed on television. He said he would love to meet her and wished she could visit the boatyard. "She's responsible for our new way of building boats," Ed said. "Suddenly she discovered, by accident, a material that was so strong we couldn't believe it." Ten years later DuPont sold vests that stopped a bullet at ten feet. Later uses included fiber-optic cables, fuel hoses, helmets, composites for aircraft, spacecraft parts, and of course boat hulls.

It's possible that many shipwrights who build and repair wooden boats know little about the Cutts Method, perhaps never having examined a boat made that way, nor having tried out the actual technique. Some may have seen a diagram illustrating the use of Kevlar in the Cutts & Case brochure that was reproduced in *WoodenBoat* (Oct. 1987), and still have unanswered questions. Many may have serious doubts about the strength of the new Kevlar-and-epoxy technique. But, it is being used at Cutts & Case for rebuilding and for new boats. The strength and reliability of this method should be seen and experienced in order to be understood.

Ed repeatedly said he wasn't trying to get rich on the patent, which expired in 2000 and is now in public domain. "All they have to do is buy the material from Eddie, and it's not expensive," he said. This was just for the braided Kevlar cord, which is made up for Cutts & Case. The boatyard also recommends the correct epoxy most suitable for this process.

But, there are no instructors out there as this book is written. Dr. Crile Crisler and Lee Casper had the benefit of observing the process at Cutts & Case before building with the Cutts Method. Hanno "Allan" Savolainen, the Finnish trainee, was actually there working on *John's Boat*, which prepared him to use the technique and train other builders in Finland.

Many who have heard of Ed's building method may consider it too experimental compared with standard plank-on-frame construction. Even with occasional magazine and newspaper articles, this building method may appear mysterious.

Most boatbuilders and boaters don't know much about Edmund A. Cutts who, after all, was a regional designer/builder with no class boats to his name. For example, a Connecticut man, Philip Teuscher, who is a maritime writer and blue-water sailor, had never heard of Ed or the Cutts Method. This boater, who has owned eight classic wooden vessels including two steamboats, asked, "Is it something like cold molding?" The answer is no.

The boats built or rebuilt with this Kevlar-cord technique should say something about its reliability, strength, and conservation of the hull. Time will tell if *Curio*, *Millennia*, *John's Boat*, and *Souvenir*, Ed's last boats built with this new technique, have greater longevity — and if they reach the hundred-year mark or more that Ed shot for. *Ocean Gem*, the experimental skiff built in 1982 using braided steel wire and epoxy, also belongs with this group. By 2012, Eddie said that Cutts & Case had done major refits using the Cutts Method on ten yachts.

In 1988, Jon Johansen, publisher of *Maine Coastal News*, met Ed Cutts at the Newport Boat Show. Ed welcomed him aboard *Foto* and cruised around so he could take photographs of the boats. Johansen spoke about Down East boat building in a 2008 interview. "Maine boatbuilders say a boat is a compromise. You can design a boat several different ways. Our boats, of course, are lobster boats. They're not hard chine, but round built," he said. "Some of them are what we call 'skate boats,' so it's a flat bottom going into a skeg. And there is the built-down boat that is more rounded as it goes into the skeg. And there's always an argument which one's better. Which one pounds, which one doesn't? Which one's better in a following sea? Basically, it ends up a compromise," Johansen said.

"We have a slew of wooden boats up here. There are probably five to ten builders that would love to build wooden boats," he said, "but most were doing repair work." He named Richard Stanley and Peter Kass who were building traditional boats that year. As for the cold-molded boats being built in Maine, he called them "high-tech wooden boats."

In many places, cold-molding comes to mind when someone speaks about building a wooden boat. Some builders believe that Cutts & Case used this technique. Ed Cutts denied this forcefully, like a storm-warning wind gust. "Cutts & Case does not build cold-molded boats. We plank boats. Cold-molding crosses layer after layer at right angles so planks crisscross like the figure X. As you can imagine, this is not as strong linearly as our method," he said, "which has a result like solid lumber, because all the lumber goes fore and aft.

"Cold-molding is so ridiculous," Ed said, gesturing with both arms, "because it has a greatly reduced longitudinal strength. If you take a piece of ¾-inch plywood 3 inches wide, you can break it over your knee, but if you took the parent material, you couldn't break it over your knee. But to get this across to people's thinking is hard to do. The plywood has panel strength, and you don't want this in a boat. You don't want the boat to break in half. So then you must make sure that the scantlings are great enough to handle it."

Ronnie Cutts had walked into the kitchen at the end of his work day. He stood and listened to his father, who asked what he thought. Ronnie knew the technique because the yard had repaired some cold-molded boats. "It's an easy structure to build," he said slowly, "with a lot of gluing, screws, grinding, and epoxy. It's not as clean building as the Cutts Method, or as strong, or as light." He paused. "But we do not build with cold-molding."

Asked about the weight saved when he used the Cutts Method, Ed said, "Twenty percent or more. It's all according how the boat is laid out inside, how much accommodation is required — how spartan or how complicated."

Convinced of his Method's value from years of good results, Ed would like to see wider acceptance. And he would like to see it used properly in building and repair. At times, Ed could make firm pronouncements, like a professor. Or at other times, he could be in his relaxed, persuasive, public-relations mode. The last was the more effective, of course. Either way, his words would be brief, clear, and finely honed — like his mind.

Fred Hecklinger, an Annapolis marine surveyor, spoke about the "Cutts Method." "Ed thinks it's the best way, and there are many advantages to it, but it's not been generally accepted. In many ways, Ed is too enthusiastic about it. When he is talking to other people, he sort of acts as if they're dimwitted for not jumping at his method."

Some people had another view of Ed. They had trouble believing everything Ed told them. Richard Scofield had doubted some of Ed's statements he heard when working at Cutts & Case. Ed had talked about early Cutts arriving in this country from England. "If you listen to Ed," Scofield said, "if you believe everything he says, every boat built in North America derived from the first Cutts, who was the first boatbuilder. Well, I don't know about that." Sitting in his office at the Chesapeake Bay Maritime Museum in 2005, Scofield smiled and took a breath. "So I think everybody who knows Ed says, 'Yeah, that's Ed talking.' A lot of what he says is actually true, including some great stories. But some people say, 'Ah, I don't know about that one.'"

Early in his career, Ed told Francis Herreshoff he was trying to find historical material on his own family. "I too am interested in genealogy," Herreshoff said. He had seen the Cutts name somewhere in his reading, so he encouraged Ed to look into it. With the help of his son Eddie, Ed did some research on three ancestors — John, Richard and Robert Cutt (the S was dropped), who had arrived from England in the mid-1600s.

"John and Robert started a shipyard near Portsmouth, New Hampshire," Ed said, "and records show that Robert later moved it across the river to what became Maine." Ed had an aura of authority while speaking for a magazine interview. "John remained on the New Hampshire side and, using his brothers' ships, established himself in the mercantile business." At the end of his summary Ed dropped a zinger: "John Cutt was made President of the American Colonies by William and Mary." With a relaxed face, he watched his interviewer for a moment before adding, "George Washington wasn't our first president, John Cutt was." He smiled triumphantly and leaned back. (Brown)

With new research for Ed's biography, the Cutts name turned up in the Library of Congress, at libraries in Kittery and Saco, Maine, and at the Maine Maritime Museum. Census records had shown that Ed's grandfather, John Henry Cutts, was born and worked in Derby, England. Roughly 140 miles south is Bristol where Cutte families were living three hundred years earlier. They were also at Bath, about twenty-five miles southeast of Bristol.

Cutt brothers did come to New England in the mid-seventeenth century. According to the *Genealogical Dictionary of Maine & New Hampshire*, "Their ancestry has been traced no further than their father's grf. [grandfather] Mr. John Cutte, a Bristol merchant, at times Mayor of the City." It also stated, "St. Michael's Church in Burnett, England, between Bath and Bristol, has a memorial brass representing the Mayor" He died May 21, 1575. (Noyes, Thornton, Davis)

His grandson John Cutt was born in Burnett where his father and grandfather had lived, and in 1613 was living in Bath, England.

He was a Member of Parliament when he died in 1625, according to 1700s historian Joseph Whipple. His wife, Bridget Baker Shelton Cutt, was married previously and had twenty-three children in all. There are records of six Cutt children, five sons born by 1619, and a daughter Ann born in 1625. (Ibid.)

John, Richard, and Robert Cutt landed at Boston in 1646 with bank letters of credit. We know Richard had been apprenticed ten years to a Bristol merchant. They traveled to Strawberry Banke, the settlement by the ocean that later became part of Portsmouth in the Province of New Hampshire.

"Richard right away was buying and selling land and ships, and he and John began importing English goods at 'the Banke.'" Another brother, Baker Cutt, visited and returned to England, and a fifth brother, Walter Cutt, was a London merchant by 1659. (Ibid.)

In the 1640s, there was an ongoing civil war between King Charles I and a rebellious Parliament. The Royalists took Bristol in 1643, but the Parliamentarians reclaimed it in 1645 — the year before the brothers embarked for Boston. An historian wrote, "It is not known if the final 'S' was dropped when they came to this country for political reasons or some other cause." But, at some point, the final "S" was added. (Howard)

The Massachusetts Bay Colony was the seat of New England's Puritan government under the authority of England. Oliver Cromwell and the Parliamentarians, who governed England, finally captured Charles I and executed him in 1649.

One of the three brothers, John Cutt, was an active Puritan, which was fine when trading with England. In 1662, he married Hannah Starr whose father was the well-known Puritan, Dr. Comfort Starr of Cambridge, who became President of Harvard College. They lived at Strawberry Banke, but his two brothers didn't remain long.

As a merchant Robert Cutt sailed to St. Christopher (now St. Kitts) and then to Barbados. He stayed awhile, got married, and

returned to New Hampshire as a "mariner and merchant navigator of his own ships." (Prugh)

We learn from another historian that in 1650, "Robert Cutts was
building fishing boats at Crooked Lane, Kittery, on the Piscataqua,
and vied in importance with John Bray as a pioneer in shipbuilding. Cutts launched more vessels, but they were smaller than the
deep-sea trading craft built by Bray." (Fairburn)

Robert wasn't a shipbuilder but he ran the shipyard, which
also turned out boats for the West Indies Trade. For this trade,
which had started around 1640, the ships were about 90' to 100',
beam 26', and weighed 400 tons. Fishing boats were lighter and
smaller, but strong enough for heavy seas. "Ketches were used a
great deal in the off-shore fishing until about 1700 when they lost
their popularity." (Chapelle)

The brothers took an active part in government. Richard was
a Justice of the Court of Associates in Maine Province in 1664,
and in five years commanded the Kittery Fort. John Cutt, at first a
selectman, became a deputy to Boston.

When Charles II came to the English throne, the Province of
New Hampshire appealed to England for help to govern itself. "In
1679, when New Hampshire was separated from Massachusetts, the
King [William] appointed John Cutt as President. The royal charter
then given was the only one ever granted to New Hampshire."
(Brewster)

Noyes wrote that John Cutt was called "President of the Prov.
Ct." This could read "Provincial Court." Another historian noted,
"He died 27 March 1681; was president of the council at the time
of his death." (Pope)

Ed Cutts was on the right track. His ancestor John Cutt had
been council president in the Province of New Hampshire whose
inhabitants were mostly Native American tribes. In 1680, John
Cutt called a general assembly that brought representatives from
Portsmouth, Dover, Hampton, and Exeter. "The whole number of

voters in the four towns was 209." John died the following year, 1681, and left his great house to his son Samuel. (Brewster)

Col. Richard Waldron succeeded John Cutt and is officially regarded as the first Governor of New Hampshire. He married John's daughter Hannah, whom Indians killed in a raid on their wooded property up river. As shipbuilders and logging operations moved further north on the Piscataqua and other rivers, uprooted Native American tribes became an increasing hazard.

William Pepperell and his sons were among the early shipbuilders on the Piscataqua and Saco Rivers where trees were floated down stream from the great forests. At first there were a small number of shipbuilders. "The first William's father-in-law, John Bray, was well established there as early as 1660. Upriver at Crooked Lane, Robert Cutts — who lived like a lord, it is said, and employed slaves in his yard — built for the fisheries and the West India trade." (Rowe)

When Robert Cutts died, his son Richard ran the Kittery shipyard and built fishing boats for William Pepperell. (Fairburn) Richard's brother Robert Cutts rose from being a shipwright to command a ship from 1712 to 1715 for Col. William Pepperell. (Noyes)

Shipyards weren't necessarily situated next to deep water. "The country well inland from Sanford . . . built some ships 'among the timber,' and tradition tells of the hauling of vessels by oxen over snow as far as twenty-five miles from the building berth 'on the farm' to tidewater where they were first put into the water." Some ships were floated a ways, hauled out above the falls, and then pulled a few miles on the packed snow to tidewater for re-launching. As many as a hundred teams of oxen were sometimes needed. (Fairburn)

Shipbuilding kept increasing in the Maine yards. In 1742, forty topsail vessels, square-rigged schooners, were being built at one time. Many present-day Maine families carry names of ancestors who were shipwrights, sailors, captains, and merchants.

Richard Cutts and Eunice Foxwell Cutts of Kittery were parents of Thomas Cutts, born in 1736. He worked as a clerk for the Pepperell family, which had huge land holdings. He opened a successful shop in Saco, and, in 1759, he bought a share of Indian Island. He put up a large house and store, warehouses and a wharf. The island became Cutts Island, and he prospered being a good business man. He traded lumber for a cargo of molasses that he sold on a high market for a $100,000 profit. (Folsom)

Rum and molasses were major West Indies imports for Maine. "Rum played a role in many daily activities of early America. It fueled the terrible labor of felling trees and pulling stumps. An eighteenth-century settler swigged rum as a mid-morning pick-me-up in the fields, and his wife sipped a bit to cure whatever might ail her." (Sheehan)

Maine and Portsmouth continued their trade voyages at the beginning of the War of 1812, when there was an embargo on trade with England. To circumvent this embargo, merchants shipped lumber and spars to Spain and the Canary Islands, where the English could pick them up. In exchange, merchants received certificates for British goods.[3]

The British hoped New England would remain neutral and therefore allowed New Hampshire and Maine some shipping privileges. "The captains of British warships along the coasts allowed vessels to pass and repass, and for a consideration they even acted as convoys for smuggling craft." (Rowe)

In order to smuggle goods, both import and export, merchants had to take secret measures. These can be seen in the Portsmouth mansion built in 1805 by Edward Cutts. A great-great-grandson of the original Robert Cutt, he graduated from Harvard College where his mother's father, Rev. Edward Holyoke, had been president. Edward Cutts headed the corporation that built the first bridge over the Piscataqua River in 1819.

Edward Cutts, a Harvard-educated lawyer, built this impressive house in Portsmouth over Cutts Cove of the Piscataqua River in 1805. It had two secret tunnels to the water that survived for about two hundred years.
Wayne Brown

Edward had built his large house high above Cutts Cove in Portsmouth on land owned by the first John Cutt. As recent owners and occupants discovered, two tunnels ran down a steep bank to the water at Cutts Creek. With the Federal embargo on wartime trade and surveillance at major docks, secret tunnels allowed merchants to smuggle goods.

The lenient British policy encouraging smugglers swung 180 degrees when the British began blockading New England in April of 1814. Fishing boats and smugglers' trading craft were stopped, captured, or destroyed unless they could outrun the larger British warships. One of these was the 74-gun *Bulwark*, sent to destroy all shipping she could reach in the Maine Province. "On the 14th, she sent a landing party to the establishment of Captain Thomas Cutts at Biddeford Pool near the mouth of the Saco River. One of the vessels they had chased from the sea they burned. The frame of another on the stocks was cut into pieces, and they carried off a third . . . in retaliation for an insult the Saco Captain hurled at the British." (Rowe)

Later, Thomas Cutts was able to ransom the ship the British had taken. He and his brother Foxwell Cutts were owners of large ships that visited ports of the world, and they were not building the fast privateers like other shipbuilders. Maine was surviving despite the destruction and hardships of the war, but men began mobilizing. A day after attacking the Cutts boatyard, the *Bulwark* came in to Kennebunk where the local militia prevented any destruction.

After peace was proclaimed, the Marshall of Maine, Thomas G. Thornton, according to an historian, "gave a magnificent ball at the John Cleaves' Tavern in Pepperell Square. The Cuttses, Nyes, Scammans, Hartleys and a dozen other leading families joined in the cotillion, danced to the music of a well-known Portland fiddler." (Fairfield)

Machias Ship Registers at the Maine Maritime Museum in Bath lists Cutts captains. These records indicate that captains, like merchants, held proportional shares of boats. Hiram Cutts is listed as one-sixth owner of a 74.5' schooner *Oriole* in 1832. And in 1846, Thomas Cutts went from a one-quarter share to a one-third share of the 89' brig *Girard*. Another relative William Cutts captained four different ships starting in 1834.

Cutts Genealogy traces the family's different lines. Ed Cutts, it seems, had only scratched the surface. It's evident the family had played their part, along with many others, in America's early shipping, trading and boat building.

Lawyer William Wentworth Cutts, a member of the Maine Historical Society, was living at Kittery Point in 2006. His grandfather was Joseph Williams Cutts, related to the original Robert Cutt and his son Richard who lived at the Whipple Garrison House, standing near the present Navy Yard. William W. Cutts summed up his heritage when he said, "People who do title searches tell me you can barely research a property back three hundred years without running into a Cutts."

Early ship owners and merchants, wanting to safeguard their investments, made certain that someone regularly inspected their ships. This was often the master builder, or the captain. When a ship returned to home port, the ship's logbook described damage, repairs, leakage, and any accidents. Today, before buying or selling, boaters hire a marine surveyor to go over it.

When *Curio's* owners asked for a survey in 2004, Ed Cutts contacted Fred Hecklinger, who had twenty-five years experience. He surveyed the raised-deck cabin cruiser, which resembles a 1930s custom yacht. Hecklinger wrote in part, "This vessel was built to unusually high standards and has been maintained to unusually high standards. All of the equipment is suitable and of the best quality. The hull is constructed of wood using the 'Cutts Method,' which is unique. This method is proven to be remarkably strong and unusually resistant to deterioration and the corrosive effects of a marine atmosphere. Suitable woods are bonded together with epoxy, and all is reinforced with Kevlar to create a hull with no seams." On the exterior and interior surfaces the surveyor found "not the first suggestion of any cracks or of any type of weakness." And the report describes the topsides as "wonderfully fair and glossy."

Hecklinger hadn't known whether this pristine boat had been in the water or used at all, but thought it had been kept in the Cutts & Case boat shed. In fact, Ed verified that the six-year-old boat had been in the water four summers. This report pleased the owners as well as Ed. "I read surveys of boats all the time because we repair them. It's the best survey I ever read." He mentioned the surveyor's hand-written note, which he pulled out of an envelope and read. "How refreshing it is to inspect such a neat and clean boat." He paused smiling and proud of the professional praise.

In Annapolis, Hecklinger learned that Ed Cutts said that this boat had been in the water and used for four summers. He was silent for a moment but didn't seem surprised. "The Cutts power boat *Curio* is in such good condition," he said, "because she spends so much time in the showroom in the Cutts yard where she is relatively dry and protected from the sun."

The marine surveyor talked about damage to wooden boats. "A marine atmosphere is corrosive to metals and supporting or encouraging of rot development in wood. Water must be present for the development of rot in wood." He called this a fungus that is basically dormant in temperatures below 55 degrees. "When anything is frozen," he said, "it does not rot. That, of course, is why we keep meat or fish in a freezer. If wood is protected by epoxy coatings or any coatings, the water cannot get to the wood," he said. "However, if the epoxy coatings are in the sunlight, the coatings will break down. All coatings will break down when exposed to the sunlight, but some last longer than others." He paused.

"So if you want to keep a wood boat for a long time," he said, "you should keep it in the Cutts showroom."

Speaking of metals, he said "Classic cars are best kept in a heated garage and not driven on salted roads or exposed to the sun. Salt water is more corrosive than fresh water. Cutts tried to eliminate the possibilities of rot and deterioration. It's a time-consuming process, but if you don't have any metal exposed to salt water, you don't have corrosion."

Hecklinger didn't know of any ocean racers built with the Cutts Method. "Those ocean racers are all custom-built, and they are trying to achieve lightness." Sometimes, they use wood and carbon fibers, and don't have any frames either, he said. "Some types of wood like Western cedar glue well, suited to laminating these high-strength fibers to give it extra strength. The stem and stern is where you don't want weakness. However, a lot of these composite boats are not resistant to impact. They may be strong as a shape, but for a direct impact they're quite fragile, and embarrassingly so, because they don't flex like straight wood."

Surveyor Chuck Wiley shared his views on interior damage in older boats. "The problem with boats that were built in Maine compared with the type of work Ed does is the ventilation in them. You can build a wooden boat and do a great job, but if it's completely sealed on the inside and doesn't get proper ventilation, it will rot. With the way that Ed Cutts builds and rebuilds boats, they have ventilation, so that just doesn't happen.

"Ralph Wiley was another who saw that his boats had interior ventilation," Wiley said. "Way back, the thing at the time was to make a boat interior pretty, so you put all that ceiling on the inside. These are narrow, in most cases, mahogany or cedar strips that were fastened on the inside of the frames horizontally fore and aft. They started right up on the deck with one next to the other all the way down. And you left a little bit of a notch at the top, and at the keel there was another one," he said. "Now fresh air was supposed to circulate down behind that little thing, all the way beyond the ceiling, and go down and turn around and come back up — but it didn't happen.

"The boats my father built," Wiley said, "and the boats that Ed Cutts builds or rebuilds, are open boats, if you can get right down to the skin of the boat. And they just don't rot."

Ed Cutts explained one way that water penetrates a hull. "The bottom paint is not impervious to water going through it. You're not keeping water out completely," he said. "You can paint a board, measure it carefully with a micrometer, and put it in a pan of water. Come back a few days later, and you will be surprised at the increase in size. If you put it in an oven, it will decrease in size. But all those things will have an effect on the seams. Our boats' seams don't move." Ed likes to describe his Cutts-Method boats as "seamless." Aside from normal bottom painting, *Curio* had never been painted, he said, except when it was new.

After discussing *Curio*, Hecklinger said, "If I had unlimited money and I wanted a classic power boat for day usage, I would go to Ed Cutts. I wouldn't go to him for a large cruising sailboat because he doesn't understand about cruising sailboats. His active boating has been quite limited because he has been running the boatyard. He's never been long-range cruising or off-shore sailing."

It's true Ed never had the deep-water experience of sailing ocean-going yachts like Hecklinger, who once captained the *Pride of Baltimore I*. While Ed never emulated Captain Slocum's circumnavigation, he did sail and motor along the Atlantic coast.

Chapter Thirteen

CLASSIC DESIGN
AND HEALTH

A CLASSIC SPEEDBOAT was the order of the day, following the tradition of the Chris Craft, Gar Wood, Hutchinson,
and Hacker designs — smart, open-cockpit, sporty speed-boats
with brightwork and brass. In 2005, a couple asked Ed to build
them one for a Pennsylvania lake. "How did you happen to come
to us?" Ed asked.

They said that they had talked to custom boatbuilders in
Europe who didn't want to build just one small boat. Either they
could build a number of small boats, or they could design and
build one large boat.

Ed understood this. "The reason is, there's too much ground
work in a small boat, especially of a type that the European yards
weren't used to." The foreign builders had essentially told the
couple, as Ed remembered, "You have a small company in the
United States that does fine work, and they can produce the boat
you want." They named Cutts & Case.

Ed sketched a profile of a classic two-cockpit speedboat of
22' to 23', which they discussed, but he also drew a modern boat.

"Perhaps," he said later, "they didn't know what a newer model with nice lines might look like, so now they have a choice." The clients chose the classic, said it was exactly what they wanted, and asked Ed to start on it.

"I can't give you the cost yet," he said, "but I want you to know it will be about six figures. Is that all right with you?" That was fine with them, and they offered then and there to write a sizeable check.

Ed held up one hand. "I couldn't accept this now, but thank you. There are reasons for this. For one thing, I can't tell exactly how much the boat is going to cost. For another thing I don't like to take money for something I haven't done."

He had a third reason — diabetes — which he didn't mention to the couple. To friends he said, "I have a healing problem. You get a cut or something in the extremities, like the end of your foot, and it can be years healing." The previous year a foot operation removed part of his left foot and all the toes. It was painful walking, even with a cane or crutch. But, he didn't want everyone to know, so he tried to walk normally. A golf cart took him around the boatyard.

In 2006, his doctor said he needed another operation at the ankle to prevent the infection from moving up his leg. "What are you going to do, just cut off a little bit of me at a time?" Ed asked the startled doctor. "Why not cut higher so you won't have to operate again?" The doctor agreed and amputated at the mid-calf.

The professionally-fitted prosthetic lower leg was painful. Ed's response to this was decisive and active. He would cut away a little of the metal and plastic at a time while leaving enough support for walking. As he continued this, the pain lessened.

Complicating Ed's health concerns, his right foot now developed an infection and started to become numb, so he couldn't stand for long. "I can't take a pain killer, because that dulls the senses," he said matter-of-factly, without self-pity.

The prosthetic leg was still uncomfortable, so after two months his doctor suggested getting a leg from a different manufacturer. With this new prosthetic leg, Ed noticed a slight improvement. But he would have to work on it.

After deciding he would have to turn down the speedboat, Ed phoned the Pennsylvania couple. "I never go back on my word," he said, "and so this hurts me to the quick, but I can't do this boat. Something happened that I never expected, so I am devastated. But I can't do it."

The clients were sorry to learn of his diabetes, but said they still wanted the boat. "Could you follow through on the design? We'll wait."

When asked later why he couldn't just design it and then let his sons build it, he said, "That's easy to say, but I'm hurting half the time. If I could just walk back and forth without agony — that's all I ask." He nodded toward his prosthesis, sitting against the wall by his knee. "This thing won't do it, and it's the new one."

As for possibly turning his speedboat design over to another builder, this was out of the question. "Never," he said. "I have to be there." This had been Ed's mantra since he stopped being an active boatbuilder. He had to be there, to check the work, and make sure it was perfect.

He continued to make adjustments to lower the pain in his left leg while maintaining support for stability and safety. "I keep cutting it down and fitting it better," he said. "When I started, I could only wear it for an hour and it began to hurt. After 2½ hours I couldn't stand it any more and had to get it off. But, I kept working on it and now I tested it for 11½ hours, and it didn't hurt at all. So that was very interesting to me," he said with an upbeat tone. "Big difference from what the doctor and the action-prosthetic people had done. They have both their legs, so they don't really know what the problems are. I aim to tell him there are certain things he should watch for, as someone with experience." Two weeks later, he saw the doctor and explained in detail what he did and why. Ed didn't know if his input was relayed to the manufacturer.

In early August 2005, he walked with some effort to the living room and sat in his Governor Dewey chair, putting his metal cane on the arm. "I'm still going to cut it down even more," he said. "I have no feeling in my right foot so if I bump into something I won't know it so I'll go down on my face."

After speaking of his parents with love, he stood up suddenly and said, "I found some old pictures." Ignoring his cane, he lurched partway across the room, his right leg aiding his left in an uneven rhythm. He bent over the center table, and suddenly leaned too far left and again recovered while ignoring his footing, his eyes on the photographs in frames. He returned rapidly, trying to keep his six steps even, and sank into his chair. With pride and enthusiasm, he held out his mother's theatrical photos, showing her in costumes. "My mother was very talented. She sang in Carnegie Hall and did musicals and even opera." He said she had understudied a role in *Aida*. She was in a touring musical review when Vernon Cutts met her.

Months later with even more prostheses modifications, Ed had improved maneuverability, his energy was returning, and his thoughts turned to designing. "I embellished the speed boat-drawing into a three-cockpit, center-engine speedboat," he said. "I keep stretching the length because I know they will be happier with a boat that you can put six people in and not make a sluggard out of her. That takes power to weight again, and if you add 350 pounds per couple, you have to take great care. I had made her a little lighter, carefully saving a few pounds here and a few pounds there." Putting over a thousand pounds of extra weight into the short boat was detrimental, he said. "The trick then is to get a good power-to-weight ratio and to make the boat big enough so that it can accommodate the weight gain. This is only a small part of the problem."

Having made detailed drawings of the larger boat, Ed then needed the customers' final approval. Although their marriage had broken up, the man came to Oxford and studied the three-cockpit design. This was the speedboat he wanted. He said he would be patient and wait for Ed to begin building.

"I was astounded," Ed said about one month later, "because people usually don't wait like that. Certainly not people who can afford whatever they want." He was grateful for the man's extraordinary patience. At this time, however, the yard didn't have a building schedule, although a month had gone by since the client meeting. Ed projected a subliminal feeling he didn't want to go ahead with it. Eddie said he lost his enthusiasm for the project after the couple's breakup.

In 2005, Maggie suffered a heart attack and went to Shore Memorial Hospital in Easton. "The doctors said there was evidence of a previous attack," Ed said quietly, looking serious. "So this was number two." Maggie recovered and returned home to resume her busy life.

One day, a Hollywood representative arrived in Oxford. Troy Waters, a marine coordinator for Paramount Pictures, visited many boatyards including Cutts & Case, scouting locations. The next thing Ron and Eddie knew, a director named Tom Dey appeared and joined Waters looking over the boatyard. When he spotted the ketch *Spellbound* at the dock, the director studied the beautiful boat and checked out its suitability for the scripted scenes.

Then, Dey and Waters walked to the Byberry House. The director told Ed he would like to film a sequence using the ketch for a Paramount feature titled *Failure To Launch*. That sounded fine to Ed, but he felt he should give these westerners a little advice. "I'm not fond of the title. I wouldn't put the word 'failure' in it. It's a downer."

The director didn't think Paramount would approve any title change. He brought the conversation around to *Spellbound*. "It's exactly what we want for this picture. We'll need it for four days to do all the scheduled shots."

Ed agreed it could be used for the film and named a rental figure of $3,900, which was accepted. Ed was flabbergasted to receive a check promptly after contract signing. A week later, Eddie Jr. appeared at the office door opening into the living room where his father was sitting. "They're asking about the insurance on *Spellbound*, so what should I tell them?"

From his favorite red-leather chair, Ed considered this. "I wouldn't take less than $250,000 for it," he said firmly. Eddie disappeared into the office. Then Ed learned that Dr. Hedger who owned *Grizzly Bear* predicted it would cost nearly half a million to build a boat like it — a more-than-slight exaggeration. Ed smiled at this. When asked if it could be duplicated for $250,000, he said, "Probably not. It would be more now because everything's higher with material and labor." As Eddie was opening the outside door, Ed called, "Oh Eddie, make it $300,000." Eddie repeated the amount and returned to his desk.

The first filming was at a nearby boatyard, but on the scheduled date the Hollywood production crew arrived with the stars Matthew McConaughey and Sarah Jessica Parker. Ronnie Cutts saw that the production had their own flotilla of seven chase boats. These shifted positions like gulls trailing a trawler.

Director Dey and the cinematographer were in a large boat with a camera crane. With a lengthy metal arm and elbow in the air, it had a boarding-house reach while holding film and video cameras. In other boats were: art director and staff, actors' doubles, wardrobe, property department, gaffers, and more — a naval armada of Hollywood professionals. But, the film sequence would just show the couple.

Ronnie was surprised the name on the transom read *Miss Paula*. He sailed the yacht for the filming and recalled there were twenty people aboard, most of them out of sight below deck. There were cameras and crews below as well as radio people, wardrobe, makeup and hair departments.

"We went out and did jibes," Ronnie said. "There's a scene where the lead actor is hit by the boom and knocked overboard. I had to set the whole boat up and put it on auto pilot and then go down below, and they would do all the shots. When it was off auto-pilot, we'd say, 'Turn left,' and the actress did the turn. In the cabin we were low on the floorboards."

The crew took steps to prevent the boom from injuring the actor. Ronnie said, "We had a stunt man for this, and we put a preventer on the boom, so it looks like it comes all the way over. And we lowered the sail so the boom would catch him in the chest. He comes out of the companionway with a bottle of champagne, and Sarah Jessica Parker, looking great, is sailing the boat. He's on the windward side of the boat looking towards Tilghman Island. She says, 'Look, there's a lighthouse.' So she turns to port, and he's looking to starboard during the jibe. When he turns around, the boom knocks him overboard." As the boat continues to turn, she spots him and looks for a life preserver.

"They photographed us from a 50' steel boat with a telescoping crane," Ronnie said. "Sailing along at about 7 knots, there is a 2½ by 3-foot camera coming over the transom and checking out Sarah Jessica Parker."

Ed and Maggie sat in a bench at the water's edge and enjoyed the preparations until the boats moved out sight. From Ronnie, he received reports of each day's filming, which included Matt McConaughey in the water patting a remote-controlled dolphin.

After the production wrapped, Ronnie took Tom Dey, his wife, and assistants out on *Spellbound* for a sail. "That boat goes fast in a light wind if you get it right," Ronnie said. "She's just like a motor boat, and she motors at nine knots!" He and Eddie felt that a 44' ketch cruising at that speed under power was remarkable.

The following day he took Carl the Art Director and his department out for a sail. The weather appeared a little squally to Ronnie as it started blowing harder. "I kept looking back and saw how dark it was, so I knew a squall was coming in here. We dropped the mizzen and kept the working jib. The wind was west northwest, so from the Tred Avon Yacht Club to Benoni Point was pretty much a broad reach for us.

"We'll do one last lap," Ronnie shouted as the squall hit. "It was exciting," he said, "because there were guys on board who had never been sailing before. We had a nice downwind run. The rain drops felt like steel, so we would squint and hold a hand in front of our eyes." Some were below, feasting on chicken, beer, and some champagne left by Tom Dey.

The following day, Art Department members brought over a throw-ring life preserver with *TO THE CUTTS FAMILY* printed on it, and with their signatures. Before leaving, Tom Dey stopped over to thank Ed. "I've made documentary films," he said, "and I'd like to do a movie of your life."

Ed was amused. "Sure if you want to, but I don't know why you would pick me." Later, Ed shared some thoughts, "He thinks I'm an oddball, you know? It's OK with me. I'm getting out of the picture in a year or two, I'm sure. But we'll see." He sometimes mentioned in a cheery fashion, "I'm ready to meet my Maker."

Ed tended to ignore health suggestions and could become argumentative about diets, but in a pleasant way. "I don't like apples or oranges," he said, "so why should I change my habits now?" He appeared to eat three good meals a day, and to his credit he started taking vitamins. Ed often prepared gourmet dishes for himself and guests. One dish featured large shrimp in Italian bread crumbs with marinara sauce, prepared speedily on a gas stove with the skill of a chef. He enjoyed sweet wine in moderation, despite sugar warnings. He enjoyed a blending of Manischewitz with Christian Brothers red wine, which might have been a religious statement.

If doctors were mentioned in conversation, Ed would make a few derogatory statements in an amusing, half-serious way. He wanted to be rid of them all, but admitted there were some good doctors around. In the enclosed porch behind the kitchen sat a new rowing machine that he said he used, but after three months it disappeared.

Maggie continued as office manager, while answering the phone and keeping up Ed's membership in organizations. When anyone would ask how she was, her answer was usually, "Fine, thank you." Never did she mention that she had diabetes in one leg.

Once again Ed sold his first sailboat to her sixth owner Fred Wise. "Fred was one of our top builders here in the yard," Ed said, adding he had worked on Wellman's *Jeanne*.

When Maggie mistakenly thought *Cygnet* was headed for Maine, she said to Ed, "Now maybe the people up in Maine will see what a nice boat you can build."

"Maybe," was all he answered. He seemed depressed at the thought of the sloop so far from Oxford. On learning that Wise berthed it near Chestertown, Maryland, he visibly brightened.

After Dr. Crisler had sailed his Cutts-designed *Hummingbird* sloop for a number of years, he gave it to the Chesapeake Bay Foundation, which auctioned it off. Robert Muir, a Texas photographer, bought it and sailed out of Cutts & Case. Crisler's name *Molly Hubbard* had been changed to *Hummingbird*, her original name as well as her class name. The yard did some sprucing up and replaced the outboard propeller with a two-blade racing model.

One afternoon Muir and his brother-in-law set sail for Annapolis. "We were going in wing and wing," Muir said, "as the fleet came out for the Wednesday evening races, so we rounded up and stayed with the fleet. We kept up very nicely." This racing group included J-24s and other 30-footers, he said.

Muir asked Cutts & Case to ship *Hummingbird* Down East to Paul Luke's yard in East Boothbay. He planned to enter races for classic wooden boats, but it turned out that he couldn't because she was a new design. He did, however, have a racing-type thrill when he was watching a race between recently-built 70' sloops. He found himself sailing next to the racers. "It was kind of drizzling with light winds," he said. "*Goshawk* had an enormous genny. Of course, we didn't have a genny but I passed her to the leeward. The next thing I knew, people began appearing at the rail taking pictures of our boat.

"I always get comments on what a beautiful boat she is," Muir said. This was as true in Maine as in Maryland. The sloop carries two masthead jibs on her shorter-than-usual raked mast like the Chesapeake Bay Skipjack — designed for towing power needed to rake up oysters. *Hummingbird* can move smartly, however, for he sailed her at up to 9 knots. "Nat Herreshoff." he said, "liked a shorter rig with a big boom." Unable to race officially, he sent the boat to Old Greenwich for his daughter to use. Later, it would appear on a yacht broker's list at $82,000, with a new Genoa jib.

In September 2005, Ed answered a phone call from someone he hadn't seen in years. "This is Colin Case," the voice said, "and I want to come see you."

Ed said he was always welcome at the boatyard. "I really felt that. We thought the world of his father and also his mother who was Fanny Moore, a lovely lady." The last time Colin Case had visited the yard was for the launching of *Spellbound* in 1970. "I liked him," Ed said, "but he soon disappeared to California. He was unhappy with the way the family was operating its various businesses, so he decided to go off on his own. He was a terrifically wealthy young man." His grandfather, Judge Moore, had owned Republic Aviation, Ed said. He was a founder of Bankers Trust in New York City. Later, his mother and uncles owned the companies. And there were California companies, too.

When the tall visitor walked into his house, Ed looked in amazement and was speechless. The man was about 6 feet 2 inches tall and a double image of John Case. "It felt to me as if we went back forty years, and here was John coming through the door. I was shocked. Colin spoke with me a couple of hours, and he spoke with Maggie separately a few hours. And he spoke to Eddie for three and a half hours, and an hour or more with Ronnie. He was trying to decide, 'Why did Dad like these people? Why did he trust them?'"

Colin Case appeared to be in fairly good health, but they noticed he sometimes had a dizziness. He went all around the sheds observing work in progress and spent time in the museum where he admired *Foto*. Out on the docks he looked over *Spellbound* and his father's former boat, *Rebellion*.

After a night at the Robert Morris Inn's cottage, Colin met with Ed. "I'd like to talk about what you were doing for my father when he died," he said, and then began discussing the large unfinished white hull.

Ed recalled how the dialogue went. "It really wasn't for your father. It was for your father's understanding of what he wanted in a boat," he said. "The boat is 65 feet, and we wanted to demonstrate this new method of boat building in a large boat. We somehow had to produce this large boat to show the possibilities."

Colin, experienced in running several companies, asked, "Well, what's holding it up?"

"Two things," Ed said, glad to be direct with him. "I don't have as large a crew as I used to have, but we are busy enough to keep my crew at work. There are times when we can spare some hours on another project. That's why it's a long-term, slow-to-finish type of thing. Also there's considerable expense."

Colin wanted specifics. "What kind of expense are you talking about?"

"Well, I guess it would cost 75,000 to 80,000 dollars just to put the engines in and the engine room costs." Colin listened, asked insightful questions, then left to catch his plane.

Two or three days later, he was again on the phone to Ed. "I'm sending you 75,000 or 80,000 dollars, whatever you say it will cost, so you can put engines in that boat."

"Don't do that, Colin," Ed said, "because what I tell you is incumbent upon others. I don't know how much time I have left on this planet, so I don't like to make promises others are forced to carry out. My boys could follow through, but I would like to talk to them. I'll make sure they are amenable to that."

Ed remembered Colin saying, "OK. Just talk to them. And there's no need for a contract. I'll just send green cash." Ed said he would get back to him with an answer.

Once again, Ed had hesitated when offered a generous payment. Was he a contrarian? Many boat-building outfits would have accepted this provided the numbers worked out. How long could it take to talk this offer over with Eddie and Ronnie? Perhaps, Ed didn't want to be pressured.

In a conference, Ed and his sons agreed that the engines and engine room could be done for that amount. It was encouraging to think the yacht *John's Boat* or *Americana* would once again be moving forward. Ed waited a few more days — he wouldn't say how many — as he prepared to call Colin. Here, as at other times, he avoided rushing. Before he could make the important move, another California call came in for him. Colin's wife, crying on the phone, managed to say, "Colin has suddenly dropped dead."

A few weeks later, Ed sat in his two-seat sofa in the kitchen wondering why this happened to Colin who was just fifty-five. "We liked him," Ed said. "He was just like John." As he thought over the recent visit, he speculated about Colin's motivation. "Did

Colin feel it had been a mistake to leave his father years before? Maybe, he wanted to help complete the boat for his father, to make up for something in the past?" Never did Ed blame himself for the delay and missed opportunity.

Ed retold how John Case supported building the large yacht. "That's why it's called 'John's Boat'. That's why I call the place Cutts & Case. I never changed the name because I wouldn't be here if it wasn't for John. He was as important as I was in a different way."

After many days of trying to find the correct phone number, because Colin had so many business activities, Ed was able to reach Colin's widow. "I told her how sad I was about the whole thing and how much he reminded me of John." She told Ed that if she visited the East Coast she would like to see him and his family. But, this never happened in Ed's final years.

In November 2005, Maggie Cutts had another attack. She went to an upscale nursing facility and then to Deer's Head Hospital in Salisbury, where she died on December 1st. "The night Maggie died," Ed said, "when I visited, she feebly raised her hand and said, 'I love you, Eddie.'

And he told her many times that he loved her. "I am so very glad I did that. I did it over and over through the years." At the Oxford cemetery internment, Ed had them turn the casket. "I did that so that she would face toward Town Creek and the boatyard she loved." He regularly visited her Oxford grave.

Maggie's presence remained around the house in many photographs: with her two brothers, at her daughter's wedding, with her children when they were young, and together with Ed in pictures taken over the years.

Ed spoke of Marguerite Cutts in the slow cadence of controlled grief, while sitting on his kitchen sofa. "She was a very special person. I never heard her say a bad thing about anyone." He was lost in thought for a moment, looking toward the Michelangelo Pietà relief sculpture. "If someone sounded a little raunchy, she would just fade away. But she wouldn't take issue, and she was never argumentative — never swearing one word." He reflected a moment. "I never knew anyone like her. She was just wonderful. I couldn't have picked a better person. I loved her more at the end than I did when we were young."

Just beyond the kitchen-dining area were two large bedrooms Maggie and Ed had used. Ed decided to move his design table and desk into the first room, because of his limited mobility.

At night, he often watched the military and history channels. Seeing military planes like the ones he worked on gave him a veteran's exuberance, so that he seemed to be younger. Adding to this, an occasional shock of tan hair sometimes fell over his forehead. Ed spoke of planes he worked on, like Grumman Hellcats, with their "improved armor and wider wheels."

His favorite plane, he said, was "the indestructible P-47 Thunderbolt built at Republic Aviation. The only way to bring it down was to hit it head on through the engine. They built 17,000 P-47's, which I believe was the best airplane that ever was." It did have a fine war record, but Ed's friendship with John and Fanny Case influenced his opinion. Whether talking of planes, motorcycles, or boats, Ed admired anything that was beautifully built and performed well.

To discuss in detail the ongoing building of *Souvenir*, Ed held morning meetings with Dennis Risher. They met in the kitchen over coffee, weekdays at 8 a.m., with Dennis at the round table and Ed about four feet away on his couch. Without daily trips to the shed, Ed was keeping track of each day's work. It was obvious he enjoyed these meetings because he liked Dennis, liked being creative, and liked talking about *Souvenir*. He learned what Dennis had accomplished the previous day, and the planned work, and possible problem areas. With the plan in his head, Ed listened carefully, while he visualized the joinerwork or the construction details being described. Occasionally, he explained just what to do for any difficulty, which Dennis understood after a brief exchange. Ed had a real need to be in supervisory control, even though the mood was friendly, low key, and conversational.

After the building matters were settled, they habitually migrated to topics that might be: philosophy, religion, or health. Dennis sometimes loaned him books and videos, such as one on selecting qualified doctors. Ed could sound critical and even irascible about the medical profession, but he did respect doctors who had proven their worth to him.

One day Dennis, a Methodist, offered to lend Ed, a Catholic, a book about St. Paul. "I'd be happy to read it," Ed said. There were no debates or quarrels on religious matters in these meetings. Open to spiritual teachings from many sources, Ed often watched television evangelists, such as Joel Osteen, Frank and Billy Graham. "I don't completely agree with Graham on everything," Ed said slowly, "but I think he's one of the greats."

Since being slowed down by ill health, Ed seemed to do more reading, except when at his design table or with clients. His usual kitchen spot was the right side of his well-used couch with his legs up on a chair. The prosthetic left leg with its shiny metal strips and plastic in padding lay on the floor, handy for quick attaching if he had to walk anywhere. Overhead was an L. L. Bean clock, and beside him on the glass wall to the porch were clippings, photos, and notes. He had to lower himself carefully, for on the sofa's left was about a foot-and-a-half, precariously-balanced hill of papers, books, and oddments.

Ed often said, "People give me more things to read than I have time for." He cautioned others not to give him anything they want back, because things could and did disappear.

At this time, the pile contained: letters, boating equipment spec sheets, clippings on health, and material from the NYYC. The local *Star Democrat* newspaper, his early morning reading, was on top, and in front at the bottom were pliers and a small hand drill with bits. Among the many books and paperbacks were: *How to Clean Practically Any Thing, Reversing Diabetes, Good News New Testament, the Layman's Bible Dictionary, Unleash the Inner Healing Power of Foods,* and a *Consumer Reports Buying Guide.* There was a video of John Houston's *The Bible* and a CD titled *Living the Life of Excellence, Have the Courage to be Different.* Also there were boating and technical magazines: *Boat Works, WoodenBoat, Prop Talk, American Machinist, Machine Design,* and *Marine Technology & SNAME News.*

This unwieldy filing system, with daily additions and changes, was significant. It revealed a lot about Ed Cutts and his curious, inventive, searching mind — searching for new solutions. Like his greatly-respected Thomas A. Edison, he believed in keeping up to date with self-study, and with ne'er a thought of impressing anyone.

Chapter Fourteen

HALF-HULLS AND THE NEW YORK YACHT CLUB

FROM HIS EARLY TEENS Ed often saw the name of a famous New York club in boating magazines and newspapers. "I loved the New York Yacht Club, because they fostered the very finest in sailing, yacht design, and boat building," he said. "So I grew up with a reverent feeling for them." Ed didn't expect to become a member.

Fanny Case thought Ed should belong to the NYYC, so she persuaded John to propose him for membership. According to Ed, John thought he was slightly "rough-hewn" to fit in with the wealthy members. They probably talked it over. John followed through, and Ed became a member in 1980. "I was deeply gratified," Ed said, "to be included in the club."

He enjoyed telling friends how J. Pierpont Morgan had donated three lots in the middle of New York City to build the magnificent clubhouse at 37 West 44th Street. Pedestrians recognize it by the nautical architecture, facing the street, with the three ship's windows.

The NYYC's Model Room, truly awe inspiring, was Ed's favorite place when visiting the Club. The thick door opens into a 45'

230

by 96' interior that dwarfs an individual. Among larger-than-life dimensions is a 47-ton fireplace with an oval painting of the first transatlantic race. Overhead, seemingly higher than its 26 feet, is a magnificent Tiffany stained-glass skylight. Half-hulls of the members' sailboats surround visitors on fabric-covered walls. In 2012, the hundred-year-old collection numbered about 1,300, but it is constantly growing. The magnificent visual display shows yacht-design changes over the years. In cabinets are larger models that have played a part in yachting history. On the street side of the Model Room are three finely-sculpted bay windows, resembling the stern of a seventeenth-century Dutch *Jaght*. This became the English word "yacht." All around is dark carved oak with a polished glow. (Sydnor)

On occasional trips to New York City, Ed visited the Club to see the half-hulls. These inspired him as he studied famous yachts by leading designers. "I was always interested in the boats that were the best performers," he said. "Shapes stay in my mind. I can reconstitute a shape in my head of some boat I had seen. I'd make mental comparisons because many times there were things that were not good about a certain boat. I'd ask myself why the designer did this or that."

Ronnie Cutts stayed at the Club when he went up for the premier of the film *Failure to Launch*. He and his brother, whenever in New York City, have enjoyed the experience of eating at the Club dining room. "You would think," Eddie said, "that you are between the decks in a ship like a square rigger or a man-o'-war. There are deck beams overhead, futtocks, knees, and frames. You are in a ship."

"Most of Nat Herreshoff's models are in museums," Ed said. "One of his most successful was a one-footer." Ed smiled — actually bursting to share something important. "I have the very model that he carved — the Herreshoff 12½."

There is a story behind his valuable model. Ed once owned a 32-foot cabin cruiser named *Footloose*, carvel planked with a flying bridge and inboard engine, built by the Baltzer-Jonesport Boat Co. of Medford, Massachusetts. The Cutts & Case yard had worked on the motor, in addition to garboards, caulking, and stem work. In 1989, she sat at the boatyard dock in Bristol fashion. She had a "For Sale" sign.

One day a man visited the yard, liked the looks of the spruced-up boat, and took it for a run. Then, he sat down with Ed to discuss the price. The man was Bob Fox, and Ed knew his background. His wife had been the daughter of Rudolph Haffenreffer, who had bought the Herreshoff Company in 1924. When this boatyard closed in 1946, the family took artifacts and whatever they wanted.

Ed surprised Bob Fox by asking, "Do you have anything from the old Herreshoff yard that you might trade for the power boat? I would love to have something of Nat's."

Fox said his deceased wife had retrieved from the front office, "a classic half-hull which is in my collection. It is Nat Herreshoff's 12½."

That was all Ed had to hear. "If you own Nat's model, I'm ready to trade." Fox was agreeable, so they shook on it and drew up a sales agreement. Though contrasted in size, the values were equal to Ed. "I wouldn't reverse the trade for anything," Ed said when he was seventy-nine. He was tight-lipped about the half-hull's location, but a month later he admitted it was in his design studio, serving as an inspiration.

"I like to work the way Nat did with a half-hull. You can't beat three-dimensional stuff," he said. "I work out the boat and the configuration, such as how deep, the ballast, and the shape. Then I make a half-hull."

Nat Herreshoff had men offset lines from a model, but Ed didn't like offsets. "His loftsman couldn't picture the shape of the boat until he had laid the offsets down," Ed said. "Nat had to take vertical offsets every six inches and then write the number down, so all the loftsman had was a booklet full of numbers. My method produced the actual lines in the boat no matter where you wanted to take them. You could take them angularly across the stern to find out what the stem flare should be," he said. "You could take them anywhere you wanted, and it gives you the full shape of the boat exactly. With my method, I had the whole set of lines right in front of my face. It had never been done before."

Ed kept his lofting equipment secret, but one day he talked about it in a general way, knowing it would later turn up in his biography. It began when he had bought, from war surplus, three high quality wartime lenses made by Fairchild for aerial photography. "The lenses must have cost a fortune to make. They were superb. I made my own projection equipment. I had to start studying what the hell I was doing, for it was an entirely different field for me." After several months, Cutts & Case had a projection system from scale to full size. "I worked right from the model. It magnifies according to its scale," he said. "Therefore, a ¾-inch section times 16 becomes one foot of boat measurement. I tell you the machinery is spectacular. I am amazed at the super accuracy. If you blow the lines up twenty times, it's within 1/1000th of an inch. I never told a soul about it, but my boys know how to do the lines this way."

Eddie Jr. had come into the room while his father was talking. "This is done now with computers," Eddie said. Then he watched and waited for the expected reaction.

"Bull," replied Ed, at full volume. "You can't use a computer for a brain. The computer is making comparisons with other things that have already been done, whether they're good or bad." He began speaking softer but with plenty of emphasis. "You can't get Michelangelo out of a computer. If you want to do beautiful work, it's not coming out of a computer." He gestured to a white, bas-relief sculpture, about two feet high, in front of him by the porch door. "That's Michelangelo's sculpture, an exact copy taken right off *The Pietà*. It's gorgeous. You could study it for half a day. Look at the expression. It's exquisite, and it's cut out of stone. A computer just doesn't have that. The art is in a person's head and heart if he's good at it."

Getting back to the subject of precision, Ed said, "Grumman had me making nose-cone patterns (for NASA), so I was used to being accurate. If it was 1/1000th inch, I made them within that tolerance. I was used to that, and I still am today, but my eyes are not as good as they were."

This admission was a surprise, for one might describe them as keen. But there were signs of this change. Eight pairs of reading glasses were here and there around the house, on drawing board, seats, desks and tables. These were mild drug-store models, selected for magnification. Ed laughed at the suggestion that he should see an ophthalmologist. "These glasses suit me fine."

Sitting at his drawing table, he looked studious in his half glasses. Ed leaned slightly forward and slowly drew a condensed drawing of the main spar for the new sloop, using a spring batten. He held it in shape by small black objects suggesting small whales. "Designers have spline weights," Ed said, "to hold battens in positions on the drawing boards. When Francis Herreshoff was drawing, he would never use a ship's curve for producing the sheer of a boat. He would use a batten and do it by his sense of eye and proportion. Then he would draw it when he was satisfied. That's how the lines of a boat are drawn." And that's how Ed draws them.

In 2006, Ed Cutts sat in the living room looking up at a 2½-foot oil painting in a gold frame that had recently appeared between

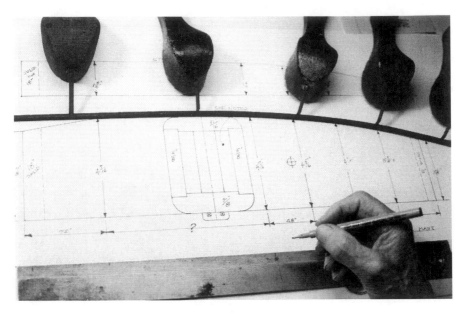

Ed drawing the mast for *Souvenir*, in a compressed plan.
Wayne Brown

the windows, above the model of *America* in its glass case. He had commissioned a local artist to paint his mother in costume from a theatrical photo. As he pointed to the painting, he had a warm, remembering smile. "I think it's rather good," he said. He admired it quietly for a moment before he continued with a new thought. "We're all of us temporary. We tend to forget that, and some people think that they can go on forever. Boats can and should last longer than people. Boats we build can go on for a hundred years, and more, if they're well cared for. They'll outlast all of us," he said cheerily with a grin.

One day, Ed apologized for his memory, getting a date wrong in his seventy-ninth year. "I'll tell you one thing today, and then at a later time I'll tell you something completely different." With a raised pitch on the last two words, he made it humorous. This was an exaggeration, but he probably saw he made mistakes in short-term memory. While he could err on dates, or forget all the details that others remembered, his long-term memory for key events and conversations had been fine.

After five years of interviews for this biography, he said, "I don't know why you want to write about me. I've only turned out a comparatively small number of new boats compared to some other designers." This comment had a self-effacing quality and showed his humility. He built many boats at Long Island boatyards before going on his own. All told, his sons said he designed over seventy-five boats and built around fifty.

Outside the Chesapeake Bay, Ed Cutts is something of an enigma and a man of mystery, although articles on him have appeared. *Rebellion* may be his best-known design because of the fine photo by Benjamin Mendlowitz and the description by Maynard Bray in *The Book of Wooden Boats*, 1997. This 33' double ender has plank-on-frame construction like all of Ed's boats built before 1981.

Boaters around the country may know little of his other boats. For one thing, Ed was never interested in creating a racing class, which can promote the designer's name. In the future, boaters may know more about Ed Cutts as owners sail his designs into boating centers further afield from Oxford.

Ronnie Cutts, slightly overweight and relaxed, was in his home across a lawn in front of Byberry. The cottage is shipshape with cabinets illustrating his good joinerwork and with many family photos. In the living room is a photo showing fourteen-year-old Ron on his own small motorcycle. He spoke of his dad with low-key sincerity. "He's the best designer alive today. I can remember during my whole childhood and growing up here, that there was always a boat being built. My dad's very artistic. He doesn't build a lot of boats, but his boats are right on target. He's got imagination like nobody I've ever met. It works as if he's on the boat sailing.

In his head, he has the whole image of the boat, of what it should be like, how it's set up, and how it's going to act."

Once, Ed spoke about the way he liked to work. "I have a reclusive mind and I like to be left to think. I can sit in a room and people might say, 'What in the hell is he doing looking at the wall for six or eight hours?' Well, I'm not looking at the wall. My mind is racing with interesting concepts on how to do something." After this, he said, he goes to his design table.

"When I am about to draw or build it, I have already seen that boat in my mind," he said. "I see it with its paint work and varnish work and glistening and sailing the way I expected. Or operating the way I expected it to operate. I draw it then to do that exactly and to meet those specifications that were in my head," he said. "And I try to emulate that in the drawing. If I concentrate on a certain thing, which doesn't take much effort, I would see the layouts of the foredeck, the cockpit, transom, all those things," he said. Visitors won't hear background music when Ed is designing. "I don't like background anything," he said. "I just like to look at a wall with a blank stare and have my brain working. It's interesting that if we search with the right attitude, God will give us revelation, if what we ask is proper. I absolutely believe it."

"Of course, you have to transfer your thought to others. That requires that you put it on paper the way you want it to be. And I also give instructions to make it correct."

Known for his strong opinions, Ed spoke about the new look of large cruise ships. "If I want a hotel, I'll go to a hotel. A boat should look like a boat," he pronounced. "I see a boat sometimes, and I'm horrified. It can be the shape or the weight of the boat, and things done wrong like the propeller angle. We see things that we can't believe."

Ed never attempted to patent his earlier inventions, realizing that someone somewhere could be doing the same thing. His sons said he invented an oil extractor. "It was difficult to get oil out of an engine," Ed said, "so I came up with the idea to make a little hand tank and put it on the suction and compressor to get the air out of it. It had a valve on it so you carried the little tank out, inserted the tube, opened the valve, and drew the oil out of the man's boat."

On a visit, retired boatbuilder Donald Wilson told Ed he invented this oil changer, and added, "Every boatyard has them now."

Eddie reminded his father he had started the drop-in rack for pick-up trucks. "There wasn't one of them anyplace when you came up with that."

"Those things happen when you have original ideas you don't patent," Ed said. "You'll find no one has a patent on them because they were already being done."

Ed was then researching a project to benefit boating. "I've been working on a new type of propulsion system for a year," he said. "Something constantly troubled me about the idea, but the solution was easy. I started to make a model of it, small but full size. I have it pretty much all thought out." Ed thought he might build it if he had help with the steep stairs to his shop.

"The outboard motor is as good as we've got with propellers, because it drives parallel to the boat's course. But when a boat has 12 or 14 degrees of down angle in the shaft, it's heading for the sky instead of straight ahead," he said. "You get good efficiency from the propeller but poor efficiency from having to use the transmission in making the right-angle drive, which the upper motor requires. The propeller has been accepted worldwide for the last 150 years, but it's a terrible thing with a 30-percent to 40-percent loss of efficiency in it. There's a big knuckle where the blades are attached that has to be dragged through the water. There's a spinning shaft in front of it. The circumference of that shaft is the square of its diameter, and it is increasing in resistance at the square of speed.

So this is a great loss. And the prop has centrifugal force that goes at right angles to the direction that the boat wants to go. And that's a loss. And then there's a frictional loss." Eddie and Ronnie plan to continue research on this — someday.

"Now I'm working in my head on the fast runabout," Ed said in May 2006. It was nine months since he had spoken with the Pennsylvania couple who wanted a classic speedboat. Eddie thought his father had lost interest when the couple divorced. But, Ed enjoyed talking about the project. It illustrated his thinking.

"I'm concerned with the bottom of this boat so that she will bank correctly in the turns. She will be a hard-chined boat. Round-bottomed boats bank further in turns. I'm thinking of the unusual attitudes that the boat may be put in, and these can be dangerous. You can't do it with an airplane, with a car, or with a motorcycle, yet someone may try to do it with a boat — full speed and a right-angle turn. If you do that with a car, you're going to lose the car and your life," Ed said.

"So I'm always worried about people blaming me for what can be their stupidity. I don't want to get myself into a mess or any kind of litigation," he said. "That's why a boat should be very carefully shaped in the designer's head so that it will at least accommodate most of the bad-handling worries. The whole business of designing a boat is choices," Ed said. "If the designer has a subtle knowledge of what the hell is going on, then he will make more correct choices. That boat will be a much better boat for those excellent choices.

"Nat Herreshoff didn't need a tank to test models," Ed said. "He knew what the hell the shape was going to do full size, and that's how he went through life. He had a super sense of proportions that comes from upstairs. You can't give that away to anyone. He designed the finest America's Cup boats that ever raced in the history of the world, and they were never tank tested — the 140' boats. His tank was the Atlantic Ocean. And his models were

40-footers he used to determine what to do when it was 140 feet." Ed was warmed up and on a roll.

"I feel I know what goes through water fast and why, and if you know this, you don't have to tank test. A difference in structural design makes a boat go faster. It's all kinds of little things: what the bow shape should be? Should we do this or do that? All those things are important, and Nat knew.

"There are modern designers today who have finally caught on to the business. When I see a picture of a boat cruising along, I can tell you if it's correct or not. I don't have to go to the tank and see. I know what that wave pattern should look like, and if there is too much or not enough, I can tell." He pointed to the photograph of *Millennia*, at his side, planing at about 50 mph with a bare minimum of wave action. Visitors to his living room will see this favorite photo of Ed's near his favorite chair.

"I would know what I expected the boat to do, and then I would make that boat meet it," Ed said. "If the boat will be 30 feet and I expect it to go 40 mph, I would determine how much engine I will need, and the boat would be designed to take that." Although the Pennsylvania man never said what cruising speed he wanted for the open-cockpit boat, Ed made some assumptions. "Of course, he came to us to get performance out of it. This means speed — a fast boat." His eyes had a glint. He was enjoying the creativity of designing.

Which leads to some questions: Did Ed intend to follow through and build the boat? Was Ed just living the dream? Was he prolonging this with his biography in mind? Or, was it for his inner needs as a boat designer wanting to create, in less-active, senior years?

Typically, Ed did not procrastinate when a client ordered a boat, but he had endured foot and leg operations, a painful prosthesis, and effects of earlier surgeries, including eleven hernia and other intestinal operations.

"It's difficult to do any work when you're in pain all the time," he had once said with a quiet voice, as he slowly shuffled his feet to enter his design room. With this change from his usual vigorous, exuberant nature, he came across as a tragic figure who had been hiding his pain.

In July of 2007, it was then one year and ten months since the initial speedboat order. When questioned about the progress on the speedboat, Ed hesitated, looked off, and thought for a moment. "They didn't call me about it," he said in a faint, far-away voice. He sounded surprisingly weak and depressed. He said nothing further. Eddie Jr. said they probably went elsewhere, for they had the necessary funds.

Ed spoke about the boatyard in 2006. "You know some people do love this business. I was one of them. Money was not my thing. The boatyard had to make us a living, and it had to sustain itself," he said. "I would forfeit the great work I get out of it if I sold. I love it, and I think the boys do too. I think they'd be fish out of water if we weren't doing it. We feel it is a duty."

At seventy-nine, Ed was proud how his sons were managing Cutts & Case. One might wonder whether he had told them this. For working sons with large responsibilities, having their father call major decisions wasn't easy.

"Eddie is academic, working in the shop, more into engineering problems," Ed said. "Ronnie is more of a get-it-done guy. I'm glad they're like that. After this happened," he gestured to his left leg clamped into the prosthetic extension, "Ronnie directed the whole damn crew, and he's got it going to this day." He paused, "Don't forget that we have fifty or sixty boats here that have things to be done to them. Somebody has to oversee it. Ronnie supervises the crew. Ronnie knows much more than we give him credit for, and so he delights me.

"It's a difficult business to run a boatyard," Ed said. "We don't make much on the rentals. It's the repair work that matters." Ed as always was cautious about expenses, from experiencing the Depression years, his mother's advice, and John Case's financial expertise. Anyone could see the yard was run conservatively with Ed as CEO. "People have no idea how expensive it is to operate shipyards. When you're finished with the payrolls, insurance, the overheads, maintenance, machinery and operation, all this is expensive as hell. And you end up with hundreds of thousands of dollars in payrolls. So you have to be careful." He let this sink in. "Last year I paid $59 thousand in insurance. I'm running this yard to pay the insurance company."

Eddie didn't completely agree with his father on yard matters. After college courses in accounting and business, Eddie had an objective view of managing the boatyard. "My dad has always focused on the design work, and his boat building, and what was in front of him. He maintained the place the best he could at the time. But, times are moving along, and I've got to move along with them," he said. "The buildings and stuff are very old. On one side I enjoy this, and on the other side I realize that they're tremendously inefficient. You could revamp and end up with very-insulated, heated buildings with good light."

Already, Eddie had made some improvements on the business side. "Basically, we modernized the invoicing system and improved the cash flow, upgraded the docks. So you end up seeing which individual areas are profitable and which ones aren't. In this kind of business the margins are so slim that you really have to understand where you break even, where you lose, and where you make money. Because if you don't, you won't be in it for long," Eddie said.

"I want to be working smart and doing great quality work. I've seen too many great boatyards that produced fine work that didn't last very long." Eddie had heard of a man who ordered a 100' boat, and later went to jail. "The boatyard has this project sitting there half finished. What do you do? The problem is you find yourself stuck in a big hurry with those big projects."

There's no telling who will run Cutts & Case in the far future. Ronnie has remained single as of 2013, but Eddie has three daughters. "It takes a very unusual type of character," Eddie said, "to run a successful designing and building boatyard. It's extremely difficult." It is not known whether one of his daughters might want to learn the business. At the Oxford Boatyard, near Cutts & Case, a woman had been successfully running the large boatyard.

Boatbuilder Tom Morris, in an interview from Maine, remembered one experience with Cutts & Case in 1971. "I consider myself fortunate for a few things that happened in my life. One of them was meeting Ed and keeping a boat in his yard. My wife and I were on a vacation in Europe. I never had any insurance on the boat, which developed a leak and started to sink." On returning home, Morris found a message from Ed Cutts and phoned him. "There was a leak around the rudder post," Morris said. "Ed spotted it and took care of it. That's the kind of a yard he ran."

Morris had successfully expanded his own business in Maine. He then owned service boatyards in Northeast Harbor and Bath and a building yard near Mt. Desert Island. In 2007, he reported he was still driving the black Volkswagen he had used for commuting to Oxford in the 70s. Morris sailed his boats, like the Payne-designed Morris-46, to East Coast boat shows and as far as Scotland. He Crossed the Bar[4] in 2008 at far too young an age. Ed and his sons remembered him as a good friend. Tom Morris is in the Maine Boatbuilder's Hall of Fame.

As work on Grasberger's sloop continued, Ed thought he would do something special with the lumber. He read that some white oak trees, planted by George Washington at Mt. Vernon and Claymont Court, were taken down because of overgrowth. He contacted the logging company. Kent Smith, head of the timber company, said they did quarter sawing which brings out the tiger stripping for this custom order. He brought this over to Cutts & Case and met

Ed. "Mr. Cutts was so gracious," he said, "and invited me into his home where he showed me a piece of wood from the yacht *America*."

In building work, Cutts & Case used oak for soles, keels, and keelsons, as do other yards. Ed wanted this oak for the sole or cabin floor. According to Kent Smith the oak came from another nearby property Washington worked on called Claymont Court, but Ed preferred to say it came from Mt. Vernon. He was elated at acquiring wood planted by the Father of our Country. Ed revered the first President and often spoke of him.[5]

Ed considered a centerboard for the sloop, but chose a keel. "The drawing has less than minimum lateral plane," he said, "but this is a chine boat and doesn't require the amount of lateral plane needed in other boats. If I were a racing lunatic, I might like a small centerboard so I could adjust pinching the boat closer to the wind." In May of 2006, Ed said, "I hope to have her sailing sometime this summer."

His scheduling was way off. It was the following January, after Dennis completed the cabin, that Ronnie began to make Sitka spruce spars.

Nick Grasberger said, "It's taken five years since we agreed to build the boat, and at times I have certainly been impatient." When boat people had said the sloop would never be finished, he had replied, "Well, I'm a young guy. This will be a boat I'll have for the rest of my life, and I'll pass it on to my kids. So I'm going to be patient. It'll be one of a kind." He knew his Cutts-designed sloop would be something very special. Nick understood the delay caused by Ed's health problems, Eddie's divorce, and the regular repair work.

Ed thought the deck design was a first, and he was pleased with it. "We just invented a new kind of deck, and it's just as strong as any or more so. I'm using it on the 23-foot sailboat and any boat I build from now on. Once it occurs, it's in your mind like a light bulb, you can't disregard it any more. It does away with all the deck beams in the boat and gives you tremendous strength. It does away with all the weight of the former structure, and that's very important to us. The deck comes up and continues to the cabin top."

Eddie Jr. said they had seen boats where the deck came up to the cabin as a fiberglass-molded deck. "I cannot say this is totally unique to us, but I will say it was very artfully executed. The cabin sides are tapered down to a point where the cabin top becomes the foredeck surface. The cabin top is made strong by the crown, and the cabin sides are acting as a standing beam to both the side deck and the coach roof. It is a unique and artistic means of handling the cabin to deck, providing increased headroom, an interesting look, and a lighter arrangement."

In the boatyard's South Shed, the new sloop sported a Cutts hatch. "This doesn't ride on two tracks, one on each side," Ed said. "It runs on one track in the middle. I've done it on a few boats, and it's very successful. It's the best hatch there is — it'll never stick on you."

Eddie said they had built these hatches since the early 80s, beginning with a boat called *Surfbird*. "I believe this is unique to us. It does have its advantages, but is rather different and probably not for all."

Ed never applied for a patent on this. "No use patenting stuff that's going to cost a lot and that's not going to make much money. These ideas come into my head constantly, and I can't help it." He spoke, not in a bragging manner, but quietly as stating a simple fact.

"This will be a family boat, but it will be fast," he said. "It will have a Genoa to increase the sail area. Mostly, with a whole family and young people, you don't want to be changing sails all the time, so she'll have a rig that will be pretty much self tending, except if you put the big headsail on. It will be a mast-head rig, and it could also have a spinnaker."

With the cabin completed, Dennis carved a wooden mold for the chocks. "Ed's always given me the ability to do the best job I can do," Dennis said. "We've never hurried up because of expense and costs. It's all about the boats."

Nick Grasberger talked about the weight advantage in his future boat. "Ed claims the Kevlar cording between the double planks of white cedar will enable this sloop to sail much better than a heavier boat constructed with the traditional method. My boat will displace 3,000 pounds, but the keel will weigh about 2,000 pounds. The A/B ratio, above and below the waterline, is over 2x, and will contribute to the boat's performance.

"I've always thought when sailing to windward," Nick continued, "that the amount of tension on the tiller and the ability of the boat to maintain its course indicated the quality of the design and materials. I've sailed some Cutts & Case boats, and I've been very impressed with these features and how well they handle."

Perfectionists usually take longer to complete a task. Psychologists have said perfectionists have an element of procrastination and sometimes a third "P," standing for phobia — an exaggerated or unreasonable fear. These three characteristics fit Ed like a custom boat cover. But what did he fear?

"I know I'm paying for perfection," Nick Grasberger said, "but I haven't complained. If Ed believes something is not quite right, and Dennis has to spend two hours to fix the problem, that is fine. But all these slight adjustments become very expensive. Most supervising builders would never make such minute changes, but I certainly respect Ed's eye, his experience, and his judgment," Nick said. "If he wants the boat to be perfect, I do not have a choice but to yield to him. In the end, I believe it will all be worth the time, trouble, and expense."

One of the little neighboring kids whom Ed took for short motorcycle rides back in Northport, Mary Ellen Waszczak, had visited him with her family each year until her parents broke up when she about fourteen. She visited him on her own regularly in her thirties and forties. After marrying in 2000, she brought her husband Dwight Campbell, so he could get to know Ed and Maggie. The couple had met working for an oil company where she was a production foreman.

Mary Ellen had once owned Sting Rays for fishing but admits not knowing how to sail. In 2003, the couple were looking at small fiberglass power boats, so on a visit they asked Ed for advice. Ed bristled at the thought of *fiberglass*.

"The only kind you should buy," Ed said, "is a Herreshoff 12½." That was all he would say. He wouldn't talk any further about this. Mary Ellen said she found it amusing, but the couple never did buy a boat.

Ed had a special place in her life. "He was what I wanted in a father," she said. "To me Mr. Cutts was the quintessential — I just looked up to him. As I got older and visited him as an adult, I found him as magical and as childlike as he was when I was a kid. He had the same quality that never got old. He always had the impish, fun-twinkle, and his genius. But on top of that he had that beautiful spirit — that ageless, fun-loving zest for life that was so inspiring."

"I think that the place that he inspired me the most was the way I am with little children. Ed loved people, who were not his own, the same way as his family." Although childless, she follows Ed's example while interacting with children in her life.

After the Campbells had made a recent visit to Byberry House, Ed spoke with affection of the little girl whom Maggie didn't see, at first, when opening the door. "She was the cutest little kid." Ed was beaming and had some news. "She, like her husband, has a sea captain's license! Can you imagine?" He repeated this again with more inflection, looking amazed and joyful. But, Ed wouldn't discuss what size boats they captained and their routes.

On the phone from British Columbia, Mary Ellen Campbell laughed lightly at "sea captains." She explained, "That was his terminology for that, because I was out on an oil platform — over the water in the Gulf of Mexico. So I was a captain." Her husband, an engineer in the oil fields, also made captain.

Ed designed and made this 1695 sign as well as others for historic buildings. In the bottom 2007 photo, he stands in front of *Byberry,* Oxford's oldest house.

Wayne Brown

Chapter Fifteen
SUMMING UP

"DRAWING CAME EASY TO ME — from above. You can't cultivate it," Ed Cutts said. "It all begins with a drawing." He often said this, but he did many sketches before the detailed drawing. "My sketches were pretty close to what I would draw. I didn't want to get way into all the work if I didn't receive the client's message right, to see if we were on target."

In the spring of 2007, Ed decided to look over his collected sketches. Rolling easily around the house in a power chair, he navigated through tight doorways. He had to get up and walk through a narrow, almost secret hall behind the kitchen to his former design studio. Compact, constricted, with one window by a medium-sized desk facing front foliage and trees, it offered privacy. Bookshelves sat on a cabinet, half models of his boats hung on the walls, and a large model of his favorite fighter, the P-47 *Thunderbolt* hung near the window. This last was a tribute to Fanny Case, Republic Aviation co-owner.

"I took out all the drawings of many boats, boats that even now I have never built," Ed said. "One of them caught my eye, and

I said to myself I ought to go back and do that and find somebody to buy it. She was a power boat and a pretty little thing."

Ed carried the profile drawing of a 27' runabout to his new roomy studio and tacked it on his drawing table. To get some opinions, he showed it to visitors and his sons. Ronnie had thought the design looked terrific when his father had first drawn it, and he still felt that way. "Dad, that's beautiful. I've got to build it."

"I don't know, Ronnie," Ed said, "because if we build it, we'll be building on our own." Ronnie still wanted him to go ahead with a drawing and a half model.

Ed liked the sketch but was ambivalent about whether or not to proceed with it. His hesitancy to go forward with something was more pronounced in recent years. Physically, Ed had slowed down, while his mind cruised along with creative concepts.

He finished the powerboat drawing and, with Ronnie's help, carved the half-hull model to scale. In previous years, Ed had done this on his own.

Eddie Jr. spoke of the runabout as a boatyard president with a weather eye. "The model is a small part of it. Somebody's got to lay out the timing, the planning, and line up finances. And somebody's got to have all the drawings, so the price list can be made. I really want to have a damned good idea of what's going on," he said. "I have to, if I'm going to tell somebody what it will cost and project a time frame on when it's going to be done. I can't be running around unaware of what's in someone else's head." Ed talked about a shorter 23' runabout, and made new drawings.

Ed said somebody was interested in completing the 65' motor yacht. "If I go ahead with that, it will take the crew to finish it." He was relaxed and speaking calmly, without the expected enthusiasm. A month later, Ed was in good spirits and with more variety in his voice. "Nick Grasberger wants us to go ahead with *Americana* — he preferred this to *John's Boat* — after his boat is finished. I'm amazed." Just a few weeks after this pronouncement, Ed sounded

Ed, at age 79, drawing the runabout at his design desk. Spline weights are holding the curve for the sheer, which he is doing by eye. He never worked with a computer which he strongly criticized. He was following in the steps of the classic designers he admired.

Wayne Brown

tentative. "I don't know how it will turn out. It may or may not. I would like to see somebody complete it. It's a handsome boat."

Nick Grasberger clarified the situation. "I would love to see that boat finished. I would be willing to invest in it. My interest was not to buy the boat outright, but to value Ed's investment in the boat and then put in a like amount of capital, so we'd have a 50-50 interest, and to finish it."

Ed estimated the completion cost, but Grasberger found it unrealistically low. The building of his sailboat was about $1,700 a week. As the financial head of a major company, he wanted accurate cost projections for the 65-footer.

"I hope it will be finished in Mr. Cutts's lifetime," Grasberger said. "This would really be the crowning achievement of his career to see that boat finished. He lights up when he talks about it."

Eddie Jr. was surprised to hear any discussions had taken place on completing the motor yacht. "It's the first I have heard about that. Dad doesn't keep me informed on what deals are structured." Like many others, Eddie would like to see *John's Boat* built and in the water. "The only difficulty," he said, "is we don't have drawings of the cabin interiors. Dad will tell you he has it laid out, but it's not on paper. You can't start four or five guys jumping into a project and then stop because the designer is off on a whim. Unless it's on paper so everybody can say, 'This is what we've got to do,' you can't even guess how long it will take."

On the cover of *WoodenBoat* (Jan.–Feb. 2007) was a photograph by Benjamin Mendlowitz of *Foto* cruising off into a low-angled sun. Many friends recognized Ed Cutts at the helm with Maggie sitting next to him. A Washington State man phoned Ed and said, "It's just the kind of a boat that I want. I called to ask if you can build me one like it."

"It's a lovely little boat, but we could do much better," Ed replied. "You know we've learned a lot in 75 years." Nothing developed from this conversation, because the caller never pursued it by visiting Cutts & Case. Perhaps, it was Ed's attitude over the phone.

Grasberger's new boat was nearing completion in March of 2007. Ed thought the sloop might be launched in late April or May. But on June 26th the sails were not ready. Ed had phoned a major Annapolis sail loft, but they never showed up. So he sent drawings to Potomac Sails, who soon arrived to check the spars. The sails would soon be ready.

The July 4th launch date was moved, and Ed predicted the end of July. "I've got to do the mast hardware today," he said. His cardboard patterns would be transferred to metal. "We can do it here, unless Eddie decides to give it to somebody with a laser cutter. You can't buy the hardware for wooden spars anymore. You can't buy a gooseneck or masthead equipment."

Although there are bronze cleats and chocks in a wide range of sizes available, Eddie Jr. had watched the decline in mast hardware. "The whole industry for the most part has gone over to aluminum spars and stainless-steel hardware," he said. "But the boats are not, for the most part, hand-made boats." Cutts & Case had made the hardware for *Millennia* and *Curio*.

"*Rebellion* was built back at the time when there was lots of wood construction," Eddie said, "so boom hardware was available." Her cleats were purchased, but Cutts & Case built her chocks. Ed Cutts preferred to use his own hardware as they did at Nevins. "When hardware was available to meet the mechanical function," Eddie said, "Dad wasn't inclined to accept their quality or design. And the truth of the matter is that he comes up with things and wants them his way."

Nick Grasberger phoned Ed to ask, "Can we have the boat done by Labor Day? We're having family and friends, and we want to buy them plane tickets to come for the launching."

"You're really putting a lot of pressure on me," Ed replied.

Nick didn't want last-minute changes for his forty guests. "You guys have to tell me. First, it was going to be Easter, then Memorial Day, and then the 4th of July."

"Well, I'll let you know," Ed said.

This deadline led to a father-and-son conference characterized by frankness and many questions. Eddie told his father what parts that they would have to make at the yard. Moving rapidly, Eddie organized things, talked with Ronnie, and listed what needed to be done. He called a boatyard meeting that took the men by surprise, for meetings were rare. Eddie gave out lists and made people accountable for work, so the sloop would be completed on schedule in seven weeks.

"At that point, Dad indicated how he expected it to go," Eddie said. He and his father had dinner together, the first in a long time. "It was the best dinner I've had with Dad in years," he said.

When Nick phoned Ed each week for an update, Ed replied, "Nick, you're driving me nuts. I'm staying awake, every night, trying to figure out how we can get this boat finished."

"On one hand I felt bad about this," Nick said at a later time, "and on the other hand we needed to do this to get it done. I think, since that dinner, that Eddie Jr. and Ed Sr. have had a better relationship."

On Wednesday, before the Labor Day weekend, Ed Cutts discovered that the tiller hadn't been started, and that they only had the rudder's outside form, "Can you imagine a boat without a rudder or tiller?" he asked with a self-justifying air. "It's a good thing I checked. "He took credit for the discovery, overlooking his share of the oversight.

Eddie said his father didn't have a plan for the rudder. "Maybe he did, but he didn't give anybody any drawings. I had to figure out how to make it myself, which was no problem."

On the Saturday, the sloop sat on the ways minus a rudder, which was drying. Eddie and his daughter Sophie applied polyurethane to the tiller until Sunday at 2 a.m. When the rudder was in place, Dennis attached the tiller at 8:15 a.m. Sunday, the day of the launching.

As the crowd built up, Ed sat in his golf cart near the ways, greeting friends, guests, and family members, thoroughly enjoying everything. His daughter Linda, taller than her dad, sat with him, talking to guests. A half-hour later, Ed's red-haired, eleven-year-old granddaughter Sophie also sat next to the grandfather she loved. She was reserved but had a proud look. She recalled finishing not only the emergency rudder with her dad, but also her grandfather who had designed and then supervised every detail in building the graceful sloop.

Ed was pleased with the sailboat, which had taken over five and a half years to complete. This construction had been fuel for

Ed and his granddaughter Sophie share time together as the gathering crowd enjoys champagne and crabcakes, before the christening of *Souvenir*.
Wayne Brown

his mind, body, and spirit. Perhaps, unconsciously, he didn't want to finish it.

The group of about eighty, half being family and friends of Nick Grasberger, milled around, enjoying Eastern Shore crab cakes, hors d'oeuvres, and champagne. Launch time neared, and the Cutts & Case builders, some from past years, lined up before the sloop. Someone called for Ed who actually sprang out of his Power Chair by the rails. He walked with surprisingly rapid steps to join them, followed by his two sons.

In front of the boat shed above the sloop ready for launching, Nick Grasberger made a short speech, surrounded by his family. Dennis Risher, an assistant Methodist minister, said a prayer. Nick's wife Michele said, "I christen you *Souvenir*," as she swung the champagne onto the bow. A nearby cannon fired, and crew members ran down the docks with lines attached to the cradle. Dennis, at the rails with a sledge hammer, knocked out the chocks. *Souvenir* slid down the ways, with fourteen-year-old Maddie Grasberger in the cockpit.

Sophie Cutts had just fired the breaches-buoy cannon. In a low-key, professional manner, she later explained, "You just hold one hand over an ear, turn sideways, and with the hammer in your other hand you hit the pin." Ed Cutts had rebuilt the breach to take a 10-gauge cartridge and had added brass trim to the barrel. The cannon was a smart-looking piece of ordnance.

As sails went up on *Souvenir*, Ed drove his indoor power-chair onto the dock and bumped, at what appeared full throttle, over the spaced boards for about 50 feet to reach the boat. He pulled himself up and held onto a piling until Ronnie and Nick helped him into the cockpit. They sailed out, with a light breeze, into the mouth of the Tred Avon River.

Back on shore, Ed Cutts officially turned the sloop *Souvenir* over to new owner Nick Grasberger. Ed had tears in his eyes. Eddie and Ronnie also felt the deep emotions of this event, as Jack Sherwood reported in *Soundings*.

Following sunset, the boatyard was once again tranquil except for locusts calling in the high pines and elms. In a new kitchen armchair, Ed was happy with the way *Souvenir* handled in spite of the light wind. "Now I wish I had put a little more square footage in the sails," he said.

He became serious when he said, "I nearly fell in. Michele tried to lift me and wasn't strong enough. Nick and Ronnie grabbed my arms and pulled me up." Ed gave Michele credit for being the best sailor in the Grasberger family. Looking resigned, Ed said quietly, "I don't think I'll be getting on a boat again."

The next morning, Ed rolled up the path to the dock where he saw Nick and his family hoisting sails with Ronnie. The golf-cart wheels were too wide for the dock. Suddenly, without speaking, Ed was up on his feet and lurching toward the sailboat. To a shouted offer of a cane or power chair, he called, "No," over his shoulder. He accelerated his stiff-gaited strides, as if pushed by wind at his back — actually his determination. As Ed approached the boat, keeping to the center of the dock, Ronnie and Nick looked up in surprise and apprehension. Ed took a final step, grabbed a piling by the boat, and hugged with his full strength, becoming still. Eddie termed this his "trademark iron will."

With final advice to Nick Grasberger, Ronnie climbed off the boat, and released the dock lines so they could get underway. He turned to his dad, speaking quickly, "Just stand there and don't try to move. I'll bring the boat to you." Ronnie trotted off and soon motored up in a center-console *Slickcraft*. He helped his father onto a woven-rope chair on the forward deck. The chair was a few inches below the low gunwale, and the freeboard seemed to be

Ronnie Cutts at the helm of his center-console boat. He gave his father a gift of a 52-mph ride.
Wayne Brown

Ed Cutts turning to face aft on Ronnie's boat before going out to observe *Souvenir.*

one foot. The motor boat had neither stanchions nor lifelines. Ed wasn't wearing a life jacket in his collapsible chair, nor was Ronnie, standing behind the windscreen at the helm where he exuded joy on this special occasion.

Ronnie's boat gained speed, sometimes made sharp turns, and was smacked by waves, so there was bouncing and buffeting. Unconcerned by his somewhat perilous position, Ed focused intently on the sailboat as it picked up the brisk breeze.

Running parallel to *Souvenir*, Ronnie called advice, "Take up slack in the halyards. Tighten the mainsheet."

Nick and Michele Grasberger took turns boarding the powerboat. Sitting next to Ed, they observed their new sloop tacking or on a reach, as it made good headway.

While heading home, Ronnie opened the throttle on the 13-hp V-4 Yamaha outboard, and shouted, "We're doing about 52 mph."

Nick Grasberger on the foredeck making adjustments to halyards and lines on *Souvenir*. Ed Cutts is observing this from Ronnie's boat which is running parallel.

Wayne Brown

He based this speed on timed runs over a course. Ed Cutts was oblivious to any danger, sitting just above the water and without a flotation device, as occasional chops hit the hull. He wore a big grin as did Ronnie, who was delighted to take his father out on the water after a lengthy absence. There was a bond of love in the rush of wind and surface spray. Ronnie was bringing speed and joy once more to his dad who all his life had loved speeding. For father and son it was an experience to remember.

That evening, Ed explained his rapid walking along the dock. "I had to walk fast to get to a piling, which I could hold on to for balance." After a pause he said, "There is no feeling in the right foot, so I don't know what it's doing." As an afterthought he added, "And the left leg sometimes gives out. A few days ago I was going out the front door and fell forward on the ground — flat as a pancake." There was no hint of self pity. "The woman who cleans for me tried to help, but she couldn't lift me. I crawled along and pulled myself up on the golf cart." Self-reliant at eighty years of age, Ed Cutts had no intention of slowing down. His infirmities were a challenge.

That evening, Ed had more to say about his health. "I've had an awful pain in my lower back," he said. "Today I did something I never did before. Eddie told me to pray directly to Jesus and ask for help. So I said, 'With everything going on now, Lord, I don't need this awful back pain. Please help me now.' And, do you know, five minutes later it was gone, just like that. And it's still gone." He paused with a content smile.

"Ever since I was a little guy," and he held out his hand, "the Lord has been good to me. Even when I was knocked down, I would get picked up again — all my life."

Nick Grasberger described Ed Cutts succinctly. "Ed is an artist and a romantic, but his mind also has tremendous technical capacity. He possesses a gift to simply look at a boat, or any engineered product, and determine if the design is optimal, and if not how to make it so. Others need computers and mathematical calculations, but not Ed. I imagine most of the great inventors possessed a similar gift."

Eddie Jr. summed up working with his father over the years. "He's a funny guy, a nice guy, a great artist, a great engineer, but he's very much in his own world and his own head, and he always has been. If you tell him he's great, you're sticking with him — that's fine," Eddie said. "But, if you ever offer arguments for discussion's sake, he won't like you, and he'll shut you out. That was my problem, the problem I always had with him and the difficulty that arose between us as father and son.

"I started working with my dad when I was five, so I was with him a lot when I was very young. He taught me how to think, and as I grew older, I would think of things. He would say, 'We're going to do this and do that,' and I'd say, 'Just wait a minute. I think you could do this like that.' He didn't want to hear anybody's thinking in the sense of a challenge or anybody else's thinking but his own. But, he did teach me how to think," Eddie said, "so I was getting to the point where I was thinking stuff myself. And I'd say, 'We could do this. This could go like that.' And he'd do it differently — it seemed for the sake of it. But, the truth is he taught me how to think, and it does me good every day." Eddie paused a moment to reflect.

"I don't know if he ever understood that," Eddie said. "Often we would feel like we were in an argument. We'd get at it, and then find out we were both closing in on the same point but from two different angles."

In 2008, after Eddie Jr. received an invitation from officials in Finland, he flew over to attend the opening of the Finnish WoodenBoat Center in Kotka. The new building, sheathed in heavy copper, displayed some pristine 6-meter sloops. "The Nordic countries," he said, "still build a nice percentage of wooden boats.

As in all countries, the fiberglass ones are production oriented, hence their sheer numbers always make fiberglass the most built."

One of the Finnish builders, Hanno (Allan) Savolainen who had worked on *Americana*, telephoned Ed Cutts. "Allan said that he was building a 32' power launch using the Cutts Method," Ed said. "It will be put to heavy work, but it will have some bright work, so it will look nice. Just think, he doesn't have to do any steam bending of frames." Ed was in his public-relations mode and throwing in a zinger.

Because of increasing problems with his right foot, Ed went to the doctor in March 2008. The physician said he might have to remove part of his right leg. Ed, who had been feeling pretty well, wasn't ready for this. "If you're going to take the other leg," Ed told the doctor, "you might as well shoot me in the head." He knew it would be impossible to drive his truck into Easton without a right foot. On a return visit, the doctor decided Ed was doing all right without the operation.

As a patient, Ed didn't follow what diabetics are supposed to do, such as monitoring blood levels. Also, he enjoyed sweet wine and plum preserves in moderation.

At this time a dealer in Delaware was fixing Ed's 4-cylinder Suzuki motorcycle. "It's old but I always took good care of it," Ed said. One day he polished his Kawasaki *Ninja*, and then sat astride it, wishing he could cycle again.

Ronnie walked up. "You shouldn't be on a motorcycle."

"I'm all right as long as I'm sitting down," Ed replied. The following day he said, "I would like to go 100 miles-an-hour on a motorcycle again. I really miss it." He had a thin smile on his face, but overall he appeared disheartened.

Sharing some good news, Ed said, "I built a beautiful little boat almost fifty years ago, *Joie de Vivre*, and recently someone bought that boat. It was put away in the shed and hadn't been out for almost twenty years." A Cutts & Case customer who admired the 28' 10" sloop had asked about it. Ed went to the owner who said she would sell it.

Ed gathered together some drawings and sail plans for the biography, and said, "It'll give the flavor of boat design for people who know nothing about it." Would his boys worry that they could be copied? "Ah hell, I don't give a damn!" he exploded. "Why do we worry about such stuff? If they copy it so much the better, because some of the boats we see are awful." It was fine with him if the using of his designs "promoted better work." Ed's attitude of a lifetime had swung about to the opposite compass heading.

In May 2008, an enthusiastic group of seventy-five tourists came into the Cutts & Case boatyard in two buses from an American Cruise Lines ship docked in Cambridge. They spent time in the museum and looking over the boats. After they walked through

Joie de Vivre sits in the water, after many years in storage. She is "taking up" preparatory to fitting out. Ed began building her in Northport and completed her in Oxford for Abe Oberlin.

Wayne Brown

the boat sheds, Ed invited them to his house, saying, "It was built forty years before George Washington was born." They were packed into his living room and spilled into the front hall as Ed told of building with wood and about his unique Cutts Method. "They were the most intent audience and had good questions," he said. "They went back to the tour company and raved about having come to this yard. The tour company called me up this morning, and they want to arrange tours here, so I said sure."

The touring group turned out to be members of the Stanford University Engineering Society. They showed their appreciation by sending Ed an official cap with their society's name, which Ed wore. Since this visit, tours have been coming to the yard during warm weather. Their enthusiasm motivated Ed to go to his desk where he typed the many benefits of his Cutts Method. He intended these notes for a future handbook on building, which he never wrote. (See the Appendix.)

The poor national economy in 2008 affected Cutts & Case too. Ronnie had once said, "We have never laid a man off in over 75 years of business, and this includes when Ralph Wiley had the yard before. Some of the old timers left to catch oysters and crabs for two or three months and then came back to work."

Eddie explained to two builders he would have to let them go at Christmas 2008. "If I run the business down, then there'll be nothing here when the economy picks up, and you may want to return." They understood. On their last day Eddie gave them the usual Christmas bonus plus vacation pay. "It's all I could do," Eddie said.

In early January of 2009, Ed was unaware of Eddie's conversation. He spoke quietly and seriously. "I did something I've never done before. I had to let two men go, and I feel awful about it." He sat motionless and silent for a few minutes. He had broken a life-long principle.

Ed had a surprise when Discovery Productions arrived in June 2009 to tape a documentary about him for a television series. Ed probably played the accordion for them as he did for tour groups. In fairness, he was not skilled on the keyboard and only played chords, but this fit a sea-captain image. He enjoyed performing for visitors. But when he sat motionless with a sad smile for a photo-op, he looked weak and frail. It didn't match the active, alert, forceful speaking, gesturing Ed — decisive, persuasive, and strong — as was Franklin D. Roosevelt in his chair.

Ed Cutts remembers the people in his life in a rather special way. Writer Jack Sherwood, who sailed his sloop to Cutts & Case to cover *Souvenir's* launching, spoke of this. "Whenever friends die, Ed puts their anchors outside his house."

"At first," Eddie said, "the anchors were placed there as an element of the garden. Then, a customer dropped an anchor off, and later that year he passed away. Someone wanted to buy the anchor, but Ed wouldn't sell it. Then it became a kind of memorial. People started coming in and dropping off old anchors."

"We put the anchors out there," Ed Cutts said, "as a sign that these people are still anchored here. The big anchor is from a tremendous boat we took care of — Slade Dale's boat. We have had some wonderful customers."

Two years before, Abe Oberlin had phoned that he would be arriving from Oregon for a visit. "Abe," Ed said. "you'll be surprised that we got older, but *Spellbound* didn't. She looks just like the day I gave her to you thirty-seven years ago." Whenever that ketch was being discussed, Ed often said, "*Spellbound* never had a repair of any kind."

Ed paused a moment looking serene, thoughtful, at peace with the world. "I've been surrounded by wonderful people all my life, I really have. I mean everybody including John Case," he said. "Now that must come from upstairs, don't you think? Abe is a wonderful man — one of the people I love dearly."

Ed said he gave to some charities now and then. "I recently sent $1,000 for the Jews in Russia, who are having a difficult time." He had never before mentioned any charitable gifts, a subject he kept private. Ed was generous by nature and took pleasure in treating guests to meals.

Customers of the yard speak well of Ed, and many have special stories. Boat builder Tom Morris once said, "I've described him to people as my Babe Ruth of the boat building business. You know how you look up to people you think really set the highest standards? That's how I feel about Ed. He sets the standard," Morris said. "It's great that his two sons are there — Eddie and Ronnie."

Dr. Crile Crisler, who built two of Ed's designs, shared his opinion of the Oxford designer-builder. "In my mind, Ed's particular talent has been a remarkable ability to combine grace and beauty of form with function in a boat. He has a profound understanding of how materials work and just how strong something needs to be. He really knows how to minimize the weight and waste of materials, while providing sufficient strength to the structure."

In striving to continually improve his skills, Edmund Cutts developed a lifelong philosophy he applied to his work. "If you feel that what you are doing is excellent, then you are finished with your improving. You have to feel that your work by God's standard is poor," he said. "The things He made on this planet are exquisite. So what can man do? — Not much.

"The greatest of all men probably was Michelangelo, and his work was exquisite. But he was only chopping out of a rock what God made alive. He did a beautiful job, but I don't think he was ever finished. I don't think a person who strives for excellence can ever be finished," Ed said. "Once you're satisfied with yourself, you stop. But, not if you're still saying to yourself, 'It's not good enough, there's more to know, and this could have been slightly different.'

"I was just thinking about who was the most important person in my career," Ed said, "and I came to the conclusion that it was Al Meyer. It was he who introduced me to important people at the early stages of my career, like the Fontanes, Abe Oberlin, and John Case.

"They were people who were connoisseurs of boat building. One of the greatest was Al Meyer. He was fantastic. Of all the hundreds of people I have known, he was the most knowledgeable, yet he couldn't screw a piece of wood together. Sometimes I would drive with Al Meyer up to New England to look at boats he wanted to check out. He had a tremendous knowledge of boats." Ed was probably aware that much of this rubbed off on him during these trips, in dockside conversations, and while sailing on Meyer's boats. Ed acknowledged that Al Meyer was in effect his third mentor, along with Francis Herreshoff and Nils Halvorsen.

In late summer of 2009, Ed Cutts went to Easton Memorial Hospital where doctors performed two operations on his stomach. Ronnie and Eddie took him to an Easton nursing facility for supervised physical therapy. When they noticed that their father was growing quieter and weaker after two and a half weeks, they spoke with him about going home. Ed said he was ready, so they took him to Oxford after notifying Hospice.

"We spent the night with him," Eddie said. "He died in the morning at about 8 a.m." Ed Cutts was eighty-two, and the date was November 11, 2009, when he Crossed the Bar.

Family, friends, and boat builders gathered November 30th at a funeral home and the next day at Oxford Cemetery near the water. Officiating was Monsignor Thomas A. Kane of Annapolis, who helped children in his parish build kit boats. The US Navy assisted with flag folding and a distant Taps. In his closing remarks, Kane said Ed Cutts believed that Jesus was a boat builder and then quoted Ed, "He hung around with fisherman who repaired their own boats. What do you think he was doing in his father's carpenter shop — building chairs?"

As the service ended, three spaced cannon shots rang out from Cutts & Case across the water. Then everyone gathered at a restaurant luncheon to share memories of Ed Cutts. At the boatyard, Eddie and Ronnie put *Rebellion* up on a cradle out front. Following lunch they took all the assembled family members for a sail on *Spellbound*.

"Ed Cutts was a very humble man who never really sought the spotlight for himself," said Nick Grasberger in 2013. "Given the talent he had and the degree of some of his innovations, I strongly believe that if he had wanted to be more aggressive and commercializing, on a larger scale, Ed could have made a much bigger name for himself. That just wasn't what Ed Cutts was all about. He simply was never out to promote himself." Nick reiterated Ed was humble "and did really world-class work."

In 2007, two years before his death, Edmund Cutts was sitting in his 1695 living room surrounded by boat photos, paintings, and half-hulls. On a large coffee table were magazines and books with articles and photos of Cutts & Case, and Ed Cutts himself. Old ship lanterns, photos of *Spellbound*, *Curio*, and *Millennia* were all there, as was the Nat Herreshoff half-hull he treasured. A foot-and-a-half white metal *Chris Craft* sat on a piece of furniture near a photo of young Ed on a motorbike. A framed photo of Ed and Maggie at a CBMM event sat on the mantle. "It was an interesting life," he said then, "but it went by so fast, which happens when you enjoy what you're doing. I don't know where thirty-five or forty years went.

"When I was a little boy, my father recognized something in me." Ed was speaking slowly from his heart, emphasizing key words. "And he enhanced it by taking me, as the smallest kid, to different boatyards. And it made an impression that lasted all my life: to watch the way things are done and to know how they're done. And maybe there were better ways.

"I knew from about eight years of age what I wanted to do," Ed Cutts said. "There was something intriguing about boat building. It wasn't finished. I thought I would spend my life to find out what the ultimates were."

Appendix I

CUTTS METHOD

E~D~ C~UTTS~ wrote out nineteen benefits for boatbuilders who build with the Cutts Method in comparison to plank-on-frame wooden boat building. He sometimes spoke of putting this into a book called *God Was the First Boatbuilder.* Ed would say, "I plan to begin with Noah."[6] When reading these out loud, Ed made some comments, which are included.

CUTTS METHOD ADVANTAGES
By Edmund A. Cutts

1. If we do the design on your boat, there is no lofting required on your part. We give you full-size patterns so all you have to do is cut it out like paper dolls. I have equipment that you can't believe.

2. There is no mold ribbanding[7]. It's when you take 2 x 2s, or something else, and put it around a boat. You cut the molds back 2 inches, or you cut grooves and then cut back for the thickness of the frame. Then you bend the frame over those ribbands, which are longitudinally fair strips. There is no ribbanding, the inner plank does it.

3. There are no keel rabbets[8] required, because instead of rab-beting, the planking comes right down to the end of the keel. This is allowable because Kevlar cords go completely around the boat, and the tensile strength of a cord might be 6,000 to 10,000 lbs. Before, the edge of the planking would have been submerged inside the deadwood and ballast lines. If there were trouble, you couldn't get at it. But, the cords go completely around it, and there is no way for that to happen.

4. No frame beveling is required. You had to put a batten around and make sure they are fair. If you want perfect fits, you have to bevel them. It's a tough job, and that bevel is changing all the way up the boat.

5. No frame fairing is required either.

6. No steam bending is required. Imagine cooking up a big bunch of steam. You've got the whole building steaming.

7. No screws are required. Do you know how much bronze screws cost? Very expensive. Hundred and hundreds of holes, and they're bigger because you put a bung in bigger than the screws.

8. No electrolysis problems because there are no screws in the outer hull.

9. No caulking of any kind required.

10. No seam treatment required.

11. No cross planking if used in round-bottom boats. All [plank-ing] is longitudinal for strength, because if you cross a plank, that's half the strength.

12. No water migration in the planking. There's a groove and epoxy barrier every 4 inches or whatever measurement is decided on.

13. No buttocks required because we specify that planks be scarfed together. If you have a 30' frame, you can't buy 30' lumber so you have to join it.

14. No more yearly painting required.

15. Far greater ballast-to-weight (ratios) for a sailboat.
16. Far greater power-to-weight (ratios) in a power boat. So you have a lighter, faster boat.
17. There is far greater room in the boat because you have taken out the frames and ceiling.
18. There are far fewer throw-away building materials.
19. The tensile strength of white oak is 10,000 PSI (pounds per square inch). The tensile strength of Kevlar is well over one half million PSI (per DuPont).

Appendix II

EDMUND A. CUTTS
DESIGNED BOATS

	Built	LOA	LWL	Beam	Draft
Launches	3	23'4"	22'8"	7'3"	1'7"
Simplex	1	32'10"	29'9"	8'5"	2'8"
Cygnet	1	23'	17'4"	7'6"	2'6"
Cabin Yacht	1	31'	27'4"	9'9"	2'8"
Cabin Yacht	3	33'	29'8"	10'2"	2'2"
Joie de Vivre	1	28'10"	22'5"	7'7"	4'9"
Rebellion	1	33'	23'8"	7'7"	4'9"
Grizzly Bear	1	33'	23'8"	7'7"	4'9"
La Mouette	1	37'4"	30'4"	10'6"	3'9"
Spellbound	1	46'	36'	10'8"	3'9"
Jeanne	1	42'4"	33'10"	10'7½"	5'2"
Ocean Gem	1	13'6"	8'	4'	3'1½"
Americana (hull) (aka John's Boat)		65'	63'	10'4"	N/A

	Built	LOA	LWL	Beam	Draft
Curio	1	27'	26'1"	7'3¾"	1'2"
Hummingbird	1	33'	24'	8'6"	2'4"
Crisler *garvey*	1	24'6"	19'	7'6"	1'2"
Millennia	1	28'	27'3"	8'2"	1'2"
Souvenir	1	24'½"	18'3½"	7'9"	3'1½"

⚓

ENDNOTES

1. The numbers tell the story. In the 1894–95 season, watermen harvested from the Chesapeake Bay 15 million bushels of oysters — an incredible amount. In the 1950s the harvest count was 2,878,756 bushels, but, in 2000, the total for the Bay dropped to 347,968 bushels for Maryland and Virginia.

In 2003, the Maryland Department of Natural Resources determined Maryland watermen took in just 55,832 bushels. But, as authorities eliminated some pollution in the watershed, they recognized a dangerous disease destroying oysters and attacked it. Organizations are fighting nitrate run-off in the seven state watershed, planting oyster reefs, and working on legal corrections. The tide may be turning slowly because the 2010 Maryland harvest of 185,000 bushels was the best in nine years, said the Maryland DNR.

2. Lowndes Johnson and his brother Graham, after winning the Chesapeake Bay Championship for the second time in 1929, won the World Championship in New Orleans that same year.

3. Boats from Maine carried lumber, fish, and fur. Lumber included pipe staves, boards, shingles, and ships' timber for Europe and the Caribbean, and urgently needed masts for England. Historian William Rowe wrote that an English law reserved all white pine

measuring 30 inches or more in diameter for spars. The largest masts could have a 36-inch diameter and be 125 feet or more in length, and bowsprits measured 75 feet. Merchants shipped these on specially designed ships with transom hatches that could carry fifty to one hundred masts and spars. Most of these ships left from Portland, originally called Falmouth.

4. From the poem "Crossing the Bar" by Alfred, Lord Tennyson.

5. "George Washington liked white oaks," Ed Cutts said, "because they represented honesty and strength." Ed designed a small metal plate for *Souvenir's* port deck that reads, *Mount Vernon white oak planted by George Washington 1781.*

Sounding like a history teacher, Ed Cutts described a battle in which Washington took part. "Washington was at first an English officer, and was about to battle the French. Before the fight, he prayed, and so he had some mud on his knee. In the fierce battle, General Braddock was killed, so Washington had to take charge. He was shot in the hat, between the legs, and on two sides of his tunic, in addition to having two horses shot from under him. And not one bullet hit him."

6. In 1869, a Scottish boatyard built an iron-hulled, fully rigged vessel of 223' by 37' by 22' 3" — using the *Ark* dimensions given in the Bible. Measurements were in cubits, based on the head builder's elbow to middle-finger tip, often seen as 18 inches. She was named *Golden Fleece* and sailed the seas for fifteen years. Richard Maury wrote of this clipper ship and quoted Marine historian Lubbock who called her, 'One of the most beautiful iron clippers ever built.' Not only handsome, "Maury wrote, "she was also able, an easy ship to work, and one endowed with a good turn of speed." (Maury)

7. A ribband is a long, narrow strip fastened to the frames to keep them in place during building.

8. A rabbet is a grove or recess.

ACKNOWLEDGMENTS

Many people contributed to this book, and I wish I could name them all. My greatest appreciation and heartfelt thanks naturally goes to Ed Cutts for his total cooperation as he welcomed interviews over a six-year period. Without these frequent interviews there would not be a biography.

His sons Eddie Cutts Jr. and Ronnie Cutts provided details on living with their father up to the present and added important information on boating, boatbuilding and Cutts & Case happenings. Other family members shared important events they remembered: Bob Cutts, Virginia Erickson, Linda Cutts Featherman, and writer Jeff Durstewitz, who read an early draft. I am indebted to Debra Durstewitz and Richard Somerville for their extensive family research.

Thanks to Ed Cutts's friends, associates, and customers for their contributions: Bill Bunting, Mary Ellen Campbell, Lee Casper, Dr. Crile Crisler, Helga Fontanes, Nick Grasberger, Fred Hecklinger, Dr. John Hedger, Seth Hetherington, Bill Hingst, Ginger Martus, Tom Morris, Robert Muir, Abe Oberlin, Sakoto Parker, Dennis Risher, Joseph Ruddy, Jonathon Smith, Roger Vaughan, Chuck Wiley, and Donald Wilson.

Thanks also to: John Haug, Jon Johansen, William Wentworth Cutts, Matt Moore, Richard Rosenfeld, Jack Sherwood, and the New York YC staff. Much valuable material came from maritime

278

museums. Major thanks to: Pete Lesher, curator, Richard Scofield, assistant curator, and Lynne Phillips, collections manager at the Chesapeake Bay Maritime Museum; Melvin Hickman, curator, and Herm Kramer, manager, at the Richardson Maritime Museum; Polly Brown at the Strawberry Banke Museum; Tom Nye, historian, at the City Island Nautical Museum; Nathan Lipfert, curator, at the Maine Maritime Museum; the Mariners Museum staff; and David Tanner, PhD, formerly of DuPont Research.

Historians provided research information: Gloria Pritts, Mamaroneck, New York; Miriam Varian, White Plains, New York; researchers at Yonkers Public Library, New York; and Oyster Bay Historical Society, New York. Some important libraries were: Library of Congress, Washington, DC; Kittery Public Lib., Maine; Dyer Lib., Saco, Maine; IBM Archives, New York.

I wish to thank the editors and publishers of Connecticut, Maryland, and Virginia newspapers and magazines for publishing my work as a journalist. I am grateful to Sylvia Gannon of Easton, Maryland, for her help.

I thank the photographers, the cover designer, and the book designer team for their fine work. Thanks to Susan Schmidt, PhD, for developmental editing, and to Brian Jud for publishing guidance.

Thanks to my three sons Andrew, Evan, and Charles Jones for advice, to my daughter Laurie Anne Toback for her help, and to my brother Charles Wardell Brown who made this book possible. Finally, thanks to my dear wife — Carol Lindblom Brown — for her patience and support. She was Commander of Flotilla 88, US Coast Guard Auxiliary, in Virginia, when she Crossed the Bar.

⚓

BIBLIOGRAPHY

Bowen, Frank, and Capt. H. Parker. *Steamships of the 19th Century.* London: Samsom, Low, Marston, 1928.

Brewster, Charles W. *Rambles About Portsmouth.* Portsmouth, NH: 1859.

Brown, Wayne. *Edmund Cutts, Oxford Boatbuilder.* Tidewater Times. Oxford, MD: Feb. 2002.

Cable, Mary. *The Blizzard of '88.* New York: Athenaeum-Macmillan Publishing, 1988.

Chapelle, Howard Irving. *The History of American Sailing Ships.* New York: Bonanza Books, 1935.

Fairburn, William Armstrong. *Merchant Sail.* Vol. 5. Center Lovell, ME: Fairburn Marine Educational Institution, 1955.

Fairfield, Roy P. *Sands, Spindles, and Steeples, A History of Saco, Maine.* Portland, ME: House of Falmouth. 1956. Reprint edition: Bowie, MD: Heritage Books, 2003.

Garitee, Jerome R. *The Republic's Private Navy, the American Privateering Business as practiced by Baltimore during the War of 1812.* Pub. for Mystic Seaport by Wesleyan University Press, 1977.

Goldenberg, Joseph A. *Shipbuilding in Colonial America.* Charlottesville: University Press of Virginia, 1976.

Groom, Winston. "A Lineage of Craftsmanship." *WoodenBoat Magazine.* No. 78. (Sep.–Oct. 1987): 30–39.

Hayes, Sir Bertram Fox. *White Star Line.* London, NY: Cassell, 1925.

Herreshoff, L. Francis. *Sensible Cruising Designs.* Publisher's Preface by Roger C. Taylor. (International Marine Pub. Co.) New York: McGraw-Hill Education, 1991.

Howard, Cecil Hampton Cutts. (Member: American Historical Assoc.) *Genealogy of the Cutts Family in America.* Albany, NY: Joel Munsell's Sons, 1892.

Karaphuna. *The Last of the Karaphuna.* (Documentary film) Westport, CT: Teuscher & Pettys Productions, 1982.

Lord, Frederick K. "A Viking Ship." Reprinted in *The Rudder Treasury.* Editor: Tom Davin. New York: Sheridan House, 2003. 110–122.

Lyons, Chuck. "A Tornado of Wind and Snow." *History Magazine.* Vol. 13 (Dec. 2011): 42–46.

Maine Maritime Museum. *Captains' Index.* (2 parts) Bath, ME.

Mariners' Museum, The. *Chesapeake Bay. Native Americans. How did they travel?* (Educational brochure) Newport News, VA: April 29, 2007. http://mariner.org/chesapeakebay/native/nam004.html.

Maury, Richard. "Curious Records of the Sea." *The Rudder Treasury.* Editor: Tom Davin. New York: Sheridan House, 2003. 17–27.

Mcdonald, Gregory. "Herreshoff: Last Grandee of Yacht-Design." *Boston Globe.* June 11, 1967. Magazine section. pages: 14–17.

Mendlowitz, Benjamin, and Maynard Bray. *The Guide to Wooden Boats.* New York: Norton, 1997.

Meyer, Elizabeth. "Concordia." *Nautical Quarterly.* Summer, No. 22. 1983.

National Archives. *Ship Registers and Enrollments of Machias, Maine. 1780–1930.* Manuscript form. Rockland, ME: Prepared by the National Archives Project, Div. of Community Service Programs of Works Projects Administration, 1942. Maine Maritime Museum Library. Bath, ME.

Noyes, Sybil, Charles Thornton Libby, and Walter Goodwin Davis. *Genealogical Dictionary of Maine and New Hampshire*. Baltimore, MD: Genealogical Publications, 1972.

Pope, Charles Henry. *The Pioneers of Maine and New Hampshire 1623–1660. A Descriptive List Drawn From the Records of the Colonies, Towns, Churches, Courts and Other Contemporary Sources*. Baltimore, MD: Genealogical Publishing Co., 1965.

Port Chester Journal. "Consent Refused, Love Finds a Way." Port Chester, NY: Jan. 7, 1904.

Prough, Dallas Whylie. *Piscataqua Pioneers 1623–1775*. Somerville Printing Co. Orig. 1919, Reprint 2004.

Ridlon, G. T. Sr. *Saco Valley Settlements and Families*. Rutland, VT: Charles E. Tuttle Co., 1969.

Rosenfeld, Stanley. *A Half Century Under Sail*. New York: Addison-Wesley, 1984.

Rowe, William Hutchinson. *The Maritime History of Maine, Three Centuries of Shipbuilding and Seafaring*. New York: Norton & Co., 1948.

Sheehan, Viola. *Saco River History & Canoeing Guide. The Valley in Maine*. Pamphlet. Dyer Library. Saco, ME: Saco River Corridor Assoc. 1976.

Sherwood, Jack. "Following the Trail of the Rosenfelds' *Foto*." *Soundings*. Vol. XL. May 2003. 18.

Stackpole, Everett S. *Old Kittery and Her Families*. Lewiston, ME: Press of the Lewiston Journal Co., 1903.

Sydnor, Lucy Harvey. "The Clubhouse of the New York Yacht Club." *Antiques Magazine* (Sep. 1980): 506.

Tanner, David. "The Kevlar Innovation." *R & D Innovator*. Vol. 4, No. 11 (Nov. 1995). Winston J. Brill, 2006.

US Coast Guard. *Merchant Vessels of the United States*. (G. L. Blunt-White Library, Mystic Seaport.)

Vaughan, Roger. "Neptune's Darlings." *Nautical Quarterly*. No. 42, 1988: 86.

282

Vojtech, Pat. Relaunching of the *Foto* culminates long process. *Star-Democrat*. Aug. 13, 1989.

Wiley, Ralph Houghton. *Preacher's Son, Parish Baby, Yacht Builder, Sailor*. New York: Vantage Press, 1972.

Wilson, Jonathan A. "Editorial." *WoodenBoat Magazine*. No. 78 (Sep.–Oct. 1987): 2.

Wilstach, Paul. *Tidewater Maryland. Its History, Its Tradition, Its Romantic Plantation Mansions and the Celebrated Personages who give it Glamour*. New York: Tudor Publishing Co., 1931.

PHOTO CREDITS

Benjamin Mendlowitz © photos on pages: 59, 94, and 117.
William J. Hingst © photos on pages: 75, 83, 115, and 155.
Stark Jet © photo on page: 156.
Crile Crisler © photo on page: 165.
Michael Moore © photo on page: 103.
Providence-Journal © photo on page: 36.
Wayne Brown © photos on pages: 102, 172, 189, 207, 234, 248, 251, 255, 257, 258, and 262.
City Island Nautical Museum contributed photo on page: 44.
Cutts Family contributed photos on pages: 23, 66, 100, 120, 161, and 181.
Ed Cutts contributed construction plan: 65.
John Bildahl © Cover photos: *Spellbound* on front, Ed Cutts with *Foto* on back.

THE AUTHOR

Wayne Brown crewed on races and winning inter-club competitions in Portland, Maine, at twelve and thirteen. He chartered *Comet #2* from Ralph Wiley at fifteen and a miniature *skipjack* the next year. He has enjoyed sailing wooden boats from Maine to Maryland.

Following the Marine Corp and a University of Pennsylvania BA, he went from theatre production to film production in New York and California.

As a journalist he wrote for papers in Connecticut, Maryland and Virginia. He was a public affairs officer for the US Power Squadron and the US Coast Guard Auxiliary.

He lives and works in Connecticut.

⚓